Montana

Norma Tirrell
Photography by John Reddy

COMPASS AMERICAN GUIDES, INC.
Oakland, California

Montana

Library of Congress Cataloging-In-Publication-Data

Tirrell, Norma.
  Montana / Norma Tirrell : photography by John Reddy. — 1st ed.
    p.   cm. —(Discover America)
  Includes bibliographical references and index.
  ISBN 1-878867-13-X (hard) : $22.95. — ISBN 1-878867-10-5 (soft) : $14.95
  1. Montana—Description and travel—1981– —Guide-books.
  I. Reddy, John. II. Title. III. Series.
  F729.3.T57 1991   91-15405
  917.8604'33—dc20   CIP

Editors: Barry Parr, Don Pitcher   Designer: David Hurst
Series Editor: Kit Duane   Map Design: Bob Race

First published in 1991 by Compass American Guides, Inc.
6051 Margarido Drive, Oakland, CA 94618, USA

Produced by Twin Age Ltd., Hong Kong   Printed in Hong Kong
Cover: Horses near the Crazy Mountains

ACKNOWLEDGMENTS

THANKS ARE DUE FIRST TO STAN MEYER, for his vote of confidence, and to Barry Parr, for his encouragement and unyielding demands as an editor and writing coach. Grateful recognition goes to my technical advisers: historians David Walter and Vivian Paladin; geologist Ray Breuniger; wildlife and conservation pro Jim Posewitz; census and economic research specialists Patricia Roberts and Jan Clack; arts advocates David Nelson, Jo-Anne Mussulman, and Julia Smith; and photo archivists Becca Kohl and Lory Morrow. Thanks are also due my informal council of advisers: backroads buffs Rick Rogne, Ken Walchek, Doug Monger, and Tom Palmer; community insiders Sally Mullen, Mick Mills, Becky Tirrell, Shirley Zupan, Dale Herbert, Patty Rambo Short, and Deirdre Boggs; bed and breakfast sleuth Paula Deigert; and restaurant consultants Ila Jesme, Janet Lowe, Barb Skelton, Wdythe McCleary, Pep Jewell, Mary Tietjen, Dore Schwinden, and Ann German. I am grateful, as always, to Sherryl Vaughn for her generous proofreading assistance. And I salute John Reddy for images that speak louder than words.

The publisher wishes to thank the following institutions and individuals for the use of their illustrations: Montana Historical Society, Helena, pp. 9, 31, 32, 34, 37, 63, 70, 81, 85, 93, 95, 101, 153, 163, 171, 192, 202, 221; Bancroft Library, University of California at Berkeley, pp. 30, 126; C.M. Russell Museum, Great Falls, pp. 121-123, 129, 243; Independence National Historic Park, Philadelphia, p. 42; Travel Montana, pp. 109, 246; Douglas O'Looney, pp. 38, 71, 72, 111, 215; Don Pitcher, p. 254; and Harry S. Robins, p. 51.

The quote on pages 148-149 by Richard Ford from *Rock Springs*, copyright 1987 is reprinted by permission of Atlantic Monthly Press.

(opposite) "Buffalo Hunt," oil on mirror, by C. M. Russell. (C. M. Russell Museum)

For Bennett, with whom I share Montana's mountains and headwaters, and for Janet, with whom I walked its deepest valley.

CONTENTS

Maps

Literary Quotes

Cycles of life and seasonal change are evident across Montana's uncluttered landscape.

AUTHOR'S PREFACE

LIKE MOST GUIDEBOOKS, THIS ONE IS A PERSONAL REFLECTION of its author. If I dwell on rivers and mountains, it is because that is where I spend much of my time. What will it be this weekend, Ten Lakes or the Missouri River? Bighorn Canyon or the Big Hole River? Cross-country skiing in Glacier or Yellowstone? These are the hard, year-round choices a Montanan faces. All national treasures, they are but a handful of gold nuggets in Montana's outdoor recreation bonanza.

If history keeps bobbing up, it is because the past is never out of reach in a state so young you can still sit at the knees of wranglers, homesteaders, miners, and tribal elders who keep it alive. Visit old Jake Hoover's sod-roof cabin in the Judith River country, and you'll see where cowboy artist Charlie Russell spent his early years and derived the inspiration to create his inimitable Western landscapes. Or take a walking tour of uptown Butte to sense the magnitude of the rivalry that existed between William Clark and Marcus Daly in their quest for dominance of the copper industry and the statehouse. Clark may have built the most ostentatious mansion, but it wasn't long before Daly blocked his view with a massive apartment house next door.

No longer boss of Montana's economy and politics, copper remains the symbol of a colonial state, historically driven by outside interests. After more than 150 years of long-distance promises about beaver pelts, gold, copper, silver, oil, coal, cattle, wheat, and timber, the nation's fourth-largest state still can't muster sufficient economic vitality to support more than one-third of one percent of the U.S. population—800,000 souls in all, scattered across nearly 150,000 square miles (388,500 sq. km).

But it is the resilience and diversity of its meager population that give Montana its fresh face and big heart. Smoke rising from Crow Indian sweat lodges beside Interstate 90 and cornucopian displays of fresh produce at Montana's Hutterite colonies hint at the cultural mix. Full-tilt Western blowouts, like the Miles City Bucking Horse Sale and Lewistown's Cowboy Poetry Gathering, are brassy statements about Montana's overriding cowboy culture and its attendant mythology.

In one of his essays, Wallace Stegner speaks of the importance of "placeness" in an increasingly "placeless" society. "If you don't know where you are," he says, "you don't know who you are." Montanans may be uncertain of their future, but they have never entertained doubts about their sense of place. It means more to them than money in the bank.

Through my own subjective mix of places, people, and events, I have tried to familiarize you with this addictive place. Mine is the view of a native who loves her state, and a journalist with no formal training in history, economics, or any of the isms or ologies that would lend this text the weight of authority. With any luck, it will send you searching for many of the titles that distinguish Montana nationally as a literary heavyweight. Good reading and happy travels.

Homesteaders were told of the mild winters, prodigious crop yields, and unlimited opportunity that awaited them in Montana; what many found was isolation, dust, drought, and drudgery. (Montana Historical Society)

(following pages) A perfect rainbow crowns Walton Mountain in Glacier National Park.

INTRODUCTION

■ LAND AND SPACE, MOUNTAINS AND SKY

DRIVING ACROSS EASTERN MONTANA—from, say, Sidney to Lewistown—can be an uneasy, or an exhilarating, experience. Uneasy if you find comfort in crowds; exhilarating if space is what you seek. The trip will take the better part of a day, and still you will be only halfway across the state. You will travel through all or part of five counties (roughly the equivalent of driving from Maine to New York) with a total population of fewer than 30,000. Of those counties, Garfield has 1,600 residents scattered over an area about the same size as Connecticut, with its 3.3 million people.

If you are open to a new perception of beauty, the lunar landscapes of eastern Montana can be endlessly absorbing. This is the Earth itself speaking, but if you have been conditioned to the babel of humanity, you may not hear it. So pack along a cassette tape of *High Plains Music* by Montana native, Phil Aaberg. His high-spirited and haunting piano celebrates the landscape and beckons you to the uninterrupted stretch of highway ahead. Soon, you will realize that you are surrounded not by emptiness, but by *space*. In Montana, there is a difference.

Eastern Montana space is filled with the subtlest forms of beauty. Shifting light and shadow play on coulees, badlands, and breaks. Western meadowlarks remind you with one astonishing trill that it's good to be alive. Neutral earth tones of ocher and sage magnify a 180-degree backdrop of sky that broods and shimmers in primary colors.

Driving south from Lewistown, the space becomes more immediate, more dramatic. It is defined by solitary mountain ranges that appear as islands in an ocean of grass—the Big Snowies, the Little Belts, the Castles, and the Crazies. Keeping to themselves in the distance, these isolated ranges are your signal that the landscape is about to change dramatically.

■ FROM PLAINS TO MOUNTAINS

Turning west at Big Timber, you might as well be in a different state. In fact, you have reached Montana's mid-point. Yet to come are the mountains that gave

Montana its name. First, the Absarokas and the Bridgers, then the Madison Range, the Tobacco Roots, the Pioneers, the Sapphires, and on and on, range after range, until they meld into one hazy ridge floating on the horizon. These views need no introduction; you've seen them on movie screens and travel posters. This is the Montana that outsiders know about: the mountains and trout streams, guest ranches and ski resorts, national parks and wilderness areas. You may have missed where the Dakota plains ended and the plains of eastern Montana began, but the imprint of the Northern Rockies will stay with you forever.

Scooped out of each range of mountains is a glaciated valley fed by rivers and streams that begin as snowfall on peaks that range from 7,000 to 12,000 feet (2,000 to 3,600 m) above sea level. But for an occasional town or small city, these timbered valleys and granite ranges are the domain of wildlife—abundant populations of elk, deer, moose, mountain goats, bighorn sheep, waterfowl, upland birds, and trout. The roster includes endangered and threatened species like the bald eagle, gray wolf, and grizzly bear. A popular Montana guest ranch offers this comparison to illustrate the company Montanans keep and the space they enjoy:

PER SQUARE MILE IN MONTANA
1.4 elk or antelope
3.3 deer
896 catchable-size trout
6 people

The conventional view of a remote, sparsely populated state like Montana is that there is nothing going on out here. Just land and space. In his *Montana: High, Wide, and Handsome,* Joseph Kinsey Howard wrote: "Montana is a remote hinterland about as well known to the average eastern seaboard citizen as East or West Africa. But it is this space that defines Montana and shapes the outlook of its residents." The newsman and historian also said of this place:

This sums up what I want in life—room to swing my arms and to swing my mind. Where is there more opportunity than in Montana for creation of these broad margins, physical and intellectual? Where is there more opportunity to enjoy the elemental values of living, bright sun and clean air and space? We have room. We can be neighbors without getting in each other's hair. We can be individuals.

The fact that there is still a place like Montana, where humanity does not dominate the landscape, is immensely important in a world that is overrun with people and their impact. Space and an unspoiled landscape are increasingly hard to come by, and herein lies Montana's appeal.

■ LIFESTYLE

Montanans treasure their space and the lifestyle it allows. Residents of even the largest cities can be skiing, hiking, fishing, or hunting in less than an hour. The Rattlesnake Wilderness is only a mile from the city limits of Missoula, western Montana's largest city. The people of Kalispell regard Glacier National Park as their own backyard. Bozeman skiers can choose between two of Montana's premier downhill areas—Bridger Bowl is 15 miles (24 km) north, Big Sky 30 miles (48 km) south. And one of Montana's finest floating and fishing rivers, the Missouri, is a half-hour drive from Bozeman, Helena, and Great Falls.

Isolation, a harsh climate, and a fickle, resource-based economy over which they have little control are the trade-offs Montanans are willing to make for this lifestyle. Global markets control the commodities that come from Montana: grain, livestock, minerals, energy fuels, and timber. Because of Montana's isolation from the nation's commercial centers, most of these are shipped out of the state as raw materials. It is cheaper to refine them near the markets where they will be used. The result back home is what one newspaperman has described as a "niche-poor" economy that cannot provide enough good-paying jobs to keep people, especially young people, in the state.

Montana's history has been marked by uneven growth and decline, a pattern that repeated itself as recently as the last decade. Following nearly three decades of prosperity starting in the 1950s, Montana's population reached a peak of 824,000 in 1985. By 1990, it had slipped to just under 800,000. Per capita income dropped from 12 percent above the national average in the 1950s to 20 percent below in 1987. In 1983 the state's largest employer, the Anaconda Company, abandoned its mining and smelting operations in Butte, Anaconda, and Great Falls. By the end of the eighties, Montanans were also adjusting to upheavals in the state's oil and gas, transportation, and timber industries. The clincher was a persistent drought that collapsed the agriculture industry in much of eastern Montana, and kindled

When the weather behaves, Flathead Lake cherries are one of Montana's most eagerly awaited crops.

MONTANA

TO MOOSE JAW

TO REGINA

PORT OF
RAYMOND
(24 HRS)

PORT OF
OPHEIM

PORT OF
SCOBEY

CANADA
MONTANA

HAVRE

ROCKY BOYS
INDIAN
RESERVATION

FORT
BELKNAP
INDIAN
RESERVATION

24

5

16

2

FORT PECK INDIAN RESERVATION

191

GLASGOW

HI - LINE

TO WILLISTON

SIDNEY

13

FORT PECK LAKE

MISSOURI RIVER

200

NORTH DAKOTA
MONTANA

81

LEWISTOWN

200

59

GLENDIVE

94

BIG OPEN

TO
BISMARCK

12

7

87

YELLOWSTONE RIVER

MILES CITY

12

TO BOWMAN

39

BILLINGS

94

90

87

LITTLE BIG HORN BATTLEFIELD
NATIONAL MONUMENT

SOUTHEAST
TRIANGLE

SOUTH DAKOTA
MONTANA

NORTHERN CHEYENNE
INDIAN RESERVATION

BROADUS

78

212

72

CROW INDIAN
RESERVATION

59

212

BIGHORN CANYON
NATIONAL
RECREATION
AREA

87

MONTANA
WYOMING

TO
BELLE FOURCHE

CODY

SHERIDAN

0   50mi

20

0   50km

GILLETTE

90

25

massive forest fires in the west. In just one decade, Montana's economy shrunk by nine percent.

The outlook for the nineties is brighter if only because most Montanans believe it can't get worse. But *Newsweek* presented a different forecast for the upper Great Plains and northern Rocky Mountain region, including Montana, in a 1989 article entitled "America's Outback." Describing the area as a "lost frontier" prone to chronic recession and decline, the magazine pronounced it, for all intents and purposes, dead. Montanans had mixed reactions to the article, rejecting the death sentence but warming up to a new nickname. America's Outback. They liked it. In two words, it sized up what they love about their state.

No one ever said it was easy to live in Montana. But for the few who can afford it, it is the *only* place to live.

■ A LAND AT ODDS WITH ITSELF

From the high plains of eastern Montana to the Rocky Mountain west, Montana has never made much sense as one state. Physically, economically, politically, and socially, it has always been at odds with itself. Back in 1880, when Montana was still a territory, the vast majority of its residents lived in the west, as a majority do today. According to the historian K. Ross Toole, no one gave much thought to the plains at that time. In his 1959 history of the state, *Montana: An Uncommon Land,* he theorized that in 1889, when it came time to draw state boundaries, the plains were "simply marked off and drawn in."

The result is a sprawling state that is pulled in opposite directions. Endowed with adequate rainfall, minerals, timber, rivers, and abundant wildlife, the mountains and valleys of western Montana support a diversified economy of farming and ranching, mining, logging, tourism, and recreation. Most of Montana's population live in these stream-fed western valleys. (Even so, the region's largest city, Missoula, has a population of just under 43,000.)

While western Montana is considered an extension of the Pacific Northwest, it is hard to tell where eastern Montana ends and the Dakotas begin. Eastern Montana is the heart and soul of the northern Great Plains, and it has nothing to do with western Montana. Residents of Montana's extreme eastern corners travel regularly to nearby Williston, North Dakota, and Belle Fourche, South Dakota, for

The Rocky Mountain Front is where the mountains meet the plains, and where the views and the weather are always dramatic.

shopping and entertainment, and are oriented toward the Dakotas' media and public affairs. To compound this east-west schism, Montanans living along the sparsely populated northern tier are as much at home in the western Canadian cities of Regina, Moose Jaw, and Lethbridge as they are in Glasgow, Havre, and Great Falls.

WESTERN MONTANA

Topography and climate are the obvious factors that divide Montana. While the very name, Montana, is derived from the Spanish word for mountain, in fact, it applies to only a third of the state. In the mountainous west, more than two dozen distinct ranges comprise Montana's share of the Rocky Mountains. Elevations swing from 3,500 feet (1,050 m) on valley floors to the peaks of the Beartooth Plateau near Yellowstone National Park that rise above 12,000 feet (3,650 m). Many of these ranges are high enough to make their own weather, inducing precipitation that supports dense coniferous forests of fir, pine, cedar, spruce, and larch. While snow often piles up hundreds of inches, measurable precipitation ranges from 14 to 23 inches (36 to 58 cm).

The valleys that divide western Montana's mountain ranges vary from narrow, steep-sided slots to broad floors up to 50 miles (80 km) wide. Many of the state's most unforgettable mountain valleys—the Big Hole, Bitterroot, Yellowstone, Gallatin, and Madison—are named after the rivers that drain them. Beginning their journeys as nameless streams and freshets at 10,000 feet (3,050 m) and higher, these legendary rivers support agriculture, tourism, and life itself in a dry western state.

Western Montana is the land that comes to mind when most people think of the state. Powder-white peaks, alpine meadows, trout streams, and small, friendly towns. It's an addictive landscape for both residents and visitors, but not for those who thrive on the infinite sky and open spaces of eastern Montana.

EASTERN MONTANA

Unlike spectacular western landscapes, the plains of eastern Montana are regarded by many as monotonous. In truth, however, they are full of topographical surprises, like badlands and breaks, sandstone outcrops, glacial lakes, coulees, ice caves, and even an occasional pine forest and cluster of hills or low-lying mountains. Unlike western Montana, where weather arrives on westerly air flows from the Pacific

Ocean, eastern Montana is raked by arctic air from the north. January temperatures seldom exceed 10° F (-12° C) in northeastern Montana, and snow rarely stays because steady winds whisk it away. In summer, these plains bake in the sun; temperatures in the 90s F (30s C) are not uncommon. Officially classified as semi-arid, the plains of eastern Montana receive meager amounts of moisture, with normal precipitation levels ranging from 12 to 16 inches (30 to 40 cm). Drought is a fact of life here.

Other than occasional scrub-pine forests and cottonwood-lined river bottoms, the plains consist largely of short grasses that bend to prevailing west winds and starve the landscape of eye-catching color. These protein-rich grasses support a proud livestock industry, a legacy of the great trail drives that moved cattle and cowboys from Texas to Montana beginning in the 1860s. Much has changed since the days of the open range. Blizzards and barbed wire have reduced herds significantly, but cattle still outnumber people three to one in Montana. Underlain by immense coal beds and a portion of the massive Williston Oil Basin, the eastern Montana plains also conceal vast reserves of energy fuels.

Eastern Montana is hard country. Its sharp edges are branded on the weather-creased faces of its residents. It is also austerely beautiful country. If you seek a vision of what the West was like before filmmakers and fashion designers got hold of it, a trip to the high plains of eastern Montana will satisfy your soul.

THE LAND BETWEEN

No one can point to a line where eastern Montana becomes western Montana. Some say it's as far west as the Rocky Mountain Front, where the mountains literally meet the plains; some say it's as far east as the lower Musselshell River, beyond which both population and topographical relief are in short supply. Between these extremes lies Montana's middle ground—a vast area of isolated mountain ranges, buttes and plains, great rivers and small streams, a grain-rich farm belt, and Montana's two largest cities—Billings and Great Falls.

Residents of this mid-section enjoy the best of both Montanas. The mountains are never out of view; instead of dominating the landscape, however, they lend it depth and perspective. The contrast between mountains and plains is nowhere more striking than it is along the Rocky Mountain Front, seen from the stretch of highway between Augusta and Browning. To the west is a solid wall of peaks and domes, a view that changes seasonally, daily, even hourly, as clouds and storms collide above and around them. To the east is an unrelenting stretch of plains, broken only by the geometry of crop rotation and an occasional shadowy butte suspended on the horizon.

The Rocky Mountain Front is responsible for a unique weather pattern that can take the edge off winter in central Montana. Known among Indians as "snow eaters," warm winter winds called Chinooks sweep down the eastern slopes of the Rockies, raising temperatures and melting snow along the way. Montana's Chinook winds have been known to lift January temperatures as much as 47° F (26° C) in seven minutes. A meteorologist in Havre onces witnessed something even more startling: a rise of 26° F (15° C) in 45 seconds. Strongest at the base of the Rockies, Chinooks run out of steam as they scoot across the plains, but their moderating effects are felt as far east as the Upper Yellowstone Valley near Billings.

In addition to year-round recreation, the mountains of central Montana provide relief from the weather extremes that beset the plains. In summer, they offer cool refuge from the simmering lowlands; in winter, they block frigid weather systems and, in some cases, produce their own.

Besides their physical differences, east and west differ in the character and outlook of their residents, and the source of their affection for Montana. In the east, that affection begins and ends with the sky and stretches to the horizon in every direction. Although the mountains of western Montana are responsible for the state's name, eastern Montana can rightfully claim Montana's most popular nickname, "Big Sky Country." To an eastern Montanan, mountains are a clutter on the landscape, a barrier that wrecks the view and shackles the spirit. But to a western Montanan, they are food for the soul, and the trade-off that makes Montana's lackluster economy worthwhile. For it is in these mountains—along their hiking trails and trout streams, in their roadless backcountry, and on their skytop peaks—that western Montanans find the compensation that matters most to them.

While Montana's diverse landscape is inherently divisive, the land in all its contours and moods is the glue that binds Montanans together. Whether they are digging out from under six feet (two m) of snow in Red Lodge or facing their fourth heart-breaking year of drought in Wolf Point, Montanans share a camaraderie that comes from a love of the land and a willingness to take it on nature's terms.

The Pryor Mountains are a remote, highland junction of desert and ice west of Bighorn Canyon on Montana's southern border.

H I S T O R Y

■ GEOLOGY AND PREHISTORY

SOME OF MONTANA'S MOST SCENIC FEATURES and historic treasures were born in violent natural acts that place the exploits of humanity in the realm of light comedy. Fire and ice, wind and water, massive glaciers, rivers of molten lava, shallow seas, swamps, and deserts: these are the ancient forces that sculpted the mountains, scoured the plains, chiseled river canyons, scooped out great basins, and nurtured a prehistoric kingdom of dinosaurs.

While the so-called "basement" rocks that underlie the northern Rockies can be traced back 2.5 to 3 billion years, the Rockies themselves did not begin forming until some 100 million years ago. Before that, Montana was a flat plain, flooded periodically by shallow seas. The action that created the dramatic landscape we know today began when giant masses of molten rock deep within the Earth began rising to the surface. Pushing and heaving, they broke the surface to create some of the peaks that distinguish the Western mountain ranges. The action was compounded by tectonic pressure that pushed, folded, and thrust soft, upper sedimentary rocks eastward. Further tension stretched the Earth's crust east and west, allowing north-south blocks to tilt upward. The result was a massive jumble of mountains ranges, whose peaks and valleys have been further defined by rivers and glaciers over millions of years. As the mountains grew from the plain, surrounding seas drained away. Plants that had accumulated in swamps along the edge of an inland sea were added to the layers of marine sediment formed by periodic flooding. Millions of years of pressure cooked and compacted this material into thick beds of sediment containing the petroleum, gas, and coal that now lie beneath the plains of central and eastern Montana.

After the Rockies were formed, some of the peaks were buried under thick caps of ice during several ice ages. This was an era of colder climates and massive snowfall, when more snow fell during the winter than melted in summer. Gradually, these snow accumulations turned to glaciers—rivers of solid ice that flowed and slid down mountains, gouging valleys and carving the details of today's landscape. Vestiges of these ice ages are most visible in northwestern Montana's **Glacier National Park,** which gets its name not from the glistening white snow patches that cling to its mountains today, but from the ancient ice sheets that molded this magnificent park. Glacier's photogenic vistas, its sculptured peaks, chiseled valleys, dazzling lakes, waterfalls, and cascades are all testimony to the last great glaciers that melted about 10,000 years ago.

Fire and ice were the artists in **Yellowstone National Park.** Floods created by melting snow and glaciers etched the majestic Grand Canyon of the Yellowstone, and superheated water just below the crust continues to erupt from complex underground plumbing as spouting geysers, bubbling mud caldrons, hot springs, and steaming fumaroles. Yellowstone was created by a series of volcanic eruptions, the most recent of which began more than a million years ago and culminated in a blast 600,000 years ago that has no peer in recorded history. The explosion spewed tons of gases and hot ash across North America, with fragments landing more than a thousand miles away. Estimates rank this cataclysmic blowout anywhere from 1,000 to 10,000 times greater than the Mount St. Helens blast of 1980. Intense geothermal forces are still at work beneath the Earth's shallow surface in Yellowstone Park, making it the biggest and busiest hot spot on the globe.

■ THE AGE OF DINOSAURS

For 140 million years—more than twice as long as mammals have dominated the Earth—dinosaurs ruled the world. No one knows for sure why they vanished so abruptly, but research in Montana is shifting attention to how these prehistoric creatures lived. Recent fossil discoveries by Montana paleontologist Jack Horner have forced scientists to rethink old theories about dinosaurs, long perceived as solitary, cold-blooded beasts that relied more on their brawn than their brains for survival. Horner, who presides over the paleontology wing of Montana's Museum of the Rockies, made one of his field's most important discoveries in 1978. Following a tip from an amateur paleontologist, he unearthed a nest of dinosaur eggs and hatchlings on the eastern slope of the Rocky Mountains near Choteau. Later digs revealed more nests and a huge bone bed that lend credence to an emerging theory that dinosaurs were warm-blooded creatures that behaved more like birds than reptiles, traveled in herds, and cared for their young.

It is no mere coincidence that Montana is the epicenter of some of the most significant research taking place in the field of paleontology. Its prehistory makes it a perfect laboratory. As the Rockies were forming and dinosaurs were dying, sediment sloughed off the rising slopes and formed a layer over their remains. Then came the glaciers, scouring the plains and removing the layers of sedimentation that had buried the dinosaurs. Today, fossils are found on or near the surface of a land that has been largely undisturbed by industrial or residential development.

A must-see attraction for dinosaur lovers of all ages is the **Museum of the Rockies,** located on the campus of Montana State University in Bozeman. In addition to lifelike displays, exhibits, and a fossil preparation room where visitors can watch scientists at work, the museum sponsors summer field trips that enable visitors to participate in dinosaur digs with knowledgeable "bone hunters." Field training in fossil location and identification is also available at the **Old Trail Museum** in Choteau, near the site where dinosaur nests were first discovered. Visitors to southeastern Montana will be surprised by the **Carter County Museum** in the tiny town of Ekalaka. Developed by local amateur paleontologists, the museum houses an impressive collection of bones and fossils, including the 35-foot-long

A robotic Triceratops family greets visitors at the Museum of the Rockies in Bozeman.

(11-m) skeleton of a duck-billed dinosaur named *Anatosaurus*. Long recognized as an important paleontological site, this area has also turned up some of the oldest evidence of humanity in North America.

■ THE HUMAN RECORD

THE FIRST MONTANANS

Montana's human record is but a millisecond on the geologic timetable. It is believed that Asiatic peoples first entered North America between 10,000 and 30,000 years ago during a period of glaciation when sea levels dropped enough to form a land bridge across the Bering Strait. These Asian migrants traveled south from Alaska along the eastern slope of the Rockies on what has become known as the "Great North Trail." Some wandered all the way to South America.

Those who remained in the north left evidence indicating they hunted big game animals, including the now extinct mammoth. Following a major climatic change that turned the Great Plains into a desert, both the hunters and the hunted disappeared. Beginning about 5,000 to 4,000 B.C., a different crowd moved north from the desert southwest. More foragers than hunters, these migrants occupied the western valleys. About 2,000 years later, the last wave of prehistoric migrants—the so-called "late hunters"—entered Montana from the south and west. Historians believe they were the direct ancestors of today's Indian tribes. Evidence of their culture lingers in the teepee rings and buffalo jumps that still exist on the plains of central and eastern Montana.

Plains Indians as we know them today did not arrive in Montana until after 1620. Flathead Indians, the only Montana tribe living west of the Continental Divide, came about a century earlier. In a period of little more than 250 years, several tribes flourished on the plains and in the western valleys before they were displaced by non-native expansionism. By the early 1880s, hide hunters had shot the buffalo to virtual extinction, and similarly rubbed out the lifestyle and culture of the Indians who relied on it for their food, shelter, clothing, and tools. In their *Montana: A History of Two Centuries,* historians Michael Malone and Richard Roeder describe Montana's native peoples as a "highly diversified group, combining plateau-mountain peoples from the west, Great Basin Indians from the south, hardy plainsmen from the north and east." They sum up the brief rise and fall of recent Indian culture in Montana this way:

HISTORIC MONTANA

ASSINIBOINE,
GROS VENTRES,
CREE INDIANS

FORT ASSINIBOINE

CHIEF JOSEPH
BATTLEFIELD (1877)

KID CURRY

FORT
MUSSELSHELL

FORT MAGINNIS

NEZ PERCE TRAIL

ASSINIBOINE
AND
SIOUX INDIANS

FORT UNION
(AMERICAN FUR CO.)

FORT BUFORD

LEWIS & CLARK TRAIL

MISSOURI RIVER

YELLOWSTONE RIVER

CLARK'S RETURN ROUTE   FORT KEOGH

POMPEYS PILLAR

BATTLE OF
THE LITTLE BIGHORN (1876)

BATTLE OF
THE ROSEBUD (1876)

CROW
COUNTRY

NORTHERN
CHEYENNE
INDIANS

TEXAS LONGHORN TRAIL

TEXAS LONGHORN TRAIL

BOZEMAN TRAIL

*P*rior to 1800, Montana was the eye of a cultural hurricane, where Indians migrating from all directions, bringing horses and guns with them, met to create new and unusual societies. These Indians would share a common fate in the years following 1800, as Americans and Canadians drove them from their lands, reduced them by war, disease, and alcohol, and shattered their native cultures.

By the 1800s, international interest in the North American fur trade was threatening a cultural showdown between natives and newcomers. But no single event hastened the inevitable clash as did the first U.S. government contact with the Indians—the Lewis and Clark Expedition of 1804–06. Among the goals of the expedition was an inventory of the West's fur-trade potential. Shortly after Meriwether Lewis reported that "that portion of the continent watered by the Missouri and all its branches . . . is richer in beaver and otter than any country on earth," trappers and traders arrived in great numbers, and the West, as the Indians knew it, was changed forever.

Lewis and Clark hold a council with some of the Indians they met on their transcontinental trek. (Bancroft Library, University of California at Berkeley)

ANGLO SETTLERS

As a state, Montana is just a kid. Only 100 years old, it is a state where you can learn history at the knee of an elder who has lived it. Among Montana's native peoples, the "Old Ones" sustain a rich oral tradition with songs and stories about the buffalo and coyote, the seasons, "Sun Chief," and the "Above Ones." Homesteaders recount the isolation, dust, drought, and drudgery that awaited them in Montana after they swallowed the railroads' claims of mild winters, prodigious crop yields, and unlimited opportunity. Old-timers in the stockgrowers industry heard first-hand accounts of the brutal winter of 1886–87 which, together with overgrazing and barbed wire, brought an end to Montana's legendary open-range era. Retired miners can pinpoint the hour of the Smith Mine disaster in Bearcreek, when 74 coal miners were killed in an underground explosion, or the night radical labor leader Frank Little was hanged in Butte after delivering a fiery speech against U.S. involvement in World War I. All significant in the development of the West, these legends and events are still within reach in Montana, where history is a hands-on affair.

Early homestead hype promised health and prosperity to all who ventured west. (Montana Historical Society)

True to its genre, the romance of the West is a highly idealized account of great deeds and adventures, conquest, and fortune. Indeed, great fortunes were made in Montana, but always at the expense of the state and its residents. The fresh face of Montana that greets visitors today belies a past of abuse and exploitation. Since 1805, when Lewis and Clark unlocked the West for the fur traders, prospectors, miners, loggers, stockmen, and sodbusters who followed, Montana's history has been that of an isolated colony held captive by outside interests. Armed with capital to develop the riches of this sprawling land, they trapped its beaver, slaughtered its buffalo, plowed its virgin grasslands, fenced its plains, logged its timber, mined its precious metals, and removed tons of earth to expose its thick seams of coal.

Nowhere is the legacy of Montana's extractive economy more apparent than in Butte, where the environmental wreckage that began a century ago still blights the landscape. In its heyday, Butte was known as "the richest hill on Earth." The hill that produced more than $2 billion worth of gold, silver, copper, and zinc is now a crater. Underground mines were gradually replaced by a huge open-pit mine that opened in 1955. Until it was closed in 1983, the Berkeley Pit ate away at the city like a beast that feeds on its own flesh. Once the nation's largest producer of copper and silver, Butte now has the distinction of being one of the nation's largest Superfund sites, targeted by the federal government in 1983 as part of a massive effort to rid the nation of hazardous wastes.

Once the "richest hill on Earth," the copper-mining town of Butte is still known for its scarred landscape and spirited people. (Montana Historical Society)

AN ERA OF EXPLOITATION

The colossal fortunes created by Butte's concentrated deposits of metal ores never remained in Butte long enough to mitigate the damage created by their extraction. Instead, they wound up in the hands of three principal entrepreneurs, who came to be known as Montana's "copper kings," and the Wall Street investors who backed them in their mining ventures. Montanans had an opportunity to re-examine this chapter in their state's history of exploitation in 1989, the year they celebrated their statehood centennial. Residents got a glimpse of the fabulous wealth one of those copper kings amassed when the Corcoran Gallery of Art in Washington, D.C., agreed to lend a portion of its priceless William A. Clark art collection to Montana for temporary display at the Yellowstone Art Center in Billings. Clark assembled his collection of European paintings, Renaissance ceramics, sculpture, and antiquities after building a mining fortune in Butte and buying a seat in the United States Senate. Driven by political and financial ambitions, Clark had barely won election to the Senate in 1899 before he was derailed by rival copper king Marcus Daly, who engineered a Senate investigation of alleged campaign fraud and bribery. Earlier, the two went head to head and pocketbook to pocketbook over Clark's campaign to become a territorial delegate to Congress and his successful drive to make Helena the permanent state capital. Following the Daly-inspired investigation into Montana politics, Clark was found guilty of bribery and promptly unseated. Clark then formed an alliance with Butte's third rising star, Augustus Heinze, who built his mining empire by bribing the courts to settle property ownership disputes in his favor. Together, Clark and Heinze set out to discredit Daly and elect a pro-Clark legislature, which they did. Because United States senators were still elected by state legislatures at that time, Clark soon regained the Senate seat he had so long desired.

Following a single, undistinguished term in the Senate, Clark took his Montana-made fortune to New York City, where he built an elegant mansion on Fifth Avenue and filled it with one of America's major turn-of-the-century art collections, consisting of approximately 800 works of original art. Thought to be one of the world's eight richest men at the time, Clark is said to have left an estate valued at $150 million upon his death in 1925. Heinze reaped $10 million from the sale of his Butte mining interests in 1906. He, too, was drawn to New York. But unlike Clark, who built his fortune over a lifetime of studied and shrewd investments, Heinze engaged in some madcap ventures on Wall Street and lost his millions almost as soon as he arrived. Daly, who died in 1900, divided his assets between the town of Anaconda, where he built a huge smelter to process his ore, and southwestern Montana's scenic Bitterroot Valley, where he built a 42-room mansion and pursued his passion for breeding and racing fine horses on a baronial country estate.

The ultimate victor of the so-called "war of the copper kings" was Marcus Daly's original mining company, the Anaconda Copper Mining Company, which gradually absorbed the interests of all three men. At one time controlled by Standard Oil and William Rockefeller, Anaconda's Montana empire held mines, smelters, lumber and railroad operations, coal fields, and most of the state's major daily newspapers in the snakelike grip for which the company was named. The loser was Montana, which was dominated for years by one corporation.

Surely the most colorful story of conquest and development of Montana's vast resources, the story of the copper kings is not unique in Montana history. The importation of capital, exploitation of resources, and exportation of profits has been a recurring pattern since the fur-trade era, when beaver pelts left Montana by the boatload. Later in the century, Montana's "free grass" and "free water" gave rise to a cattle boom that was financed largely by British capitalists and East Coast investors, the same crowd that developed the mining frontier and stretched railroad tracks across the continent.

In his *Montana: An Uncommon Land,* historian K. Ross Toole captured Montana's historic dilemma: "Distance meant cost, cost meant capital, capital meant absentee ownership, absentee ownership meant absentee control, and absentee control meant operation in the essential interest of outsiders with local interests a very secondary consideration. And so it was with beaver, beef, sheep, silver, copper, oil, and, to a lesser extent, even with lumber and wheat."

Marcus Daly, founder of Anaconda and one of Butte's "copper kings." (Montana Historical Society)

SAVING THE LAND

Beginning in the 1970s, during an unusual period of prosperity, urbanization, and political activism, Montanans began to write a new chapter of history by fighting back to save the land they loved. Fueled by a global energy crisis, large, out-of-state coal companies were sending their lease hounds into the cattle country of southeastern Montana to secure mineral rights to the low-sulfur coal that lay in thick seams beneath prairie grasslands. In 1971 the federal government released a study calling for construction of 42 new coal-fired generating plants in the northern Plains states, half of them targeted for Montana. In addition to threatening eastern Montana's agricultural values and diverting enormous quantities of precious water from the Yellowstone River, the power plants would have obscured Montana's open spaces with a network of high-voltage transmission lines designed to carry electricity from the mines to urban markets.

Determined not to repeat their history, Montanans pulled together to keep their state from becoming what some described as a "national sacrifice area." In the end, the energy crisis dissipated and the North Central Power Study was shelved. Millions of tons of coal were stripped from the plains of southeastern Montana, however, creating a boom that gave rise to a burst of landmark environmental legislation. Some of the nation's most stringent conservation laws can be traced two decades back to Montana's legislative halls and courtrooms.

Inevitably, the prosperity of the seventies gave way to a recession in the eighties, liberals lost ground to conservatives, and jobs became the paramount issue of the day. Daily newspaper headlines focus attention on disputes between Montana's conservation community and the state's industrial giants over forest and mining practices, wilderness classification, cleanup of hazardous wastes, subdivision development, air pollution, oil drilling along the Rocky Mountain Front, grizzly bears, bald eagles, gray wolves, and a seemingly endless array of issues that won't go away.

Montanans are torn. While they wring their hands about the emigration of their youth who cannot find good-paying jobs at home, they are reluctant to let go of the reasons why they live here. Face it. Montana simply wouldn't be Montana without its bright skies, open spaces, great trout streams, and abundant wildlife.

MONTANA'S ETHNIC ROOTS

The contrary values of independence and neighborliness define the character of a Montanan. This dual personality can be traced more than a century back to the explorers, fur traders, prospectors, miners, laborers, stockmen, and homesteaders who abandoned all that was familiar to them for the promise of freedom and independence in the American West. They came, one by one and family by family, from the East and Midwest, and from ancestral neighborhoods—the Piedmont region of northern Italy, the Volga River valley of Russia, the Pyrenees, Croatia, Scandinavia, and other European enclaves. Together with relatives and friends, they brought Old World place names that still remain in the neighborhoods and towns they built. Finn Town, Caledonia, Scotch Coulee, Dublin Gulch, Belgrade, Glasgow, Frenchtown, and Amsterdam, to name just a few in Montana.

While the state's European ethnic heritage has been diluted over four and five generations as it has elsewhere in America, remnant populations of these clannish settlements still exist in the once-booming mining and smelter towns of Butte, Anaconda, Red Lodge, East Helena, and Black Eagle. The colorful mining city of Butte, which erupted in the 1880s as the greatest mining camp in the West, has the most visible ethnic mix. St. Patrick's Day is the biggest day of the year here, drawing thousands of Butte Irish and would-be Irish from throughout the state and across the nation. But Serbian Christmas and Chinese New Year are also observed in Butte, where as many as 60 different nationalities once lived and worked together.

Scandinavian immigrants left their imprint on farming communities and lumber towns, and Scottish names are still prevalent in ranching communities, like Miles City. Germans were the largest, single ethnic group to settle in Montana. They came as homesteaders and their descendants still farm near small communities throughout northern and eastern Montana. To the south, the Yellowstone River Valley attracted Russian Germans who became successful sugar beet producers.

NATIVE PEOPLES

Preceding all of these immigrant groups and later yielding to their new society were the Indians of the plains and plateau. Unlike the immigrants who settled in one place, the ancestors of Montana's present-day Indian tribes roamed the plains as hunters, relying on vast herds of bison that once ranged throughout the American West. Like the European immigrants, they left an imprint on the land in the colorful place names that honor their chiefs and perpetuate their language: Chinook, Ekalaka, Charlo, Kalispell, and Yaak.

OWNING THE EARTH

*T*he earth was created by the assistance of the sun, and it should be left as it was . . . The country was made without lines of demarcation, and it is no man's business to divide it . . . I see the whites all over the country gaining wealth, and see their desire to give us lands which are worthless . . . The earth and myself are of one mind. The measure of the land and the measure of our bodies are the same. Say to us if you can say it, that you were sent by the Creative Power to talk to us. Perhaps you think the Creator sent you here to dispose of us as you see fit. If I thought you were sent by the Creator I might be induced to think you had a right to dispose of me. Do not misunderstand me, but understand me fully with reference to my affection for the land. I never said the land was mine to do with it as I chose. The one who has the right to dispose of it is the one who has created it. I claim a right to live on my land, and accord you the privilege to live on yours.

—Chief Joseph, 1832-1904

Chief Joseph of the Nez Perce Indians. (Haynes Foundation Collection, Montana Historical Society)

Moving into Montana from the north and east were the powerful Blackfeet Indians, whose fierce war parties dominated north-central Montana and whose influence reached as far south as present-day Yellowstone National Park. Montana's largest Indian tribe, they now live on the Blackfeet Indian Reservation at the eastern edge of Glacier National Park. To the east of the Blackfeet were the Atsinas, who came to be known as the Gros Ventres, or "Big Bellies." Once allies of the Blackfeet, the Gros Ventres later aligned themselves with the Assiniboine and now live with them on the Fort Belknap Indian Reservation between the Milk River and the Little Rocky Mountains in north-central Montana. Another band of Assiniboine Indians aligned themselves with the Yanktonai Sioux; the two tribes now live together on northeastern Montana's Fort Peck Indian Reservation.

Moving into the Yellowstone River valley from the east were the Crows, enemies of the Blackfeet. Once ranging over a broad area that stretched from the upper Yellowstone River into the Big Horn and Wind River mountains of Wyoming, they now live on the Crow Indian Reservation, covering most of Big Horn County in south-central Montana. Between the Crow reservation and the Tongue River to the east is the Northern Cheyenne Indian Reservation. The Northern Cheyenne arrived in Montana later than most other Plains Indians but were here in time to join forces with the Sioux to defeat Gen. George Armstrong Custer in 1876 at the Battle of the Little Bighorn. The last Plains Indians to arrive were the Chippewas and Crees of Algonquin heritage, and the Metis or "mixed Bloods" which represent a racial mixture of Cree, Assiniboine, Chippewa, and French. Rocky Boy's Indian Reservation lies northwest of the Bear Paw Mountains in north-central Montana.

To the west of the Continental Divide were the tribes of the Columbia Plateau, which clustered in villages and relied on plants and fish. Plateau Indians living in Montana, most notably the Salish and Kootenai, combined the two lifestyles, crossing the mountains to hunt buffalo in the summer and returning to their villages in the winter. Today, the Salish and Kootenai live together on Montana's westernmost Flathead Indian Reservation. Once dominant, these native peoples now comprise only six per cent of the population. They live on seven semi-sovereign reservations. Although they coalesce on some issues, they are, in essence, seven separate nations living within the borders of Montana.

Indian teepees still cut a distinctive profile against the sky, especially at powwow time. (photo by Douglas O'Looney)

MONTANANS TODAY

With nearly 800,000 residents, Montana has been likened to a mid-size American city, each town representing a different neighborhood with a distinct personality. Helena is the government town, Miles City the cowboy town, Billings the business town, and Missoula the university town. Each of these larger cities appears in bold type on the map of Montana and is, in itself, a bold expression of what Montana is about. But for a deeper understanding of what it is like to live in a rural Western state, look to the smaller towns, like Libby, Browning, Wolf Point, and Roundup.

Small-town America is in decline nationally, and so it is in Montana. But don't be fooled by sleepy-looking towns like Malta and Big Timber, and so many others with populations of less than 2,500. Compared with America's urban centers and mid-size cities, these small communities look like the end of the line. What do they do here, you will wonder. Not to worry. Between kids, sports, church, and local government, most residents are busy every night of the week. There are 4-H programs, basketball practices, choir rehearsals, and fund-raisers for the volunteer fire department, the senior citizens' center, and the family whose budget has been ravaged by a medical crisis. Somehow, though, there always seems to be half an hour to catch up with friends over coffee, or half a day to help a neighboring farm family with harvest.

Because Montana is so sparsely settled, neighbors are valued. Without asking, neighbors rely on one another to watch their homes while they are away or fill in when help is needed at critical times of the year, like calving and branding. Here is how one rancher describes relations in the low-lying Bull Mountains of south-central Montana: "We've worked together so long, we know what needs to be done without being told. If something happens to one of our families, our neighbors know our business better than we do and the work just goes on." This is what community is all about, and it is engendered by Montana's rural demography. Montanans rely on the entire state to provide the network of friends and business contacts most Americans find in the cities where they live and work.

The difference between commuting across the state in Montana and across town in one of America's major metro areas is that in Montana, there is nothing between Point A and Point B. Nothing manmade, that is, except an occasional gas station or roadside saloon. Montanans become intimately familiar with the look of the land as they drive to Helena to testify at legislative hearings, Miles City to place a bid at a livestock auction, or Great Falls to do some shopping. And they are all too familiar with ground blizzards, black ice, and snow-packed mountain passes. As soon as they learn to drive a car or handle a rifle, Montanans learn self-sufficiency. Neighbors are to be trusted, but it is this ability to take care of one's self that defines the Montana spirit.

THE LEWIS AND CLARK EXPEDITION

Twentieth-century moon walks aside, the Lewis and Clark Expedition remains America's greatest adventure. This was its first transcontinental trek, and much of it took place across what is now Montana. The nation's third president, Thomas Jefferson, saw westward expansion as the key not only to inland commerce but also to control of a growing trade with China via the Pacific. With a single real estate deal, Jefferson doubled the size of the United States when he bought Louisiana Territory from France in 1803 for a sum of $16 million. The Louisiana Purchase reached from the Gulf of Mexico to the Canadian border through what is now the nation's midsection; its width stretched from the Mississippi to the Rockies.

To explore this vast and uncharted land, Jefferson appointed a secret "Corps of Discovery" headed by his private secretary—Meriwether Lewis—along with William Clark, younger brother of Gen. George Rogers Clark. On May 14, 1804, their party of 45 soldiers, guides, interpreters, and others set out from St. Louis, poling up the Missouri by flatboat and keelboat. They spent that winter in a North Dakota Mandan village, and continued upriver in canoes and keelboats the following spring.

The expedition crossed into what is now Montana on April 27, 1805, and followed the Missouri to its Montana headwaters, and to what Lewis described as the "snowy barrier" of the Continental Divide. Here, Shoshone Indians provided guides and horses to cross the Rockies. The party then followed the Clearwater, Snake, and Columbia rivers down the western slopes, reaching the Pacific Ocean that fall. They built a fort near the mouth of the Columbia River for winter quarters, and re-crossed the mountains the following summer.

On the return trip east, Lewis and Clark split the expedition into two parties near what is now Lolo, Montana. Lewis and his detachment went northeast to explore the Blackfoot, Sun, and Marias rivers; Clark and his group headed southeast to explore the Yellowstone River. Six weeks later, they reached their rendezvous, near the mouth of the Yellowstone River, within nine days of one another. In the words of Robert Fletcher, popularizer of Montana history: "Considering distance and unexplored terrain, they were tolerably punctual."

On September 23, 1806, the expedition finally arrived back in St. Louis, long after everyone but President Jefferson had given them up for dead. The trip proved a vital step in bringing the Northwest under the U.S. flag, and in revealing the great wealth of this land to those back east. In just over 28 months, the expedition had traveled more than 8,000 miles (12,800 km) by foot, horseback, and boat. Well over a quarter of that distance encompassed what is now Montana.

William Clark

RETRACING LEWIS AND CLARK'S FOOTSTEPS

Travelers in Montana can visit several spots along the Lewis and Clark National Historic Trail, some developed, some not. Developed sites accessible by car are: **Missouri Headwaters State Park** near Three Forks, where the expedition traced the "heretofore conceived boundless Missouri" to its birthplace at the confluence of the Jefferson, Gallatin, and Madison rivers; **Giant Springs State Park** in Great Falls, where Clark discovered a huge "fountain or spring" during a formidable, 18-mile (29-km) portage around a series of waterfalls (now altered by dams and development); and the **Lolo Pass Visitor Center** on US 12 at the Montana-Idaho border, which explains the significance of both the Lewis and Clark Expedition and the Nez Perce Indians in this part of the state. A national Lewis and Clark Historic Center, emphasizing the expedition's encounters with the Indian culture, is scheduled to open in 1993 at Giant Springs State Park.

Meriwether Lewis

Portraits courtesy of Independence National Historic Park, Philadelphia

BOAT TOURS

One of the most enjoyable ways to retrace Lewis and Clark's journey is by boat. Commercial boat tours operate on the Missouri at the **Gates of the Mountains,** off Interstate 15 north of Helena where the river flows through a narrow canyon flanked by what Lewis described as "the most remarkable clifts that we have yet seen," and also at the White Cliffs area of the **Upper Missouri National Wild and Scenic River** below Fort Benton. A canoe rental and shuttle service on the river near Loma offers floaters the option of exploring the river on their own.

MAPS

Several maps provide detailed information on the paths of Lewis and Clark. These include: **"Lewis and Clark Trail,"** a National Park Service map available from Travel Montana, tel. (800) 541-1447; **"Lewis and Clark in the Rocky Mountains,"** a map of the expedition's route through western Montana, available from the U.S. Forest Service, Box 7669, Missoula, MT 59807; tel. 329-3511; **"The Explorers at the Portage,"** a map of the expedition's portage route around the Great Falls of the Missouri, available from the Great Falls Chamber of Commerce, Box 2127, Great Falls, MT 59403, tel. 761-4434; and **"Floater's Guide to the Upper Missouri National Wild and Scenic River,"** available from the Bureau of Land Management, Airport Rd., Lewistown, MT 59457, tel. 538-7461.

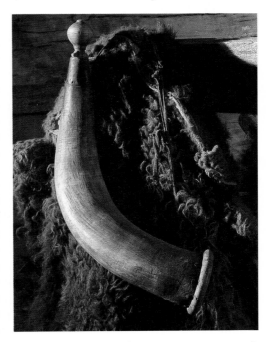

Frontier still life, displayed at Fort Benton's Museum of the Upper Missouri

THE GREAT OUTDOORS

IF HOME IS WHERE THE HEART IS, THEN THE SOUL OF A MONTANAN resides in the great outdoors. Here, it is still possible to retreat to the woods or the plains and never see another person.

Not all states were created equal—within Montana, there are two national parks and a national recreation area, 10 national forests, 15 wilderness areas, eight national wildlife refuges, 370 miles (590 km) of national wild and scenic river, and several national scenic trails, including the Continental Divide Trail. Complementing these federal holdings are 60 state parks, seven state forests, and roughly 600 miles (1,000 km) of prized, blue-ribbon trout streams.

These natural areas are the result of visionary Montanans who fought to preserve their state's rivers, forests, and open spaces. A vigilant conservation community continues this tradition by keeping watch on many fronts, ranging from forest practices and mined land reclamation to streambed protection and cleanup of toxic wastes. Priceless resources like the free-flowing Yellowstone River and the trout-rich Madison, the northern Yellowstone elk herd, and the lower 48's largest populations of grizzly bears and bighorn sheep are the reward for these efforts.

In Montana, hunting and fishing are inalienable, if not divine, rights. Montanans worship at holy places like the Big Hole River, Freezeout Lake, and the C. M. Russell Game Range. They celebrate holy days like the salmon fly hatch and the opening day of antelope season. Beyond the need to feed their souls and fill their freezers, Montanans are just plain in love with wildlife. Fishing and hunting news is reported regularly in most newspapers, and a wolf sighting or the results of a new grizzly bear study merit front-page coverage. A reporter for Kalispell's *Daily Inter Lake,* published next door to Glacier National Park and the Bob Marshall Wilderness, once told a fellow journalist, "Every time a grizzly farts, we are expected to be there."

The harmony and perfect grace of trumpeter swans in flight, the soulful song of coyotes calling, or the tonic sleep that follows a day outdoors will verify the ancient doctrine that the best things in life are free. If you have forgotten that lesson and allowed your priorities to shift in accordance with the demands of careers, possessions, and other false idols, Montana outdoors is a good place to get a fix on the planet and your place in it.

■ WILDLIFE WATCHING

The best places to observe wildlife native to the northern Rockies are the parks, refuges, and wilderness areas established for their protection. On Montana's northern border, **Glacier National Park** hosts a diversity of wildlife, ranging from a five-ounce mammal called a pika to the lower 48's largest carnivore, the grizzly bear. Glacier is probably best known for the bighorn sheep and mountain goats that grace its rocky outcrops and mountaintop perches, far removed from predators. Bands of bighorns are readily seen in the Many Glacier and Haystack Butte areas. **Wildhorse Island State Park,** surrounded by Flathead Lake, is another good place to view bighorn sheep. Bighorns have flourished on this 2,165-acre island since they were transplanted here in 1940. Other wildlife include deer, coyotes, waterfowl, raptors, and songbirds. Access is by boat.

South of Flathead Lake is the **National Bison Range**, where 400 to 500 buffalo share 19,000 acres of grassland with deer, elk, bighorn sheep, and pronghorn antelope. Set amidst stunning views of the Flathead Valley and the Mission Mountains, this refuge preserves a vestige of the estimated 13 million buffalo that once roamed Montana's plains. Established in 1909, it is one of America's oldest wildlife preserves. During the summer, visitors can explore the range by car on a self-guided tour, and in spring, they are likely to see newborn calves. The most dramatic time comes with the annual buffalo roundup of early October when visitors are treated to the drama of rumbling hooves and flying dust as cowboy rangers thin the herd.

Charles M. Russell National Wildlife Refuge on the grasslands of northeastern Montana, where buffalo once roamed, is a sprawling, million-acre refuge that protects elk, bighorn sheep, deer, pronghorns, waterfowl, and upland game. It surrounds enormous Fort Peck Lake on the Missouri River, home to trout, sauger, bass, catfish, perch, pike, and paddlefish. Together with the UL Bend Wilderness, this is the only area in Montana where elk still occupy their native prairie year-round.

Pryor Mountains Wild Horse Range near Bighorn Canyon in south-central Montana forms a unique refuge. The nation's first wild horse range, this highland desert supports about 130 free-roaming mustangs, some of which may have descended from Spanish explorers' stock. This is rugged country with year-round opportunities for hiking, birding, and fossil hunting.

NATURAL FEATURES

Although primarily within Wyoming, **Yellowstone National Park** is a major drawing card for Montana visitors. Elk and bison regularly graze alongside highways, causing traffic to back up while otherwise responsible motorists simply abandon their vehicles for a better view. September is an especially good time to visit the park, when bull elk are challenging one another for possession of harems numbering as high as 30 cows each. There are usually one or two harems lolling around National Park Service headquarters at Mammoth under the jealous gaze of the bulls.

■ BIRDWATCHING

Among Montana's best birding opportunities are the refuges at Freezeout, Medicine, and Red Rock lakes. During peak migration periods, up to a million waterfowl can be observed at **Freezeout Lake,** a state-managed refuge about 40 miles (64 km) northwest of Great Falls in north-central Montana. Snow geese and tundra swans arrive by the thousands. Other resident and migratory birds include Canada geese, mallards, teal, pintails, eagles, hawks, owls, sandhill cranes, egrets, and ibis.

Spring and fall migrations bring up to 250,000 waterfowl to the **Medicine Lake National Wildlife Refuge** between Culbertson and Plentywood in Montana's extreme northeast corner. Especially important for white pelicans and occasional whooping cranes, this refuge also attracts great blue herons, cormorants, gulls, and most species of North American ducks. It encompasses Montana's smallest designated wilderness, also named Medicine Lake, which supports a small parcel of mixed-grass prairie and a large population of white-tailed deer.

Red Rock Lakes National Wildlife Refuge in southwestern Montana provides one of North America's most important nesting sites for the majestic trumpeter swan. This largest of all North American waterfowl has made a comeback here, in Montana's remote Centennial Valley. When the refuge was established in 1935, there were fewer than 100 known swans in the entire country, two-thirds of them living in this valley. Today, about 500 nesting swans in the Greater Yellowstone area are joined by another 1,000 wintertime migrants from Canada and Alaska. The refuge's lakes, marshes, and creeks also sustain 23 different kinds of waterfowl. Other residents and visitors include sandhill cranes, sage grouse, hawks, falcons, moose, elk, deer, and pronghorns.

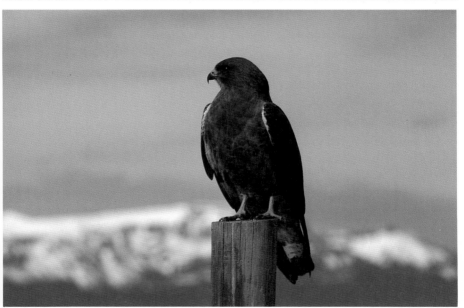

(top) Bald eagles hold fall conventions on selected Montana rivers, where they feast on spawning salmon. (bottom) Swaison's hawk is commonly seen in summer at Red Rock Lakes National Wildlife Refuge in the remote Centennial Valley. Best known for its nesting population of trumpeter swans, the refuge supports more than 200 species of birds.

■ GRIZZLY COUNTRY

Of all the animals that grace the northern Rockies and Great Plains, the one that keeps Montana truly wild is the grizzly bear. Indeed, many biologists regard the presence of the grizzly as an indicator of the quality of wilderness: where there are grizzlies, there is wilderness; where there are none, there is no wilderness.

Ever since Lewis and Clark crossed what is now Montana in 1805–06, trouble has been brewing between people and bears. Grizzlies once numbered as high as 50,000, with a range extending east to the Mississippi River. Unfortunately, rapid Anglo expansion decimated grizzly numbers and pushed them into remote Western wilderness areas where today they are federally protected under the Endangered Species Act. Gradual recovery of bear populations, especially in Montana, has stirred debate over whether the grizzly should be "delisted" as a threatened species.

Of the thousand or so grizzlies that remain in the American West, most survive in two major ecosystems: the Northern Continental Divide Ecosystem, which includes Glacier National Park and the Bob Marshall Wilderness; and the Greater Yellowstone Ecosystem which, in Montana, includes the Absaroka-Beartooth and Lee Metcalf wilderness areas and surrounding forests.

Chances of seeing a grizzly in the wild are slim. Bears do not seek human encounters. Indeed, grizzlies are so elusive that frequent visitors to bear country say they would regard it as a privilege to see one. With growing numbers of hikers visiting these wild places, however, there are bound to be conflicts. Between 1950 and 1980, visitors to Glacier Park—regarded as one of the nation's premier hiking destinations—tripled from 500,000 to 1.5 million a year. It was during that period that Glacier witnessed its first fatal mauling. Bear attacks are not always fatal to people; more often the bear is the loser. If a bear becomes conditioned to human food or cannot be successfully relocated from popular trails and campgrounds, park officials may have no choice but to destroy it. Between 1967 and 1989, eight people were killed by grizzlies in Glacier National Park. During the same period, 19 grizzlies were killed for management reasons.

If hikers are not aware of the dangers of hiking and camping in grizzly country when they arrive in Glacier or Yellowstone, they will be by the time they reach the trailhead. In an effort to keep bears and people apart, the National Park Service publishes and distributes all manner of pamphlets, leaflets, fliers, and "bear alerts," warning visitors about the hazards of entering grizzly country. Some may think the park service is resorting to scare tactics, but maulings in both parks have forced park officials to become aggressive managers of human traffic inside park boundaries.

Visitors are urged to take these precautions when hiking or camping in bear country:

- Hike in groups and make noise.
- Keep your food preparation area away from your sleeping area.
- Store food in closed containers and hang all food well away from campsites, and at least 12 feet (4 m) above the ground.
- If you encounter a bear, stay calm and give it wide berth, especially if it is a sow with cubs or a bear defending a carcass; slowly detour or quickly look for a tree to climb.
- If a bear charges, drop a pack or jacket to distract it, climb a tree, or as a last resort assume a "cannonball" position to protect your head and stomach while playing dead; never try to outrun a grizzly.

Of all the animals that dwell in Montana's spacious backcountry and federally protected wilderness areas, the one that keeps Montana truly wild is the grizzly bear. (illustration by Harry S. Robins)

Most maulings occur when people take chances with bears, by hiking alone, moving in too close to a bear, or camping away from designated camping areas. A little common sense goes a long way in bear country. So does a sense of perspective. Far more people have been killed by drownings, falls, and car accidents in Glacier and Yellowstone than by bears. Don't let the remote prospect of a bear encounter spoil your trip. For all who love the outdoors, this is a land of unspeakable beauty, where grizzlies remain a symbol of wildness.

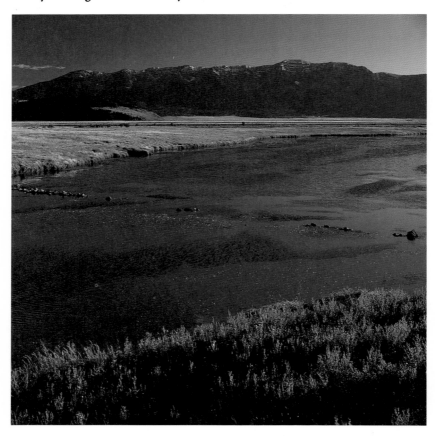

At 10,000 feet (3,048 m) above sea level, the rugged Centennial Mountains capture winter's snowfall to replenish the lakes and marshes of southwestern Montana's Red Rock Lakes National Wildlife Refuge.

TROUBLE ON THE RANGE

Montanans are happy to share their space with the kinds of animals most people see only in zoos. Most will never meet a grizzly bear or a mountain lion in the wild, but knowing they could is a source of pride. They may well be in love with the idea of wildlife, but their love is not unconditional. Livestock producers, in particular, live in perpetual tension with wildlife. While ranchers are accustomed to sharing their haystacks and grain fields with deer and antelope, they draw the line on predators that threaten their cash crop of newborn lambs and calves.

Recently, grizzly bears have begun wandering out of the mountains and onto the plains near Choteau, Dupuyer, and other ranching communities along the Rocky Mountain Front. Actual depradation along the Front has been limited to a few sheep and commercial beehives, but fear of depradation has marshalled the livestock industry against the grizzly. Troublesome bears are usually trapped and transplanted to remote mountain areas. If they stay in the mountains, chances are good that they will survive their brief encounter with humanity. But if they are tempted back to the plains by the prospect of vegetation or the scent of a fresh carcass, they may wind up as good bears, which in the minds of most ranchers, are dead bears.

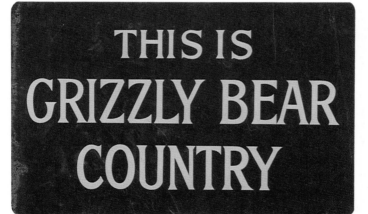

Chances of seeing a grizzly in the wild are slim. With growing numbers of visitors to Montana's backcountry, however, human-bear encounters are on the rise. The inevitable loser is the bear.

RUDYARD KIPLING GOES FISHING

*F*rom Livingstone the National Park train follows the Yellowstone River through the gate of the mountains and over arid volcanic country. A stranger in the cars saw me look at the ideal trout-stream below the windows and murmured softly: "Lie off at Yankee Jim's if you want good fishing." They halted the train at the head of a narrow valley, and I leaped literally into the arms of Yankee Jim, sole owner of a log hut, an indefinite amount of hay-ground, and constructor of twenty-seven miles of wagon-road over which he held toll right. There was the hut—the river fifty yards away, and the polished line of metals that disappeared round a bluff. That was all. The railway added the finishing touch to the already complete loneliness of the place. Yankee Jim was a picturesque old man with a talent for yarns that Ananias might have envied. It seemed to me, presumptuous in my ignorance, that I might hold my own with the old-timer if I judiciously painted up a few lies gathered in the course of my wanderings. Yankee Jim saw everyone of my tales and fifty better on the spot. He dealt in bears and Indians—never less than twenty of each; had known the Yellowstone country for years, and bore upon his body marks of Indian arrows; and his eyes had seen a squaw of the Crow Indians burned alive at the stake. He said she screamed considerable. In one point did he speak the truth—as regarded the merits of that particular reach of the Yellowstone. He said it was alive with trout. It was. I fished it from noon till twilight, and the fish bit at the brown hook as though never a fat trout-fly had fallen on water. From pebbly reaches, quivering in the heat-haze where the foot caught on stumps cut four-square by the chisel-tooth of the beaver; past the fringe of the water-willow crowded with the breeding trout-fly and alive with toads and water-snakes; over the drifted timber to the grateful shadow of big trees that darkened the holes where the fattest fish lay, I worked for seven hours. The mountain flanks on either side of the valley gave back the heat as the desert gives it, and the dry sand by the railway track, where I found a rattlesnake, was hot-iron to the touch. But the trout did not care for the heat. They breasted the boiling river for my fly and they got it. I simply dare not give my bag. At the fortieth trout I gave up counting, and I had reached the fortieth in less than two hours. They were small fish,—not one over two pounds,—but they fought like small tigers, and I lost three flies before I could understand their methods of escape. Ye gods! That was fishing, though it peeled the skin from my nose in strips.

—Rudyard Kipling, *Sea to Sea: Letters of Travel,* 1899

■ TROUT FISHING

What's so special about the fishing in Montana? All of the Rocky Mountain states are headwaters states, and all are endowed with icy, clear-running mountain streams—the kind that grow up to be legendary trout rivers. So why is it that only Montana ranks consistently with the upper Great Lakes states in terms of nonresident fishing license sales? And why is it that most trout fishermen, given a choice, would rather fish the Madison, the Gallatin, or the Yellowstone than other rivers in the continental U.S.?

The answer lies in the cooperation of visionary sportsmen's and conservation groups, and an aggressive state fish and game agency that gets high marks among its peers for fisheries management. While other states still stock their streams and rivers with hatchery-reared trout, Montana manages its thousands of miles of streams and rivers for *wild* trout. And that means taking care of the land and water that support trout.

The importance of habitat was recognized by state lawmakers in 1963 with passage of the nation's first stream preservation law. What followed over the next 20 years was a series of laws designed to protect water quality, instream flows, streambank cover, and streambed integrity. These laws provide a solid framework for the conservation of Montana's streams and rivers. Together with aggressive regulations and a growing catch-and-release ethic, they have enhanced a sport fishery of national, if not international, significance.

The rivers of southwestern Montana are the heavyweights in a statewide lineup of champions. Premier trout streams include the upper Missouri and its headwaters: the Madison, Jefferson, Gallatin, Beaverhead, and Big Hole, and the waters in and around Yellowstone National Park, including the Yellowstone itself, the Firehole, Gibbon, Lamar, Gardner, and Lewis rivers, plus Slough Creek and, just over the Idaho border, the Henry's Fork of the Snake. To the northwest are the Clark Fork and Bitterroot; to the east is the Bighorn. And in between are the countless smaller streams that feed these rivers and reward the anglers who seek them out with the promise of a day well spent.

Writer Norman Maclean in his wonderful book, *A River Runs Through It,* talks of growing up in a Montana fishing family:

> In our family, there was no clear line between religion and fly fishing. We lived at the junction of great trout rivers in western Montana, and

our father was a Presbyterian minister and a fly fisherman who tied his own flies and taught others. He told us about Christ's disciples being fishermen, and we were left to assume, as my brother and I did, that all first-class fishermen on the Sea of Galilee were fly fishermen and that John, the favorite, was a dry-fly fisherman.

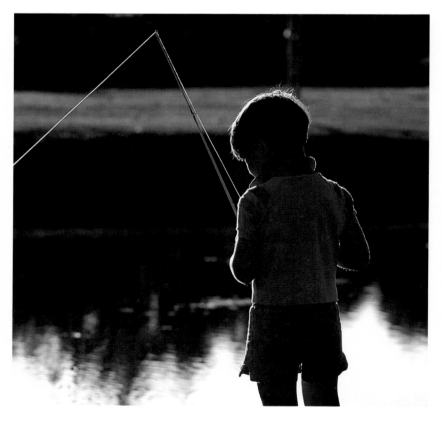

Fishing is an important part of the Montana lifestyle, and it can't be learned too early.

Montana is a headwaters state. Countless rivers are born in the snowmelt that cascades down Montana's mountain ranges.

THE RODEO CIRCUIT

The Western sport of rodeo grew out of cowboys' passion for their occupation. When they weren't movin', sortin', and brandin' cows, or breakin', buyin', and sellin' horses, cowboys were testing their day-to-day skills against one another to see who was the best calf roper or bronc rider. Before long, these barnyard contests were attracting kids and neighbors, and a professional sport was born. Cowboys began traveling from rodeo to rodeo, and the good ones won enough prize money to finance next year's circuit. Few actually make a living as rodeo cowboys, but most come away with something; if not a cash prize or a new belt buckle, often a busted jaw and a crooked grin. Some have even died doing what they loved best. But all have been lassoed by a sport that requires skill, courage, a good deal of luck, and a love of livestock. From Thompson Falls in timber country to Brockway on the plains, cities and towns across Montana celebrate their Western heritage with a weekend of rodeo, usually in summer. Popular rodeos on the Montana circuit are listed under "Top Events" in "PRACTICAL INFORMATION."

Most rodeo events fall into two categories: riding and roping. Riding events include saddle bronc riding, bareback bronc riding, and bull riding, while roping events include steer wrestling and calf roping. Women's barrel racing, along with various other sports, complete the roundup. In most events, luck has a lot to do with who wins. Much of the scoring is based on the difficulty of the ride (the toughest broncs or bulls are favorites because they mean higher scores), and times for ropers are dependent upon the speed and behavior of the calf or steer they are trying to tackle.

STEER WRESTLING

Steer wrestling, or bulldogging, involves leaping from a quarter horse onto the back of a 700-pound Mexican steer running at 25 miles an hour, grabbing his horns and wrestling him to the ground. If you think that sounds easy, try it some time! The sport originated in 1903 when Bill Pickett, a black Texas cowboy (many early cowboys were black), jumped on the back of an ornery steer, grabbed its horns, bent over its head and bit the steer's lower lip like an attacking bulldog. Soon he was repeating the stunt for the 101 Ranch Wild West Show. Others copied this feat, and though the lip-biting part has long since disappeared, the name bulldogging has stuck.

Steer wrestling today involves two men: a dogger and a hazer. When the steer hurtles into the arena, the two spur their horses in quick pursuit, with the hazer trying to force the steer to run straight ahead while the dogger gets into position to leap onto the steer's horns, wrestling him to the ground with his feet and head facing the same direction. Since they are competing with other doggers on time, every second counts. Good doggers can get a steer down in less than seven seconds.

CALF ROPING
Calf roping originated in the Old West when ropers would pull down a calf and quickly tie it up for branding. Today, this is the most competitive of all rodeo events, and there is often big money for the winners. Calf ropers chase a 200- to 350-pound (91- to 159-kg) calf on their expertly trained horses, roping it and then quickly throwing it on its side. After a quick wrap of the piggin' string around three ankles, followed by a half hitch knot, the calf is allowed to try to break free. If it can't within six seconds, the time stands and an untie man rides in to free the calf.

SADDLE BRONC RIDING
The oldest of all rodeo sports, saddle bronc riding originated from cowboys' attempts to train wild horses. Broncs are saddled up in the chutes (fenced-in enclosures along the edge of the arena) and riders climb on, grabbing a thick hemp rope in one hand and sinking their boots into the stirrups. When the gate opens, the bronc goes wild, trying to throw the rider off. The smooth back and forth motion of a good saddle bronc rider makes it appear that he is atop a rocking chair. Rides only last eight seconds; when the horn sounds, a pickup man rides alongside the bronc and the rider slides onto the other horse.

BAREBACK BRONC RIDING
Bareback riding is similar to saddle bronc riding, but the cowboy rides with only a minimum of equipment—no stirrups and no reins. A small leather rigging held on by a leather strap around the horse is topped with a suitcase-like handle. A second wool-lined strap goes around the flank of the horse to act as an irritant so that they buck more. The cowboy holds on with one hand and bounces back and forth in a rocking motion, an effort akin to trying to juggle bowling pins while surfing a big wave. Eight seconds later it's over and a pickup man comes in to rescue the rider (if he hasn't been thrown to the ground).

BULL RIDING AND RODEO CLOWNS

Bull riding is in a class of danger all its own. Unlike broncs who just want that man off their back, bulls want to get even. When a bull rider is thrown off (and this is most of the time, even with the best riders), the bull immediately goes on the attack, trying to gore or trample him. Many bull riders are seriously injured and some die when hit by this 2,000 pounds (909 kg) of brute force. There are no saddles in bull riding, just a piece of thick rope wrapped around the bull's chest with the free end wrapped tightly around the bull rider's hand. A cowbell hangs at the bottom of this contraption to annoy the bull even more. When the chute opens, all hell breaks loose as the bull does everything it possibly can to throw his rider off—spinning, kicking, jumping, and running against the fence.

If the rider hangs on for the required eight seconds (style isn't very important), the next battle begins, getting out of the way of one very angry bull. Here the rodeo clown comes in. Dressed in baggy pants and bright red and white shirts, clowns look like human Raggedy Andy dolls. In reality they are moving targets. Clowns use every trick in the book—climbing into padded barrels that the bulls butt against, weaving across the arena, mocking the bulls with matador capes, and simply running for their lives to reach the fence ahead of the bull. Frequently, two clowns work in tandem to create confusion, one acting as the barrel man, and the other as a roving target. Rodeo clowns also play another role, that of entertainer between events. Their stock of supplies includes rubber chickens, trick mules, a series of pantomimed jokes with the announcers, and anything else that might keep folks from getting restless.

BARREL RACING

One of the only female-dominated events, barrel racing is found at nearly every rodeo, and consists of a triangular course of three barrels arranged a hundred feet apart. The event requires riding a fast horse in a set pattern around these barrels, trying not to knock any over.

—Don Pitcher

Grant-Kohrs Ranch National Historic Site at Deer Lodge preserves the legacy of one of the frontier's largest and most prosperous cattle empires.

THE HI-LINE
MONTANA'S NORTHERN TIER

THE SO-CALLED "HI-LINE" IS MONTANA'S NORTHERN TIER, an immense land of cattle and grain, wildlife, waterfowl, and open space. The region's few people meet for coffee in small towns and cities along U.S. Route 2—also known as the Hi-Line—which links the high plains of eastern Montana with the Rockies to the west. Sparsely populated as it is, the sociology of northern Montana is as diverse as any you will find in the state. Scattered across this broad landscape are the descendants of immigrant farmers, ranchers, and railroad workers, the members of six Indian tribes living on four reservations, and the German-speaking residents of nearly two dozen Hutterite colonies. Adding to the mix is a regular flow of traffic to and from the Canadian provinces of Alberta and Saskatchewan, Montana's closest neighbors to the north.

■ A RESILIENT PEOPLE

The communities that dot the Hi-Line bespeak the resilience of their founders and residents. Appealing as it is, no one ever said it was easy to live in Montana, and life on the Hi-Line can be especially challenging. In addition to extremes in weather that scour the plains with arctic winds in winter and scorch them in summer, the Hi-Line has ridden out all manner of ups and downs, including the collapse both of the open range cattle industry and the homestead movement, the changing fortunes of the Great Northern Railway, cyclical drought, dust, and grasshoppers, boom and bust in the northern oil fields, and the vagaries of federal farm legislation and global grain markets. Ever since the massive farm foreclosures of the twenties, when half the state's farmers lost their land and Montana lost 60,000 residents, population along the Hi-Line has declined, due primarily to a steady out-migration from the eastern counties.

Yet, it is in the face of hardship and decline that the character of the Hi-Line reveals itself. Because people are so scarce, people matter. Neighbors are valued, and visitors frequently make the pages of the weekly newspaper. The bygone traits of compassion, good will, and humor are still palpable in communities like Malta and Glasgow. As one Hi-Liner put it: "You have to value people as the main thing when you live up here." In addition to the county fairs, church suppers, rodeos, and bull sales that bring area residents together, school sports draw passionate crowds from one end of the Hi-Line to another. It is not unusual for a Hi-Liner to drive 300 miles (480 km) from, say, Cut Bank to Wolf Point, in the dead of winter, to see a closely contested high school basketball game.

Many of the settlements along U.S. Route 2 got their start as railroad towns in 1887. Later, the Great Northern Railway Company continued west through Shelby and Cut Bank, crossed the Continental Divide at Marias Pass on Glacier National Park's southern border, and reached Seattle in 1893. Linked to the Great Lakes and the Pacific Coast by rail, these brand new towns became important storage and shipping centers for grain and livestock. **Havre** and **Shelby** are still important railroad towns along the track, now owned by the Burlington Northern Railroad. Since the discovery of oil and gas fields in north-central Montana in the 1920s and '30s, energy fuels have also been important, if fickle, partners in the local economies of Shelby and **Cut Bank.** Farther east, Fort Peck Dam and now-defunct Glasgow Air Force Base both significantly added to—then just as significantly subtracted from—the

Much of the Hi-Line was settled in the late 1880s, when Jim Hill's Great Northern Railway laid tracks across the northern Great Plains to link the Great Lakes with the Pacific Coast. (Montana Historical Society)

population of **Glasgow**. Smaller towns almost wholly dependent on farming and ranching are Malta, Harlem, Chinook, Chester, and, in the northeast corner, Scobey and Plentywood.

The Canadian border is less than an hour's drive north of U.S. Route 2 in most places. Ever since the 1920s, when bootleggers wore ruts into these and other "whiskey roads" hauling cargoes of smuggled booze into the states in defiance of Prohibition, there has been a steady flow of traffic between Canada and Montana. More than a dozen border stations are spaced along the 570-mile (910-km) international border Montana shares with Canada. The busiest border crossing between Seattle and Minneapolis is at Sweetgrass, north of Shelby on Interstate 15, which funnels traffic into the United States from the Alaska and MacKenzie highways and the province of Alberta.

■ DRIVING THROUGH

U.S. Route 2 is a relentless double lane of "oil"—in the local vernacular—that follows the Missouri and the Milk rivers from the North Dakota state line to Havre, then highballs west through Shelby and Cut Bank to Glacier National

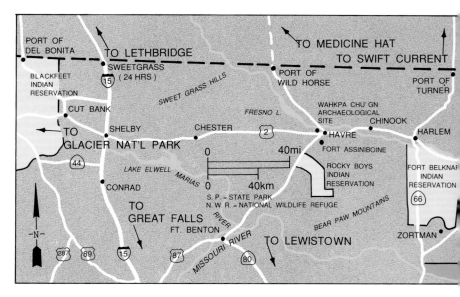

Park. The accommodations and cafés are few and far between in this remote country, but most of the small towns have all-American food and homey motels. See "PRACTICAL INFORMATION" for specifics.

Just when you think the plains will never end, the Sweet Grass Hills, the Bear Paw Mountains, and the Little Rockies appear like ghosts on the horizon. AMTRAK'S *Empire Builder*—named after nineteenth-century railroad magnate James J. Hill, whose Great Northern Railway stretched from Minneapolis to Seattle—follows a similar route across northern Montana.

Earlier visitors did it the hard way, pushing upstream against the **Missouri River,** original highway of the West. Upon first entering what is now Montana at the confluence of the Missouri and Yellowstone rivers, Meriwether Lewis noted in his journal that "we can scarcely cast our eyes in any direction without perceiving deer Elk Buffaloe or Antelopes." The date was April 29, 1805. By the end of the century, the buffalo had been shot to near extinction by hide hunters and the elk had been forced to higher ground. But the vast plains, rivers, and reservoirs of northern Montana are still home to a great variety of wildlife. Ducks and geese eclipse the moon during spring and fall migrations.

Motorists commonly spot big game and birds from the road throughout Montana, but several refuges and reservoirs along the Hi-Line assure more intimate

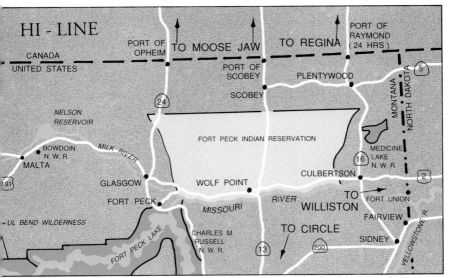

views. One of North America's largest nesting colonies of white pelicans returns to **Medicine Lake National Wildlife Refuge** each spring, along with about 100,000 ducks and geese. Get here via a paved-then-gravel road that turns east from scenic Montana State Highway 16, halfway between Culbertson and Plentywood. Medicine Lake also provides sanctuary for the threatened piping plover and an occasional endangered whooping crane. This isolated refuge in Montana's extreme northeast corner encompasses Montana's smallest classified wilderness, also called Medicine Lake, which preserves the lake's islands and waters, a small parcel of mixed-grass prairie, and a prehistoric teepee ring.

Another bird sanctuary, **Bowdoin National Wildlife Refuge,** lies about a half-day's drive west on U.S. Route 2. Spring is a busy time at Bowdoin. Starting in late March, bald eagles arrive to feast on winter-kill fish. Male sharp-tailed grouse bow and strut, coo and cackle, as they compete for mates on traditional dancing grounds in April and May. The best months to view waterfowl are May and June, as migration winds down and nesting begins. More than 200 species of birds in all, in addition to deer and antelope, make Bowdoin a favorite spot for wildlife watchers. **Nelson Reservoir,** just across the highway, is best known for its walleye, northern pike, and perch fishing, but birders visit, too, for views of its abundant waterfowl and shorebirds. Fresno Lake, Lake Elwell, and Lake Frances are also popular oases along U.S. Route 2 for fishing and hunting, wildlife viewing, and water sports.

Among the wildlife they sighted, Lewis and Clark made numerous diary entries about the "uncommonly large" and "excessively tormenting" mosquitoes they endured as they made their way up the Missouri and past its tributaries, including the Milk. Like so many other aspects of the Lewis and Clark Trail in Montana, this one has not changed. Mosquitoes are still a summertime nuisance in the Milk River valley, especially around Malta and Saco in a wet year.

■ THE FUR TRADE

Of all the wildlife reported by Lewis and Clark along the Missouri, none had more immediate impact on Montana's history than the beaver. The West presented a brand new frontier for the expanding fur trade, and eastern and European entrepreneurs lost no time in exploiting it. In 1828, John Jacob Astor's powerful American Fur Company established what was to become the preeminent fur-trading post on the Missouri River. From its strategic location at the mouth of the Yellowstone River, Fort Union dominated the northern plains and Rocky Mountain fur trade from the 1830s to the Civil War. A colorful cast of characters enlivened this lonely outpost—eastern capitalists and Plains Indians, boorish mountain men, Jesuit missionaries, artists, scientists, and European royalty anxious to glimpse America's exotic new frontier. Untold thousands of beaver pelts were floated downriver from Fort Union to St. Louis. The demand for beaver fur declined when men switched from fur to silk hats.

Fort Union Trading Post, on the Montana-North Dakota border just south of U.S. Route 2, has been preserved by the National Park Service as a historic site. Here, in this unlikely location, visitors can explore the fort's Bourgoise House, once the setting of elegant dinners for distinguished guests like the German explorer Prince Maximilian, naturalist John James Audubon, and artists Karl Bodmer and George Catlin. Newly restored to its nineteenth-century glory, Fort Union reflects one of the most colorful eras of the nation's westward expansion.

A lively chapter in Western history, this era brought death and disease to the native culture. Once nomadic, self-sufficient buffalo hunters, many Plains Indians grew dependent on the whiskey and guns they received in exchange for furs. Trappers and traders also brought smallpox, a disease that proved fatal to Indians who had no immunity. The Mandan tribe of North Dakota was almost entirely wiped out by the smallpox virus, and throughout Montana, thousands more Plains Indians died. The *coup de grâce* was the wholesale extermination of buffalo, in the mid-1870s, when buffalo hides replaced beaver pelts as the West's most profitable commodity. By 1883, the buffalo was gone and so was the Plains Indian culture it supported. Unable to provide for themselves and defend their way of life, the tribes were vulnerable to the federal government, which confined them to reservations. Even these limited reservations diminished as settlers demanded more land for farming, ranching, mining, and railroads.

■ INDIAN RESERVATIONS

The present boundaries of the Fort Peck, Fort Belknap, and Blackfeet reservations were established by the Sweetgrass Hills Treaty of 1888. The federal government created the Hi-Line's fourth reservation—Rocky Boy's—in 1916. Like Indian

A Grassy Clean Wind

*A*cross its empty miles pours the pushing and shouldering wind, a thing you tighten into as a trout tightens into fast water. It is a grassy, clean, exciting wind, with the smell of distance in it, and in its search for whatever it is looking for it turns over every wheat blade and head, every pale primrose, even the ground-hugging grass. It blows yellow-headed blackbirds and hawks and prairie sparrows around the air and ruffles the short tails of meadowlarks on fence posts. In collaboration with the light, it makes lovely and changeful what might otherwise be characterless.

It is a long way from characterless; "overpowering" would be a better word. For over the segmented circle of earth is domed the biggest sky anywhere, which on days like this sheds down on range and wheat and summer fallow a light to set a painter wild, a light pure, glareless, and transparent. The horizon a dozen miles away is as clean a line as the nearest fence. There is no haze, neither the woolly gray of humid countries nor the blue atmosphere of the mountain West. Across the immense sky move navies of cumuli, fair-weather clouds, their bottoms as even as if they had scraped themselves flat against the flat earth.

The drama of this landscape is in the sky, pouring with light and always moving. The earth is passive. And yet the beauty I am struck by, both as present fact and as revived memory, is a fusion: this sky would not be so spectacular without this earth to change and glow and darken under it. And whatever the sky may do, however the earth is shaken or darkened, the Euclidean perfection abides. The very scale, the hugeness of simple forms, emphasizes stability. It is not hills and mountains which we shall call eternal. Nature abhors an elevation as much as it abhors a vacuum; a hill is no sooner elevated than the forces of erosion begin tearing it down. These prairies are quiescent, close to static; looked at for any length of time, they begin to impose their awful perfection on the observer's mind. Eternity is a peneplain.

—Wallace Stegner, *Wolf Willow*, 1962

Northern Montana is an immense land of cattle and grain, space and sky.

reservations throughout America, these four offer a bleak insight into the conquest of one culture by another. Unemployment runs as high as 80 percent on some, and all have been ravaged by poverty and alcoholism. Cultural leaders trace a loss of pride and purpose to federal policies at the beginning of this century that outlawed traditional ceremonies like the Sun Dance and prohibited Indians from speaking their native tongues. On reservations across Montana, these people are now working with missionary zeal to heal the wounds of cultural deprivation by rescuing the language, songs, stories, and spiritual traditions of their ancestors.

Visitors can witness this cultural revival at any of the Indian powwows, where traditional dancing, drumming, singing, and games blend spirit and spectacle, reverence and revelry. The **Museum of the Plains Indian** in Browning uses Blackfeet Indian tribal artifacts and other exhibits to explain the culture and history of the tribes that inhabited northern Montana.

Assiniboine Indians at Glasgow awaiting the arrival of President Franklin Roosevelt in 1934 to launch construction of Fort Peck Dam. (Montana Historical Society)

CHIEF JOSEPH AND THE NEZ PERCE

One of the last major battles of the United States' campaign to win control of the plains took place about 16 miles (26 km) south of the Hi-Line town of **Chinook.** In 1877, the federal government tried to force the Nez Perce Indians of Oregon's Wallowa Valley onto an Idaho reservation so that white ranchers could have their lands. The Nez Perce stubbornly refused. A few drunk young men killed four whites, and subsequent raids led to the deaths of at least 14 more. The U.S. Army retaliated, but was turned back by the Indians.

Rather than face government reinforcements and certain defeat, more than a thousand Nez Perce began an 1,800-mile (2,900-km) flight in a desperate bid to reach safety in Canada. A series of running battles followed as the Indians used their geographic knowledge and battle skills to confound the inept Army. Finally, just 45 miles (70 km) from the international border with Canada, the Army of Gen. Nelson A. Miles caught up with the Nez Perce. After the fierce, four-day Battle of the Bears Paw, Chief Joseph is remembered for closing one of the great speeches in the history of the West with these words: "Hear me, my chiefs, I am tired; my heart is sick and sad. From where the sun now stands, I will fight no more forever." The Nez Perce were forced to surrender, though 300 made good their escape to Canada. Despite promises that they would be allowed to return home, the Nez Perce were hustled onto a reservation in Oklahoma, while whites remained on their ancestral lands farther west. Chief Joseph died in 1904, reportedly of a broken heart.

Now managed as a state park, **Chief Joseph Battlefield** has been proposed as part of a new Nez Perce National Historic Park.

(following pages) Costumes are elaborate and spirits are high as native dancers from throughout the country compete at Crow Fair. (photos by Douglas O'Looney)

■ ISLAND MOUNTAIN RANGES

Whether traveling north-south or east-west through Montana's northern tier, you will be struck by the sheer size of the landscape. With the exception of three small but surprising mountain ranges, there is nothing to interrupt the view for miles in every direction. Mere suggestions of the mountain landscape that lies to the west, the Little Rockies, Bear Paw Mountains, and Sweet Grass Hills add welcome dimension to the linear geometry of the plains. Buckhorn Cabins (see "Accommodations" in "PRACTICAL INFORMATION") in Zortman provide a pleasant stopping place at the base of the Little Rockies.

The **Little Rocky Mountains** are nearly as rich in Old West romance as they are in precious metals. Surrounded by a sea of grass and the rugged breaks of the Missouri River, these mountains provided refuge for outlaws, whiskey traders, and assorted scamps and scoundrels with names like Kid Curry, Butch Cassidy, Pike Landusky, Jew Jake, and the Sundance Kid. Tales of their Christmas shoot-outs, train robberies, and other carryings-on are as colorful as the gold that glittered in the gulches. Gold was first discovered here in 1884, and by World War II, the Little Rockies are said to have yielded $25 million in gold. Mining resumed in 1979 when the Pegasus Gold Co. developed a huge open-pit gold mine above the historic mining camp of Zortman. Today the mine produces 70,000 to 100,000 ounces of gold annually, and about three times as much silver.

Zortman and Landusky once fell within the borders of the adjoining Fort Belknap Indian Reservation. After the discovery of gold, however, agents of the federal government persuaded the Assiniboine and Gros Ventre Indians to give up this mineral-rich chunk of land for a mere $350,000. This land grab shows up clearly on the map as a big bite taken from the reservation's southern border.

Similarly, the Blackfeet Indians lost a precious piece of their traditional homeland in the **Sweet Grass Hills**, north of Chester, after gold was discovered there in 1885. The gold in these hills never amounted to a major strike. Nonetheless, this area, long regarded by the Blackfeet as a sacred site, is still held privately by non-Indians.

Chief Joseph Battlefield lies south of Chinook along Montana State Highway 240. The battlefield is well marked but otherwise undeveloped, allowing visitors to use their imagination in re-creating the last battle of the Nez Perce Indian War (15 miles, 25 km). The **Bear Paw Mountains** rise invitingly behind Havre—the Hi-Line's largest city—and Rocky Boy's Indian Reservation—Montana's smallest

Indian reservation. Said to resemble a giant paw print from a distance, the grassy buttes and rounded peaks of the Bear Paws offer cool refuge from summer's sun-scorched plains. Hill County maintains a 10,000-acre public park along Beaver Creek leading into the Bear Paws, south of Havre. Billed as the largest county park in the nation, **Beaver Creek Park** offers ready access to fishing, camping, swimming, and wildlife watching for local sportsmen and outdoor lovers.

Like a portent in a well-crafted novel, these isolated mountain ranges foreshadow the drama that lies ahead when the plains run headlong into the towering wall of the Rockies.

THE HUTTERITES

Montana's cloistered Hutterites are conspicuous to the outside world by the homespun skirts, scarves, and black, Western-cut suits they wear when they come to town. These German-speaking exiles are masters of the soil and devout servants of God.

The plains of Montana, the Dakotas, and Canada provided the isolation and productive land that the Hutterite Brethren sought when they fled from intolerance and religious persecution in Russia after 1870. Firm in their insistence on adult baptism, communal living, and their refusal to bear arms or participate in prevailing social and economic institutions, these Anabaptists had already been driven from Austria, Moravia, and several eastern European countries. Between 1874 and 1877, the Hutterites established a beachhead in South Dakota, where they prospered until the patriotic fervor of World War I forced them north to Canada to avoid military conscription in the United States. Government-imposed limitations on land ownership in Canada pushed some of them back over the border after the war, and in 1937, the Hutterites established their first colony in Montana near Lewistown. About 40 colonies, each with a population of 60 to 100, now dot the plains of central and north-central Montana, where a live-and-let-live attitude has allowed the Hutterite people to flourish.

Self-sufficient and isolated by choice, Hutterites do not mix with secular society. This is not to say they are secretive or standoffish. Always willing to help non-Hutterite farmers and ranchers with repairs and chores, they are good neighbors. They visit nearby towns as necessary to pick up supplies, vote in elections, or deliver fresh produce to grocery stores.

At home and in their colonies, Hutterites speak German as a first language. English is used at school and in dealings with the outside world. Hutterite men work the land and raise the livestock; women perform all household duties. Children attend school until age 16, the minimum required by the state; then, they go to work for the colony. Hutterite women marry outside their own colony and take up residence in their husband's colony. When a colony outgrows the basic farm-ranch operation, it splits in two, with half the population moving to a new site. At the heart of every colony is a philosophy of communal sharing and caring. All members work for the colony and the colony takes care of them from cradle to grave.

Visitors can get a glimpse of colony life during late summer and fall when Hutterites harvest truckloads of fresh vegetables from their large gardens. Many colonies display signs near their entrances announcing fresh tomatoes, corn, beans, potatoes, and squash. And for many Montana families, Christmas would not be Christmas without a fat, grain-fed Hutterite goose.

Wagons rutted the plains, leaving an enduring record of the hopes and hardships borne by westering homesteaders.

A chuckwagon, blacksmith shop, early barns and outbuildings provide a glimpse of the not-too-distant past at Grant-Kohrs Ranch National Historic Site in Deer Lodge.

THE BIG OPEN
EAST-CENTRAL MONTANA

I glance higher for some hint of the weather, and the square of air broadens and broadens to become the blue expanse over the Montana rangeland, so vast and vaulting that it rears, from the foundation-line of the plains horizon, to form the walls and roof of all life's experience that my younger self could imagine, a single great house of Sky.
—Ivan Doig, *This House of Sky: Landscapes of a Western Mind,* 1978

THE MID-SECTION OF EASTERN MONTANA—the lonely expanse of plains wedged between the Yellowstone River on the south and the Missouri on the north—has inspired many epithets over the years. Insiders have long known it as the "Big Dry Country" and "Next Year Country." Lately, journalists and academicians have brought their enlarged world-view to this forgotten place with such exotic names as American Outback, American Serengeti, and Buffalo Commons. But frontier photographer L. A. Huffman gets the credit for giving it the name that stuck—the Big Open.

The Big Open is exotic. Even Montanans feel like foreigners here. Barely relevant to western Montana, let alone mainstreet America, it is the fulfillment of our folklore about the West. Undoubtedly the state's most unadulterated travel destination, the Big Open has no resorts, no gourmet restaurants, no shopping centers. About the closest thing to a privately developed tourist attraction is a handful of working cattle ranches that take in guests. (See "Accommodations" in "PRACTICAL INFORMATION" for specifics.) Its two largest cities are **Jordan** (pop. 494), once described by a New York radio station as "the lonesomest town in the world," and **Circle** (pop. 805), which made the news a couple of winters back when Montana State Highway 13 north of town was clogged with tumbleweeds after a November blow. The state highway department responded, as it does to most winter emergencies, by dispatching snowplows to the site.

With roughly 4,000 people scattered over 12,000 square miles, (31,080 sq. km) the Big Open encompasses just under 10 percent of Montana's land base, while accounting for only one-half of one percent of its population. People have been quitting the Big Open ever since the homestead experiment, which failed miserably in a land that gets 12 to 13 inches (30 to 33 cm) of moisture in a good year.

■ THE OPEN RANGE

Ironically, this was a land of opportunity in the glory days of the open range cattle boom. In a New Deal-era guidebook to Montana, the Federal Writers' Project reported that "a man who could ride a horse and do his share of corral work was always sure of a job here." This was a land of big cow outfits like the Texas-based XIT, which employed more than 200 cowboys to ride herd on 15,000 head, and the CK, part of a four-state, million-acre cattle empire owned by Conrad Kohrs. This was also the land that invented the rugged individualist, a way of life that survives, even though today's stockgrowers are tethered to the land, the next weather report, cattle futures, global markets, and international trade policies over which they have no control.

Overgrazing, compounded by the brutal winter of 1886–87 and the arrival of plows and barbed wire, brought an end to the days of the open range. The end of an era, perhaps, but by no means the end of an industry. Numbering more than 300,000 head, cattle and sheep still outnumber people nearly a hundred to one in the Big Open.

On land that requires 30 to 40 acres to support a cow and a calf, it takes a big spread and a friendly banker to build a ranch "that a cow can pay for," as the folks out here would say. This is the kind of ratio that inspires Rutgers University professors Frank and Deborah Popper to carry on their campaign to rid this and other semi-arid Western lands of cattle and give them back to grass and buffalo, creating a "Buffalo Commons." Describing the Homestead Act of 1862 as "the largest, longest-running agricultural and environmental mistake in United States history," they propose that the government buy back the land, tear down the fences, replant the shortgrass, and restock the plains with buffalo. The result would be the world's largest national park, an idea whose time has decidedly not arrived in the Big Open.

■ THE PEOPLE

Those who live outside the Big Open have long questioned the rationale of those inside. But for the few who remain and the occasional outsiders who yearn for the open road, there's no place like it. Let's start with those few souls who live here. Most live on a piece of land that has been under the stewardship of one family for three, four, perhaps five generations. It is all they know, but it is more than that. It

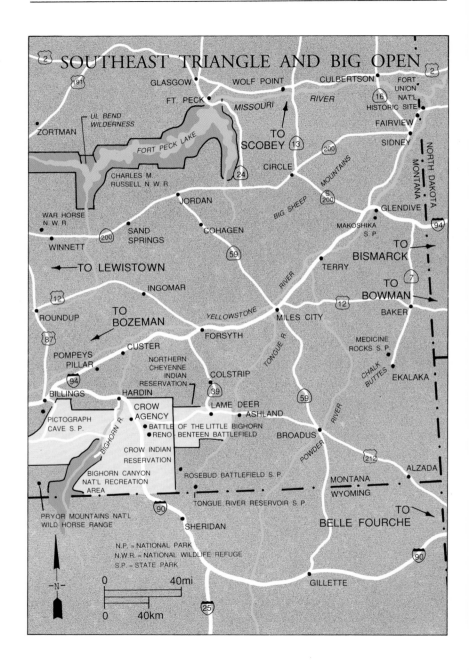

SOUTHEAST TRIANGLE AND BIG OPEN

has to do with ties that bind generation to generation, neighbor to neighbor, rancher to earth, earth to sky. In a land of infinite space, relations out here are skintight. Next door may mean 20 miles (32 km) away, but due to everlastingly busy telephone lines, neighbors know more about one another's lives here than they do in Billings or Great Falls.

In this land of isolation, people hang together. In a land of harsh winters and cyclical droughts, they sell off their herds or commute to temporary, hard-to-find jobs in Miles City or Glendive. They do what they have to do to make it through this season because things will be better next year. And, in a land of treeless plains bleached by sun, scoured by wind, and engulfed by sky, residents find unsurpassed beauty. This is the land of the long look, the unobstructed view, and they wouldn't trade it for a dozen Glacier Parks.

The inscrutable beauty of the Big Open either eludes visitors altogether or draws them back again and again. As a circuit-riding doctor from Billings describes it, "I used to think you had to have trees where you live. But pretty soon, you start seeing sunrises, sunsets, and incredible skyscapes."

Frontier photographer L.A. Huffman came west with the Army in 1878, and captured an era. His photo of a homesteader breaking the prairie is entitled "The Honyocker." (Montana Historical Society)

(top) A hopeful graingrower checks his barley crop before harvest.
(bottom) Rhythm and texture play their parts in the business of farming.

(top) Not everyone rides a horse in Montana, but they're not hard to come by.
(bottom) Grain bins form the skyline of many small farming communities.

It takes a good, long while to traverse the Big Open. Rolling ahead for as far as the eye can see, Montana State Highway 200 was made for those who travel for the sheer love of driving. Figure five hours of driving from Sidney to Lewistown, and that's with no stops. It will take at least that long to disengage from the world as you know it and adopt a new outlook. The view from the Big Open begins and ends with the sky. It has little to do with humanity, and yet it raises fundamental questions about existence. How do they make it out here, you will wonder. Wits, humor, tolerance, and style are some of the required traits, and they are visible in the weathered faces and egalitarian dress of the locals. They are audible in the no-frills dialect of the plains. When novelist Jim Harrison visited the Big Open, he had his notebook out when a cowboy blew into town and hollered that he had just "outdrove a storm down the creekbed." No need to waste time on words when there is work to be done. A soda at the general store in Sand Springs, a rib steak at the QD Cafe in Jordan, or a bowl of pinto beans at the Jersey Lilly in Ingomar (to the south, on U.S. Route 12) are all good excuses to stop, listen up, and get acquainted.

For a more formal introduction to the development of this country, plan to spend some time at the **McCone County Museum** in Circle. It took a 6,400-square-foot building to house the artifacts and memorabilia that have been assembled by this preservation-minded community. Besides comprehensive displays of the area's homestead and cattle range eras, the museum has impressive collections of firearms, Indian artifacts, arrowheads, and fossils.

■ DINOSAUR COUNTRY

Although much of Montana east of the Rockies is dinosaur country, one of the richest areas lies north of Jordan. Paleontologists and trained excavation crews comb these plains each summer for the fossilized remains of the plant and animal life that thrived here 65 million years ago, when the area was covered by swamps and shallow seas. The latest major find, discovered a couple of years ago by two amateur fossil hunters, appears to be the most complete skeleton ever found of *Tyrannosaurus rex,* largest of the predatory dinosaurs. Standing more than 18 feet (5 m) tall and weighing about seven tons, T-rex is thought to have been the most ferocious of all dinosaurs. Its six-inch-long (15-cm) serrated teeth prompted Montana paleontologist Jack Horner to describe this prehistoric giant as having had "a

Fort Peck Dam, near its completion in 1938. (Montana Historical Society)

mouth full of steak knives." Of the seven other partial T-rex skeletons that have been unearthed, five were taken from this general area of Montana. The latest skeleton has been added to the already impressive paleontology collection at the **Museum of the Rockies** in Bozeman.

More fossils from the bone beds of the Big Open can be seen at the **Fort Peck Museum**, on the northeast end of Fort Peck Lake. Salvaged from what is now the bottom of Fort Peck Lake during the construction of Fort Peck Dam, they are but a remnant of the rich prehistory of the area.

■ DAMMING THE MISSOURI

Once free-flowing and spirited, the Missouri River has been tamed dramatically since the days when explorers and mountain men muscled their way upriver to unlock the West. Several dams now control the upper river's once-treacherous current, generating electrical power and providing irrigation and recreation in the upstream states and flood control and navigation downriver. The Missouri's largest dam in Montana is at Fort Peck. Indeed, **Fort Peck Dam** is one of the world's largest earth-fill dams, and the single greatest manmade alteration to Montana's landscape.

Public policy experts now debate the wisdom of this and other dams on the Missouri, but back in the "dirty thirties," the only resistance to Fort Peck Dam came from the handful of ranchers whose lands were inundated by its floodwaters. Montana was in the grip of drought, dust, and the Great Depression. Families across the nation were desperate for work. President Franklin Roosevelt responded with the New Deal, and one of the largest New Deal projects in the country was Fort Peck Dam. When Glasgow mayor Leo Colemen learned of plans to build a dam 250 feet (76 m) high and 21,000 feet (6,400 m) across, he responded with an incredulous: "Hell, a dam like that might cost a million dollars." In fact, Fort Peck Dam cost $156 million.

Workers flocked to the site and boomtowns sprang from the plains of northeast Montana. Clusters of tents, tarpaper shacks, dance halls, and flop houses, these now-forgotten towns carried names like New Deal, Square Deal, and Wheeler. At the height of construction in 1936, nearly 11,000 workers were employed on the project. Despite the dust, danger, and drudgery, these were happy times in Montana. Paychecks came regularly and booze flowed again following the repeal of Prohibition.

Fort Peck Dam remains a monument to this troubled and triumphant era in U.S. history. Travelers today are more likely to visit Fort Peck for its recreational opportunities than its historic value, but in 1936, journalists sensed a big story here. Pulitzer Prize-winning reporter Ernie Pyle visited Fort Peck that year and described the town of Wheeler as "the wildest wild-west town in North America." Also that year, *Life* magazine was born, and Fort Peck Dam appeared on its first cover. Be sure to visit the museum located in the powerhouse at the dam, just south of U.S. Route 2 between Wolf Point and Glasgow. Besides telling the human story behind this massive public works project, the **Fort Peck Museum** has an impressive collection of fossils found during construction of the dam. The government-built town of Fort Peck is smaller and much more sedate today than it was during its dam-building days, but it offers one of Montana's finest summer playhouses, the **Fort Peck Theatre**, which features lively musicals and drama every weekend during the summer.

■ FORT PECK LAKE

Stretching 134 miles (214 km) across the northern rim of the Big Open, Fort Peck Lake covers portions of six counties and draws half-a-million visitors each year to its 1,520-mile (2,430-km) shoreline, campgrounds, and recreation areas. In recent years, however, drawdowns by the Army Corps of Engineers to satisfy demands by downstream users have dropped water levels and raised heck with the lake's recreation industry. Montana and the Dakotas have taken the federal agency to court in an effort to preserve water levels in the so-called Upper Basin states.

Between the lake and the surrounding Charles M. Russell National Wildlife Refuge, visitors can choose from boating, fishing, hiking, horseback riding, wildlife watching, and hunting. Until recently, many of the roads into the area have been impassable in wet weather because eastern Montana's clay soil turns to a greasy gumbo that grabs tires and won't let go. Today many roads have been graveled for all-weather travel, but it is always a good idea to check weather and road conditions before leaving pavement in the Big Open. Two fine drives are the gravel roads leading from Winnett (Crooked Creek Road), and Jordan (Hell Creek Road) to Fort Peck Lake—not many people, but plenty of wildlife, along with impressive badlands topography.

Every year in July, amateur and professional anglers from throughout the nation converge on Fort Peck Lake to compete in the annual Governor's Cup Walleye Tournament. While walleye is Fort Peck's best known game fish, it is by no means the only fish in this inland sea. Other popular game fish are sauger, northern pike, smallmouth bass, channel catfish, lake trout, perch, and chinook salmon. Montana's largest fish, the paddlefish, is also found in these waters, but prefers the river to the lake for its spring spawning run.

Lunkers like this chunky rainbow trout are plentiful in Montana, especially in stocked lakes and reservoirs. But a growing number of river and stream fishermen prefer to release their catch for future enjoyment.

■ CHARLES M. RUSSELL WILDLIFE REFUGE

C. M. Russell Wildlife Refuge was named for cowboy artist **Charlie Russell,** whose oil paintings and watercolors portrayed the austere beauty of the Missouri River's bluffs and coulees, badlands, breaks, and buttes. Isolated by the harsh climate, forbidding terrain, and sheer space of the Big Open, this million-acre range provides sanctuary for at least 200 species of birds, 45 different mammals, and a wide variety of reptiles and fish. Bighorn sheep have replaced the now extinct Audubon sheep that once grazed this prairie wilderness. Mule deer are the refuge's most abundant big game animals and elk are its most surprising. Together with the UL Bend, a 20,800-acre peninsula of federally protected wilderness within the refuge, this is the only place in Montana where elk still occupy their native prairie year-round. Prairie dog towns make this a good spot for burrowing owls that nest in the rodents' holes, and plovers thrive on the shortgrass and sagebrush.

The prospect of seeing strutting grouse or eavesdropping on a spring convention of Canada geese make the refuge well worth visiting, but the undefiled footprint of history makes the C. M. Russell Refuge a national treasure. Dinosaur bones, buffalo kill sites, and teepee rings mark the nothingness of the prairie like random tombstones, while abandoned homesteaders' shacks and wagon-wheel ruts reveal more recent hardships. Paleontologists and archaeologists from museums and universities throughout the country visit the refuge and surrounding area each summer in search of clues to the past.

This isolated landscape is not easily reached, but is well worth the effort. Wildlife watchers should approach the refuge from U.S. Route 191, north of Lewistown and south of Malta. A 20-mile (32-km), self-guiding auto tour starting near the west end of the refuge, off U.S. Route 191, follows an all-weather road into the bottomland of the Missouri River as it makes its way east to Fort Peck Lake. Other roads are passable only in dry weather. Morning and evening are the best times of day, when animals are moving around; spring and fall are the best seasons.

The U.S. Fish & Wildlife Service manages three outlying refuges southwest of the Russell Refuge as breeding sites and migratory rest stops for a variety of birds. Pelicans, cormorants, great blue herons, gulls, eagles, owls, and grouse are commonly seen at the **War Horse, Hailstone,** and **Lake Mason** refuges. The sage and shortgrass prairie surrounding these small lakes provides habitat for game animals, too. Located on backroads and lacking developed recreation facilities, these outposts see few visitors.

The Big Open is for nesting grebes and dancing grouse. It is for bobcats and bighorn sheep that are seldom seen in the rugged prairie wilderness of the Missouri breaks. It is for grass that needs little moisture and people who need few conveniences. The Big Open is for beasts and birds whose very existence depends on open, unpeopled places. It is for a very few people whose spirit requires the same.

THE BUFFALO DRIVE

On the north we passed a precipice about one hundred and twenty feet high, under which lay scattered the fragments of at least one hundred carcases of buffaloes, although the water which had washed away the lower part of the hill must have carried off many of the dead. These buffaloes had been chased down the precipice in a way very common on the Missouri, and by which vast herds are destroyed in a moment. The mode of hunting is to select one of the most active and fleet young men, who is disguised by a buffalo skin round his body; the skin of the head with the ears and horns fastened on his own head in such a way as to deceive the buffalo: thus dressed, he fixed himself at a convenient distance between a herd of buffalo and any of the river precipices, which sometimes extend for some miles. His companions in the meantime get in the rear and side of the herd, and at a given signal show themselves, and advance towards the buffalo: they instantly take the alarm, and finding the hunters beside them, they run towards the disguised Indian or decoy, who leads them on at full speed towards the river, when suddenly securing himself in some crevice of the cliff which he had previously fixed on, the herd is left on the brink of the precipice: it is then in vain for the foremost to retreat or even to stop; they are pressed on by the hindmost rank, who, seeing no danger but from the hunters, goad on those before them till the whole are precipitated and the shore is strewed with their dead bodies. Sometimes in this perilous seduction the Indian is himself either trodden underfoot by the rapid movements of the buffalo, or missing his footing in the cliff is urged down the precipice by the falling herd. The Indians then select as much meat as they wish, and the rest is abandoned to the wolves, and creates a most dreadful stench. The wolves who had been feasting on these carcases were very fat, and so gentle that one of them was killed with a spontoon.

—Meriwether Lewis, journal entry from Arrow Creek
along the upper Missouri River on May 30, 1805

SOUTHEAST TRIANGLE

IF THE MISSOURI RIVER IS A WINDOW ON MONTANA'S PAST, then the Yellowstone embodies its future. The longest free-flowing river in the lower 48 states, the Yellowstone is a river's river, valued for what it is, not what it could become with a little intervention from, say, the Army Corps of Engineers. From its headwaters in the mountains of Wyoming's northwest corner to its confluence with the Missouri 670 miles (1,070 km) downriver, the **Yellowstone River** is unshackled by dams. As it makes its way along a gradual northeasterly course, the river forms the hypotenuse of Montana's southeast triangle.

Born in snowmelt at 12,000 feet (3,657 m), the Yellowstone cascades down mountains, catches its breath on the Yellowstone Plateau, then gouges out canyons, carves mountain valleys, races traffic along Interstate 94, and hurries past Montana's largest, most industrialized city before it settles down to the broad and braided, cottonwood-lined prairie river that dumps four trillion gallons of water into the Missouri each year. Along the way, it flowers the plains, irrigates croplands and hay pastures, supplies municipal water needs, powers industry, builds side channels, islands, and bottomlands for wildlife, sustains abundant fish populations, and provides unrivaled recreation for floaters, anglers, hunters, rockhounds, and all who find renewal in the presence of a great spirit.

■ WATER WARS

In the early 1970s, the Yellowstone was a river under siege. Proposals to dam the river had been debated off and on for 40 years, but the real threat came after the Arab oil embargo, when the federal government, together with the mining and utility industries, began eyeing the potential of eastern Montana coal fields for powering huge electrical plants. The power plants would require unprecedented diversions of water for cooling, and the logical source was the Yellowstone and its tributaries. When it was discovered that up to 80 percent of the river's total flow might be drained off in dry years, even the most ardent boosters of economic development began to question the wisdom of selling off their river as a solution to the energy problem.

Rising like tabletops out of the plains, the Chalk Buttes, near Ekalaka, are part of the southeastern Montana mosaic.

After three years of intensive research and public debate, the Montana Board of Natural Resources and Conservation set aside 5.5 million acre-feet of water in the Yellowstone and its tributaries for fish, wildlife, recreation, and protection of water quality. Water for the sake of water. It was unheard of in the West, where once-great rivers like the Colorado and the Columbia have been dammed nearly to death. Even in Montana, with 10 dams on its main stem, the Missouri ain't what she used to be.

The board's action reversed more than Montana's traditional, consumptive approach to water use. It challenged a century of resource exploitation by outside interests and said, in effect, "This is our river and we will determine its fate." With millions of tons of coal still lying in shallow underground seams nearby, the Yellowstone's future is by no means secure. But the precedent set by state policy makers in 1978, backed by public support, and bolstered by a solid framework of water protection laws assures that anyone who tries to tame the Yellowstone will have to put up quite a fight to do it.

■ THE LAND

Like the Big Open, southeastern Montana is dramatically big country. It is a land of canyons and badlands, fossils and agates, timbered hills, treeless plains, and rivers that sustain life in a near-desert climate. Southeastern Montana is good grass country, and therefore, cattle and cowboy country. It is Indian country, more specifically, Crow and Northern Cheyenne country. It is the site of last century's most celebrated clash between native and non-native cultures and this century's most heated resource debate between ranchers and coal developers. It includes Montana's largest city—Billings—along with a cowtown straight out of *Lonesome Dove*, a string of river settlements that owe their existence to the Yellowstone and the Northern Pacific Railroad, and a smattering of one-horse towns in the middle of nowhere.

Montana's southeast corner developed in much the same way as the rest of the plains. Before the end of the eighteenth century, explorers and fur traders had discovered the Missouri's great southern tributary, which carried a French name—"la Roche Jaune," or Yellow Rock. Crow Indians knew it as the Elk River, but the French name stuck when Captain William Clark Anglicized it. In July 1806, after

Powder River roundup, framed by Army post photographer L.A. Huffman.
(Montana Historical Society)

Lewis and Clark had divided their forces to further explore Montana on their return trip to St. Louis, Clark reached the Yellowstone near present-day Livingston and drifted all the way downriver to the Missouri where he and Meriwether Lewis were reunited. The only physical evidence of Clark's Yellowstone River trip is the frontier graffiti he left on a rock outcropping about 30 miles (48 km) east of Billings. He carved his signature in what he described as a "remarkable rock" and named it Pompy's Tower in honor of Sacagawea's son, whom he had nicknamed "Pomp." The federal Bureau of Land Management is negotiating with a private owner to purchase the landmark, now known as **Pompey's Pillar**, and plans to manage it as a national historic site.

■ CATTLE COUNTRY

Later in the century, while prospectors were rushing to the gold camps of western Montana, Texas cowboys began trailing hundreds of thousands of longhorn cattle north to the rich grasslands that had once supported great buffalo herds. Growing demand for beef, not only in the Eastern cities but in Western mining camps, at military forts, and on railroad construction sites, provided the market. The northern territory's vast open range provided free grass and water. The sheep industry was not far behind, but the "woolies" never matched the numbers of Montana's open range cattle. Montana's top sheep-producing county is Carter County, in the extreme southeast corner, where the woolies outnumber people about fifty to one.

■ MILES CITY

Trappings of the stockmen's trade are readily apparent in any eastern Montana town. But the heart and soul of the livestock industry, particularly the cattle industry, resides in **Miles City,** midway between Billings and Sidney, where the Tongue River joins the Yellowstone. Long recognized as the "cow capital" of Montana, Miles City pulls on its Justin "Ropers" and Tony Lamas every morning, tunes into KATL for rock or KIK for country-western, and caps the work day with beers and bourbon ditches at the Bison Bar, the Range Riders, and a half-dozen other main-street saloons. In May, the city celebrates its cowboy culture with a three-day rodeo that fills the town with thousands of spectators and participants ranging from local ranch hands to U.S. senators. The **Miles City Bucking Horse Sale** is the season opener, and it is no ordinary rodeo. Unlike other rodeos on the summer circuit, where cowboys and girls shine in skilled events like bareback riding, calf roping, steer wrestling, and barrel racing, the Bucking Horse Sale is exactly what it says it is: a showdown between the wildest, orneriest, most ill-behaved horses, and cowboys who are compulsive enough to climb aboard because "it's there." The guys who stay on top of the meanest horses longest get the prizes, and the horses that give the wildest rides sell for top dollar to rodeo stock contractors who come from throughout the United States and Canada. At the end of each day, participants and spectators mingle in downtown saloons, where videotapes of the day's buckouts are shown on big-screen TV, and the latest fashions run to canvas dusters and teal chaps.

If you can't make the Bucking Horse Sale, there are plenty of places to soak up cowboy lore year-round in Miles City. Downtown, the scent of leather wafts from the door of the **Miles City Saddlery,** drawing you inside the way a sidewalk bakery does. Tourists delight in the racks of Western clothing, and the hats and boots stacked floor to ceiling on the main level, while working cowboys head downstairs for overalls, long underwear, bits and spurs, shoeing hammers, hoof knives and rasps, nippers, and ferrier aprons—the essential gear of their trade. A couple of blocks up the street is the exquisitely restored **Montana Bar,** built in 1902 "for those early cattlemen who stayed in Montana and parlayed a bull and a handful of heifers into herds that, when trailed, were about half the size of Connecticut."

On the western outskirts of town, the cowboys and pioneers who settled these parts are memorialized at the **Range Riders Museum,** a sprawling complex that

END OF THE FRONTIER

*K*ind fate had it I should be Post Photographer with the Army during the Indian campaigns close following the annihilation of Custer's command. This Yellowstone-Big Horn country was then unpenned of wire, and unspoiled by railway, dam or ditch. Eastman had not yet made the Kodak, but thanks be, there was the old wet plate, the collodion bottle and bath. I made photographs. With crude home-made cameras, from saddle and in log shack, I saved something.

Round about us the army of buffalo hunters—red men and white—were waging the final war of extermination upon the last great herds of American bison seen upon this continent. Then came the cattleman, the "trail boss" with his army of cowboys, and the great cattle roundups. Then the army of railroad builders. That—the railway—was the fatal coming. One looked about and said, "This is the last West." It was not so. There *was* no more West after that. It was a dream and a forgetting, a chapter forever closed.

—L. A. Huffman quoted in Mark H. Brown and W. R. Felton,
Before Barbed Wire, 1956

Cheyenne Indians being interviewed about the Battle of the Little Bighorn by journalist Olin D. Wheeler. (Montana Historical Society)

exhibits relics of the range and homestead eras, period clothing, Indian artifacts, a 400-piece gun collection, and replicas of early buildings and street scenes. The museum occupies the site of a military cantonment established in 1876 by the city's namesake, Col. Nelson A. Miles, who gets most of the credit for removing the Indian "menace" from the plains after Lt. Col. George Armstrong Custer's humiliating defeat at the Battle of the Little Bighorn. The cantonment was abandoned in 1877 when Fort Keogh was built two miles to the west. Once Montana's largest army post, Fort Keogh now serves all of eastern Montana as a USDA Livestock and Range Research Station, specializing in range improvement and the science of cattle breeding.

Lonesome Dove fans will remember Miles City as the place where their favorite cowboy, Gus McCrae, bit the dust after he and Captain Call trailed their herd of stolen cattle from the Mexico border to the grass bonanza of Montana Territory. Much has changed in Montana since those glory days, but much remains the same. Though the range is now fenced, ranches are still measured in miles, and many are still in the hands of the families that first staked them out.

While southeastern Montana is largely cattle country, the rich bottomlands along the Yellowstone River invited homesteaders to try their luck at farming. Completion of the Northern Pacific Railroad in 1883 brought another wave of settlers into the area. Russian Germans saw the climate and soil of the Yellowstone River Valley as prime sugar beet country, and to this day, sugar beet farms stretch all the way from Laurel to Sidney, making Montana one of the nation's top beet-producing states. Other irrigated crops include corn, alfalfa, oats, wheat, and barley.

■ BILLINGS

The farm and livestock industry is the first order of business for most of the cities and towns of southeastern Montana, but energy production has also played a prominent role in this part of the state. The 1951 discovery of the Williston Basin—a huge oil field that underlies eastern Montana, western North Dakota, and southern Saskatchewan—brought prosperity to small communities like Glendive and Sidney, Baker and Wibaux. The biggest winner was Billings, which emerged as headquarters for the state's promising new petroleum industry. Its claim to the title of energy capital was secured by the energy scare of the seventies, which brought major-league mining and four new coal-fired generating plants to the coal fields of nearby Rosebud County. By the mid-1980s, world oil prices had collapsed. As Montana's largest and most diversified city, Billings withstood the decline, but not without substantial losses of businesses, jobs, and people.

Located midway between Minneapolis and Seattle, Denver and Calgary, **Billings** remains a major trade and distribution hub, headquarters for the region's farm and ranch economy, medical center for all of eastern Montana and northern Wyoming, business and convention center, cultural oasis, and a gateway to Yellowstone Park and the Custer Battlefield. With its handsome, new performing arts center, two college campuses, sprawling shopping malls, high-rise hotels, and buttoned-down, pin-striped business community, Billings puts on big-city airs. But behind the neon lights and theater marquees, the symphony balls and country club shindigs, Billings is a stockmen's town at heart. From the annual stockgrowers' and woolgrowers' conventions to the Northern International Livestock Exposition and Cowboy Christmas Reunion, Billings is where cowboys go when they get all slicked up for business or a night on the town. If ever there were doubt about the city's allegiance to the cattle industry, it vanished in the dust of 10,000 hooves in September 1989. Billings residents lined city streets to cheer the riders and wranglers of the "Great Montana Centennial Cattle Drive" on the last leg of their six-day, 60-mile (100-km) celebration of the way things were, here on the range, before plows turned the grass upside down and fences got in the way.

A heroic-size bronze sculpture of a cattle drover commemorates the "Drive of '89" and welcomes travelers to the **Billings Visitor Center** on South 27th Street, just off Interstate 90. This is a worthwhile stop for first-time visitors to the greater Billings area, which numbers about 100,000 residents concentrated primarily between the prominent rimrock terrace of the city's north face and the Yellowstone River on the south. In addition to its many shops, restaurants, motels and hotels, hospitals and clinics, Billings has several cultural and historic attractions. From the Royal New Zealand Ballet to the "Cowboy Review," the curtain rises one night out of three at the **Alberta Bair Theater,** Billings' brand new, $5.2-million performing arts center. The nearby **Yellowstone Art Center,** housed in the original county jail, has the best contemporary art collection in Montana. Not to be outdone by the arts community, a dedicated bunch of Billings boosters opened **ZooMontana,** a 70-acre wildlife park and botanical garden, in 1991. The **Western Heritage Center** draws residents and visitors to its changing exhibits about the Yellowstone River Valley and the West. The **Moss Mansion** perpetuates the elegance of one of the city's early bankers, while **Pictograph Cave State Park** preserves the drawings of a prehistoric culture.

■ CROW AND CHEYENNE

Like the plains north of the Missouri River and the mountain valleys to the west, the "ground-of-many-gifts" south of the Yellowstone was Indian country long before it was exploited by fur traders and trampled by trail drives. Crow Indians once ranged across a gigantic sweep of mountains and plains from the upper Yellowstone River near what is now Yellowstone National Park, across southern Montana and into Wyoming's Wind River country and Bighorn Basin. A series of treaties with

Billings is a business town, and its Moss Mansion is a monument to one of the city's early banker-developers, Preston B. Moss.

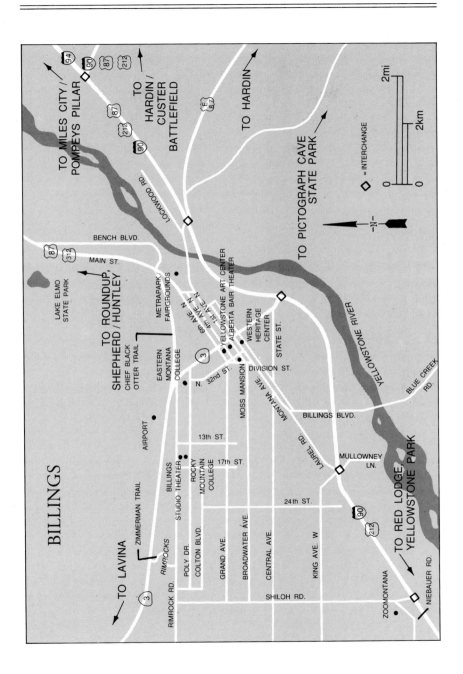

BILLINGS

the U.S. government confined them to their current two-million-acre reservation encompassing most of Big Horn County between Hardin and the Wyoming state line. Their immediate neighbors to the east, on a much smaller reservation, are their historic enemies, the Northern Cheyenne. Unlike other tribes that now inhabit Montana, the Crow developed friendly relations with the federal government before and during the Indian war years. They saw the government as a potential ally in their attempt to protect their land from encroachment by Northern Cheyenne and Sioux, many of whom had left their reservation in the Black Hills of South Dakota when it was overrun by gold prospectors.

■ CUSTER BATTLEFIELD

The **Custer Battlefield National Monument** and **Rosebud Battlefield State Park** immortalize an explosive moment and a dramatic era in Western history. The U.S. campaign to rid the plains of Indians and to open the West to development began right after the Civil War and was achieved by 1890. In just 25 years, one culture crushed another, and life would never be the same for a people whose borders were once defined by natural barriers like mountains and rivers, and whose sustenance was assured by now-extinct buffalo herds.

Scholars and Custer buffs throughout the world visit the Custer Battlefield each year in search of clues to explain the mystery of the Seventh Cavalry's misguided strategy. Casual visitors come by the thousands to walk the grounds of a battle so deeply entrenched in the lore of the American West. Some say ghosts still haunt the site, troubled visions of the violence that detonated these plains more than a century ago. A mass grave atop "Last Stand Hill" makes it a likely spot for disembodied visitors. Ironically, Custer Battlefield is also a place where all of the monuments are to the losers. Working to reverse nearly 120 years of history slanted toward Custer and his cavalry, Indian activists are promoting placement of a monument at the battlefield to the Sioux and Cheyenne victors, as well as a change of name from Custer to Little Bighorn National Battlefield.

Visitors to the Custer Battlefield are in good position to explore the culture and history of the neighboring Crow and Northern Cheyenne tribes. **Chief Plenty Coups State Park**, at Pryor, preserves the home and burial site of Plenty Coups, last chief of the Crows. The Indian leader, whose name translated means "Many

THE BATTLE OF LITTLE BIGHORN

Few events seem so fixed in the American psyche as the 1876 massacre of Gen. George Armstrong Custer and his men at Little Bighorn. The battle seems to reverberate through the years with echoes of that entire tumultuous era when whites and Indians fought over the West. Born to a middle-class Michigan family in 1839, George Custer began his military career as a rather undistinguished student at West Point. After graduating just as the Civil War was beginning, Custer proved himself an able and daring soldier, and moved quickly up the ranks, becoming a major general of the Michigan volunteers. After the war, he gained attention for his exploits in the West, and his autobiographical *My Life on the Plains* attracted national attention. There was even talk of future presidential ambitions for this rapidly rising star whose flowing yellow hair became a trademark.

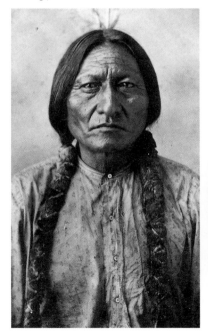

Sitting Bull, Sioux chief
(Montana Historical Society)

Lt. Col. George Armstrong Custer
(Montana Historical Society)

GOLD IN THE HILLS

The events leading up to the climactic confrontation at Little Bighorn were familiar ones, centering around the discovery of a glittering yellow rock, gold. It was the same substance that had earlier stimulated the heady rush of miners and profiteers of all stripes to California, Colorado, and western Montana. This time it was to the Black Hills of Dakota Territory.

The Black Hills had long been fought over by various Indian tribes, but the ·1868 Fort Laramie Treaty promised the land to the Sioux, for "as long as the grass shall grow and the buffalo shall roam." According to the treaty, "no persons except those designated herein . . . shall ever be permitted to pass over, settle upon, or reside in the territory described in this article." As with previous treaties, however, this one proved difficult to enforce, particularly when reports kept emerging of rogue miners emerging with gold dust. To check out these rumors, Gen. Custer was sent to head a massive expedition of 1,000 men into the Black Hills in 1874. His geologists/miners did indeed find gold, an event quickly trumpeted by newspapers across the nation. Unfortunately, the 1868 treaty stood in the way of thousands of whites anxious to get rich on the latest mother lode.

Although the government officially disapproved of whites invading the Black Hills, little was done to halt their advance. Gen. William T. Sherman commented, "I understand that the President and the Interior Dept will wink at it." Even if they *had* wanted to do something, it is unlikely that the Army could have stopped the hordes of miners clamoring to get into the Black Hills. When the government attempted to buy the land for $6 million, the Sioux responded by demanding $600 million along with a guarantee of food and clothes for the next seven generations. The U.S. then took the next predictable step: they decided to simply take the Black Hills by force.

THE BUILDUP

By the fall of 1875, Sioux on the reservations faced starvation due to negligence by the U.S. government and the corruption of its Indian agents. Many of the Sioux headed west to Montana, joining the Cheyenne on hunting grounds along the Little Bighorn River. The government issued an order that all Indians who did not reach the reservations by January 31, 1876, would be considered hostiles and subject to whatever action the U.S. Army might take. The Sioux and Cheyenne either ignored the order or were too far away to be aware that it even existed. In either case, the Army was sent out to bring them in.

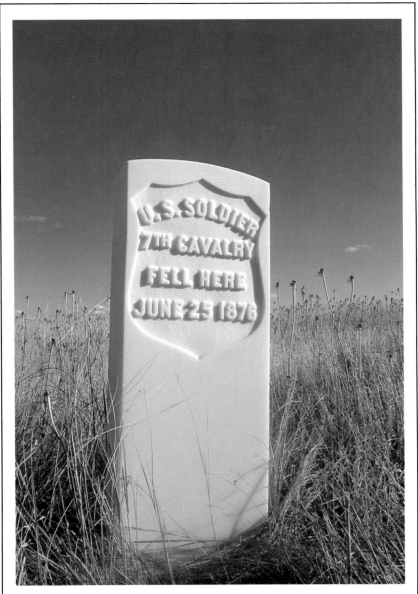

All of the monuments at Custer Battlefield are to the losers. Indian activists are working toward placement of a monument to the Sioux and Cheyenne victors.

The Army converged on the Sioux and Cheyenne from three directions under the overall command of Gen. Alfred H. Terry. General George Crook headed north from Fort Fetterman in Wyoming, while Gen. John Gibbon moved in from western Montana. The third column rode west from Fort Abraham Lincoln in Dakota Territory, headed by Gen. Terry, and including Gen. Custer's Seventh Cavalry.

Gen. Crook's column, reinforced by Shoshone and Crow warriors and scouts, met a force of more than a thousand Indians in the Rosebud Valley (south of the present-day Northern Cheyenne Reservation) on June 17, 1876. The Battle of the Rosebud was more or less a draw, but Crook was forced to retreat back to the south. Meanwhile, Gen. Gibbon was moving toward the Bighorn from the west, joining up with Gen. Terry on June 21. Custer and his men were directed to follow an Indian trail from the south into the Little Bighorn Valley while the force of Terry and Gibbon pressed down from the north.

The Sioux and Cheyenne were well aware that an attack was imminent. Not only had scouts warned of the advancing columns, but so had visions. Chief Sitting Bull had taken part in a Sun Dance along Rosebud Creek in which 100 pieces of flesh were cut from his arms as a blood sacrifice. Afterwards, he dreamed of a great victory over the bluecoats, a victory that was drawn out on the sand. Custer's scouts found the sand pictograph and understood its meaning. It was a warning that went unheeded by the blue coats.

THE BATTLE

On the morning of June 25, Custer's scouts had located the combined Sioux and Cheyenne village along the Little Bighorn River. His 600 men prepared to attack, unaware that at least 10,000 Indians and up to 4,000 warriors were waiting for him. To surround the village, Custer split his regiment into three battalions, putting one under the command of Maj. Marcus Reno and another under Capt. Frederick Benteen. Custer himself led the remaining 225 men.

When Reno attacked, his men were forced back by a fierce Indian counterattack, and were quickly joined by Benteen's force on the high riverside bluffs. Everyone knew that something must be terribly wrong with Custer and his men, for they heard gunfire and saw the smoke from a battle to the north. A messenger from Custer brought a note saying "Come on, big village, be quick, bring packs," but Reno and Benteen's men found themselves pinned down. Here they held out until the following evening when the Indians who had encircled them finally withdrew.

(Although an official military inquiry cleared Reno and Benteen, many historians place the blame for Custer's destruction on their shoulders for not moving up to help.)

Meanwhile, Custer had met up with the full force of several thousand battle-hardened Sioux and Cheyenne warriors. None of his command survived the Battle of the Little Bighorn to explain what had happened. Sioux and Cheyenne accounts varied, but seemed to point to complete chaos among the cavalry, with many apparently going insane in the battle and committing suicide. It appeared a fate better than being tortured to death. Among the 225 who died were Custer himself, along with two brothers, his brother-in-law, and a nephew. Probably fewer than 50 Indians were killed.

THE AFTERMATH

After the battle, Indian women moved onto the site, stripping off the soldiers' clothes and joining in a macabre mutilation of the bodies. Gen. Custer (whose hair was cut short at the time) was one of the few whose heads remained unscalped. His body was relatively untouched; some say because it was protected by two women who knew that Custer had taken a Cheyenne girl as a wife. It is also said that the two women punctured Custer's eardrums with a sewing awl so that he would be able to hear better in the next life. He had certainly not heard the warnings in this one. Two days later, the Army finally stumbled upon the gruesome carnage at Little Bighorn, the place that the Sioux called Greasy Grass.

A magnificent triumph for Sitting Bull, Crazy Horse, Gall, and other Indian leaders, victory was short-lived for the Sioux and Cheyenne. Back East, word of the massacre came as tragic news to a spirited nation in the midst of its first centennial celebration, evoking an immediate national outcry for revenge. The War Department dispatched a third of the U.S. Army to Montana Territory to put an end to the Indian resistance. Many Sioux and Cheyenne fled to temporary safety in Canada, but with the buffalo gone and their ancestral lands seized by American interests, there could be no return to the old days. Custer's Last Stand was in many respects the last stand of the Plains Indians as well. Within a few years, the last of a proud people straggled into the reservations, desperate for food. The death knell came in 1890 when medicine man Sitting Bull was shot by Indian policemen in a botched arrest.

—Don Pitcher

Achievements," is remembered for trying to save the Crows' beloved homeland by getting along with the white man. A museum at the site houses a cultural center for Crow tribal history.

Ashland's **Plains Indian Museum,** on the adjacent Northern Cheyenne Reservation, uses artifacts, clothing and beadwork, even a sweat lodge, to explain the culture of the tribes that inhabited this area. To this day, a careful observer driving through a reservation can detect random plumes of smoke that indicate Indians are heating rocks in outdoor lodges for a therapeutic or ceremonial sweat bath. The adjacent **Little Coyote Gallery** features hand-crafted headdresses, beaded moccasins, jewelry, leatherwork, and paintings. The reservation lies west of the rolling, pine-studded hills of Ashland Forest and north of Tongue River Breaks, an austere, wind-scrubbed landscape of red shale and juniper canyons near Montana's southern border. A gravel road parallels the river through Tongue River Canyon, providing fine views of the coulees and breaks. **Tongue River Reservoir State Park** offers good fishing for walleye, crappie, and bass. Four species of fish from the reservoir hold the state records for size.

The city of **Hardin,** on the northern edge of the Crow reservation, has an excellent visitor center to orient travelers to the area's past and present. A complex of restored buildings and rotating exhibits, the **Big Horn County Historical Museum and Visitor Center** portrays local history from the settler's point of view. With its outdoor park, well-stocked bookstore, and gift shop, it makes a pleasant stop.

■ BIGHORN CANYON

Less than an hour's drive south is **Bighorn Canyon National Recreation Area,** a scenic gorge sunk between the Pryor and Bighorn mountains on Montana's southern border. Canyon walls tower above 71-mile-long (114-km) Bighorn Lake, created by Yellowtail Dam near the park's northern entrance. Water sports and walleye fishing are the main attractions here, but the area also draws hikers, birders, and wildlife watchers. Endangered bald eagles, peregrine falcons, and even an occasional whooping crane round out the Bighorn Canyon bird list to 260 species. Backcountry camping, scenic drives, canyon overlooks, historic homesteads and ranches, and one of Montana's least-visited mountain ranges await visitors to the west side of the canyon. Boat tours of Bighorn Canyon are available from the Wyoming side of the canyon; see "Tours" in "PRACTICAL INFORMATION" for specifics.

Bighorn Canyon National Recreation Area, from the Devil Canyon overlook.

The **Pryor Mountains** are a remote, highland junction of desert and ice on the west side of Bighorn Canyon. Low-lying limestone peaks and plateaus are rutted with deep canyons and dotted with ice caves so numerous that visitors can still find some that have never been explored. The best known is **Big Ice Cave,** which tunnels into a hillside blanketed with wildflowers during the summer. But the Pryors' biggest attraction is its wild horse range, the nation's first. Established in 1968, this outback preserve is home to about 130 mustangs managed by the Bureau of Land Management. Descended from both Spanish stock and horses of local ranchers, they have reverted to truly wild animals in the sequestered meadows and box canyons of this 44,000-acre refuge. Visitors frequently see the horses from the Trans-Park Highway (Montana State Highway 37), on the west side of Bighorn Canyon.

Bighorn River below Yellowtail Dam on the east side of the canyon is a nationally renowned trout stream, supporting as many as 10,000 trout per mile, mostly good-sized browns. These may sound like great odds, but statistics are not synonymous with success. Fishing for wild trout in mountain rivers and streams is not as easy as it may appear. Beginners' luck aside, landing trout is directly proportional to knowledge of the water. And here on the Bighorn, there are plenty of fishing guides who know every inch of the river. If you are new to this or any river in Montana, it's a good idea to hire a guide the first day out. Drill your guide for information, then head out on your own the next day. One day's guide service on a new river is a good investment in any fishing vacation. (See "Useful Addresses" in "PRACTICAL INFORMATION" for the Montana Outfitters and Guides Association address.)

■ FISHING AND FLOATING THE YELLOWSTONE

Native cutthroat and other trout give the upper Yellowstone River its national reputation among anglers. Somewhere between Columbus and Laurel, however, the Yellowstone and its tributaries give up their cold-water traits and take on a prairie personality. The climate becomes warmer and so does the water. The river supports 45 species in all, including sauger, walleye, bass, pike, burbot, sturgeon, and channel catfish.

The lower Yellowstone's most exotic fish is also its oldest and largest. More than 65 million years old, the bottom-dwelling **paddlefish** has a distinctive, spatula-like snout and a hulking frame of cartilage and meat covered with a tough, leathery skin. The Yellowstone and the Missouri rivers support one of the world's few remaining reproducing populations of paddlefish. In May and June, the fish make spawning runs up the two rivers from Lake Sakakawea in North Dakota, signaling the start of one of Montana's most athletic sporting events. Anglers crowd the Yellowstone's banks at Intake Diversion Dam, between Glendive and Sidney. Because paddlefish are plankton eaters that filter microscopic organisms through their gills, they are never caught the conventional way, but by snagging. So, with a little blind luck, fishermen may snag one of these 25- to 50-pound (11- to 23-kg) beasts. The prize, besides a memorable catch and photo opportunity, is a freezer full of boneless, white, lobster-like steaks. Hoping to cash in on a resource that lies literally under its nose, the city of Glendive has even begun marketing paddlefish caviar.

■ AGATES

Other treasures from the lower Yellowstone include colorful moss agates, jasper, and petrified wood. Formed some 50 million years ago, agates are a form of quartz that contains dendritic, or branchlike, patterns in the shape of trees, flowers, and other "pictures." They range in color from yellow and orange to brown and black, making distinctive jewelry when cut and polished.

Not much for looks, the ancient paddlefish provides great sport for fishermen along the lower Yellowstone and Missouri rivers.
(Travel Montana)

Agates can be found all the way from Custer, where the Bighorn joins the Yellowstone, to Sidney, near the North Dakota state line. The best times to look are in early spring, when ice breaks up and scours the riverbed, and after June, when spring runoff has exposed new stones. Raw agates are not easily spotted by amateur rockhounds, but there are plenty of rock shops along the lower river, where tips and guidance are freely given. One of Montana's finest agate collections is displayed in Glendive's Best Western Holiday Lodge, where guided float trips can be arranged for agate hunters.

Whether searching for agates, fish, white-tailed deer, a family of Canada geese, or simply peace of mind, drifting down the Yellowstone is a lovely introduction to southeastern Montana. Unlike the upper river—where trout fishing and white water draw thousands of recreationists each year—the lower river is relatively unknown, a forgotten place where you can float for two or three days without seeing another person.

■ EASTERN BORDERLANDS

Land lovers will enjoy a similar, off-the-beaten-path experience most anywhere in southeastern Montana, but two of the more accessible sites are Makoshika and Medicine Rocks state parks. **Makoshika** is a badlands park, just outside of Glendive, that has been shaped over the past 70 million years by wind and water. Derived from a Sioux Indian word meaning "bad or stinking earth," Makoshika preserves 8,800 acres of sculpted sandstone and shale dotted with pine, juniper, and a frenzy of wildflowers. Fossilized remains of primitive plants and dinosaurs open windows to the prehistory of this area, once a vast swamp covered by giant ferns and inhabited by reptiles. During the summer, visiting paleontologists conduct "dig-a-dinosaur" tours to teach amateurs how to identify fossils without disturbing them. The **Frontier Gateway Museum** in Glendive has a fine collection of fossils from the area. The park's most popular current inhabitants are the turkey vultures that return each spring from the Southwest. Area residents mark the event, usually around mid-April, with "Buzzard Day," an excuse to get together at the park for games and activities. The park has a visitor center, campground, picnic tables, scenic drives, nature trails, and archery and shooting ranges.

Medicine Rocks is another badlands park, south of Makoshika in Montana's isolated southeast corner. As its name implies, this was a place of big medicine, where

Indian tribes came to seek strength and guidance from the spirits that dwelled here. The Sioux name for medicine rock, *Inyan-oka-la-ka,* means "Rock with a hole in it." In fact, these rocks look more like Swiss cheese than sandstone. The steady wind that sweeps the plains appears to be the master craftsman at Medicine Rocks, sculpting the soft sandstone deposits over millions of years into sand castles, knobs, pillars, and buttes. An early visitor to this quiet corner of Montana, Theodore Roosevelt, was captivated by the sight of "as singular a bit of country as I have ever seen." He described the formations as "caves, columns, battlements, spires, and flying buttresses . . . mingled in the strangest confusion." Once the domain of giant herds of buffalo, this area still hosts mule deer, pronghorn, coyote, fox, and raptors of all kinds. Relatively undeveloped, Medicine Rocks State Park provides camping, picnic tables, toilets, drinking water, and a loop road with scenic turn-outs.

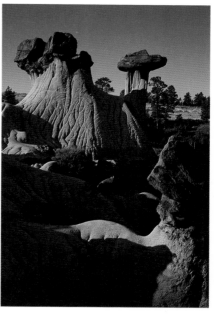

Makoshika is a badlands park near Glendive; its Sioux Indian name means "bad or stinking earth." (photo by Douglas O'Looney)

■ EKALAKA

A trip to this out-of-the-way corner of the world would be incomplete without a visit to Ekalaka, said to be founded by a bartender who was out here hunting buffalo when his horses balked and his wagon bogged down. "Hell," he said, "any place in Montana is a good place to build a saloon." Whereupon he dropped his load and built the Old Stand Bar, which still serves as the social center of this small but spirited outpost. While Carter County was named after the bartender, Ekalaka, its county seat, derived its curious name from a Sioux Indian girl said to be the niece of Sitting Bull. A town of only 400, Ekalaka has one of the most significant local museums in Montana. The **Carter County Museum** is nothing short of a prehistory bonanza. In addition to the 35-foot-long (11-m) skeleton of a duck-billed dinosaur, assembled bone-by-bone from fossilized remains found nearby, the museum houses the thousand-pound skull (455-kg) of a *Triceratops,* the remains of a giant marine lizard, a bonehead dinosaur, and artifacts from a much more recent find—an 11,000-year-old archaeological site where ancient peoples killed and butchered buffalo. All of the museum's treasures were found in Carter County.

South of Ekalaka are the **Chalk Buttes, Ekalaka Hills,** and **Long Pines,** three distinct scenic areas managed as units of the Custer National Forest. A number of enjoyable scenic gravel roads cut through this remote country, offering the chance to savor an austerely beautiful landscape. One of the nicest, Powderville Road, crosses the plains to tiny Powderville and then on to Chalk Buttes. Together with the Pryor Mountains, the Ashland Forest, Makoshika and Medicine Rocks, the diverse public lands of southeastern Montana have little in common except their isolation and the region's ubiquitous cattle crop. Canyons and mesas, badlands and breaks, limestone cliffs, terraces, pine forests, meadows, and grasslands are all part of the southeastern mosaic. Not long ago, many of these lands were regarded as sacred places where Indians gathered to seek visions and spiritual renewal. Largely overlooked by visitors who seek the grander scale of Glacier and Yellowstone, they remain an appealing destination for modern vision seekers.

(top) The post office, general store, and gas staion are the social center of tiny Volborg in southeastern Montana. (bottom) A well-placed sign beats a highway map when you leave the pavement in eastern Montana.

CENTRAL HEARTLAND

CENTRAL MONTANA IS A LAND OF TRANSITIONS. Moving east to west, from Roundup to the Rocky Mountain Front, it rises gradually from semi-arid plains and low-lying hills to fertile valleys, benches and buttes, forested mountains and isolated peaks. Along the way, grass and sage give way to cultivated fields of wheat and barley as the rainfall increases. Baseball caps outnumber cowboy hats and the people who wear them use tractors, not horses, to get the work done. If Montana has a heartland, this is it.

The tallest structures on the skyline are grain elevators, and one of the most pleasing sights in all of Montana is the inland ocean of plump, golden grain that ripples across the plains of central and northern Montana in late summer. Central Montana shares the grain-rich **Golden Triangle** with the Hi-Line. Find Great Falls, Havre, and Cut Bank on a map, and you will have traced the triangle's outline, but you will never see it named. It exists in the minds of Montanans, a perceptual region made real by the cash receipts of its annual output of grain. In a state that consistently ranks among the nation's top five wheat and barley producers, this area produces fully 50 percent of the statewide total. Indeed, it is one of the nation's breadbaskets.

Headquarters for the region's agriculture industry are Great Falls, which services the Golden Triangle, and Lewistown, a smaller city that pinpoints the state's geographic center. Dozens of small farming communities dot the heartland, remnants and survivors of Montana's homestead experiment.

Lewistown got an earlier start as a trading post on the Carroll Trail between Helena and the mouth of the Musselshell. It has served as a regional trade center ever since. With a population of about 6,000, Lewistown has the heart of a small town and a head for exploiting its assets. Its central location, together with a busy main street, the preservation of historic buildings erected by Croatian stone masons-turned-homesteaders, and plenty of outdoor recreation opportunities all contribute to Lewistown's appeal. Set against a backdrop of three mountain ranges—the Snowies, the Judiths, and the Moccasins—it is one of Montana's most attractive small towns.

■ GREAT FALLS

Great Falls, a city of about 55,000, straddles the Missouri River where a series of waterfalls once roared, giving the state's second-largest city its name. It was at this point on the river that Lewis and Clark encountered one of the most formidable challenges of their entire expedition. Meriwether Lewis described the falls as a "sublimely grand specticle" when he first saw them in June 1805, but the enchantment wore off quickly. He and co-captain William Clark were stalled at this site for nearly a month while they portaged 18 miles (29 km) around the falls before continuing upriver. Later harnessed by dams for their hydroelectric power potential, the falls also gave the city its most enduring nickname, the "Electric City." Scenic overlooks at some of the dams give visitors a chance to stretch their imaginations as they envision an earlier obstacle course of freeflowing falls and cascades.

By Montana standards, Great Falls is a large city with a diversified economy. Yet, it is in their past that civic leaders see the city's future. Through their efforts, a national Lewis and Clark Historic Center is scheduled to open in 1993 at **Giant Springs State Park,** on the Missouri River east of town. The center will emphasize the native cultures Lewis and Clark encountered on their route, and will include a dugout canoe demonstration area and an encampment along the river, in addition to a visitor center.

The city of Great Falls has assembled one of the world's largest collections of Charles M. Russell original art and memorabilia, on display at the **C. M. Russell Museum.** Great Falls is the logical spot for this national treasure because this is where the cowboy artist spent his most productive years as a painter, sculptor, and master storyteller of the romantic West. The city also celebrates Russell's life and legacy every year by throwing a colossal birthday party for him in March. Artists, art lovers, and collectors of Western art from throughout the world come to Great Falls to immerse themselves in four days of seminars, exhibits, and auctions at the **C. M. Russell Auction of Original Western Art.** Over 20 years old, the event has raised more than $1 million for the Russell Museum, which includes several galleries, Russell's turn-of-the-century home, and his original log cabin studio. Covering 46,000 square feet, the museum features the work of Russell and his contemporaries, and houses 7,500 works in its permanent collection. Not to be missed!

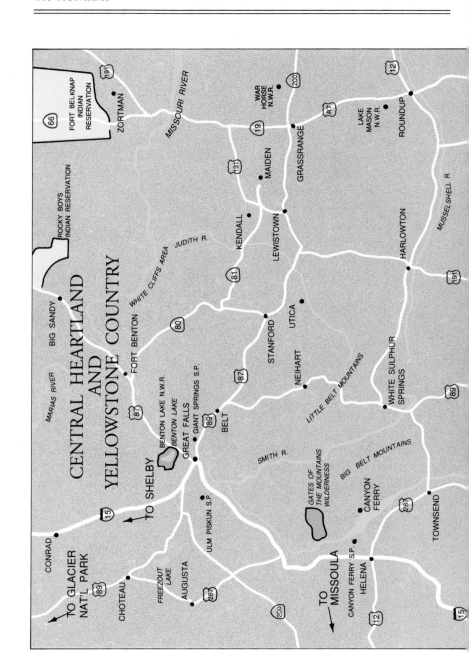

CENTRAL HEARTLAND
AND
YELLOWSTONE COUNTRY

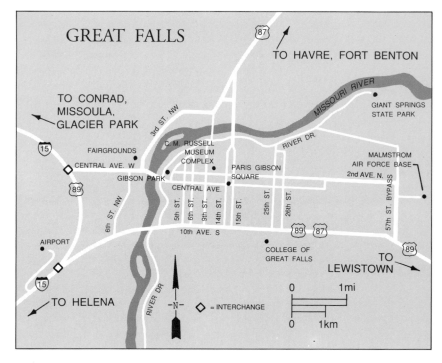

GREAT FALLS

87

TO HAVRE, FORT BENTON

TO CONRAD,
MISSOULA,
GLACIER PARK

MISSOURI RIVER

GIANT SPRINGS
STATE PARK

15

FAIRGROUNDS

CENTRAL AVE. W

GIBSON PARK

3rd ST. NW

C. M. RUSSELL
MUSEUM
COMPLEX

RIVER DR.

89

PARIS GIBSON
SQUARE

CENTRAL AVE.

MALMSTROM
AIR FORCE BASE

2nd AVE. N.

6th ST. NW

5th ST.

6th ST.

9th ST.

14th ST.

15th ST.

25th ST.

26th ST.

57th ST. BYPASS

10th AVE. S

89 87

AIRPORT

15

TO HELENA

RIVER DR.

-N-

= INTERCHANGE

COLLEGE OF
GREAT FALLS

TO
LEWISTOWN

89

0   1mi

0   1km

■ NUCLEAR HEARTLAND

If Russell condemned his nation's early incursions, he undoubtedly would have had some salty comments about today's military presence in Great Falls and the surrounding plains and grainfields of central Montana. Beneath this quiet, life-sustaining landscape lie 200 long-range nuclear missiles, each equipped with one to three warheads capable of producing a nuclear firestorm up to 100 times greater than the blast that incinerated Hiroshima in 1945. Installed in the early 1960s at the height of the Cold War, they comprise a portion of the 1,000 Minuteman missiles (some now being replaced by MX) seeded in the plains of seven Western and Midwestern states. Aimed at the Soviet Union, they are similarly targeted by that nation's ground-based, nuclear missiles. Residents and visitors rarely comprehend the fact that they are traversing Ground Zero when driving through central Montana because the missiles are housed—out of sight, out of mind—in underground silos. Covered by concrete slabs and surrounded by tall, chain-link fencing, they resemble

C. M. RUSSELL, COWBOY ARTIST

Cowboy artist Charles Marion Russell was born in 1864 to a wealthy St. Louis family, but spent his childhood in rebellion against the strictures of society. In desperation, Charlie's father sent the lad to Montana at age 16 to give him a dose of reality. His family expected to see a chastened young man return to their doorstep, but instead, Charlie fell in love with the wide open spaces of the West. His first Montana job—as a sheepherder along the Judith River—proved a disaster when Charlie lost the entire flock of sheep. Shortly thereafter, mountain man Jake Hoover found the shivering kid hunkered beside a flickering fire. Under Jake's tutelage, Charlie learned to survive on the open range. The small, sod-covered cabin he shared with Jake still stands along the South Fork of the Judith, an unmarked but unmistakable shrine to the romance and freedom he sought out West.

Eventually, Charlie landed a job as night wrangler for a cattle outfit. The job provided a perfect outlet for his pent-up creative energy; it meant his days were free to paint, draw, or make models from clay or wax. Russell continued to wrangle cattle for more than a decade, gaining first-hand knowledge of the cowboy life that became a central feature of his art work. Our most enduring reminder of the disastrous winter of 1886–87 is a small watercolor of a starving steer painted by Russell, who titled it "Waiting for a Chinook." Stalked by coyotes, the dying animal portrayed the end of an era.

Russell was a humorous, lighthearted man given to good times with good friends. Those who knew him were delighted by his marvelous, long-winded tales of the Old West. But Russell was saddened by the changes and injustices he saw during the rapid development of the West. A cowboy at heart, he had no affection for the homestead movement, which turned the plains "grass side down." Writing to a friend in 1913, he said, "The boosters say it's a better country than it ever was but it looks like hell to me. I liked it better when it belonged to God. It was shure his country when we knew it."

Russell spent a winter with the Blood Indians, a branch of the Blackfeet, and learned to speak Piegan. Using sign language, he could communicate with any of the Plains Indian tribes, and lamented the demise of their culture and the government's policy of displacing the West's native inhabitants. "Those Indians have been living in heaven for a thousand years," he once told a friend, "and we took it away from 'em for forty dollars a month." Russell was one of several prominent Montanans who lobbied for creation of the Rocky Boy's Reservation in 1916 for landless members of the Chippewa and Cree tribes.

Russell documented the West he loved in more than 4,500 oil paintings, water-colors, sculptures, and illustrated letters. In later years, he gained an international following for his self-taught artwork, commanding up to $20,000 for a single painting. Despite national acclaim, he continued to live in Great Falls, working in an artifact-filled log cabin studio next to his home. Russell died in 1926, but left behind his passionate legacy of paintings documenting the American West, many of which are on display in the outstanding C. M. Russell Museum in Great Falls.

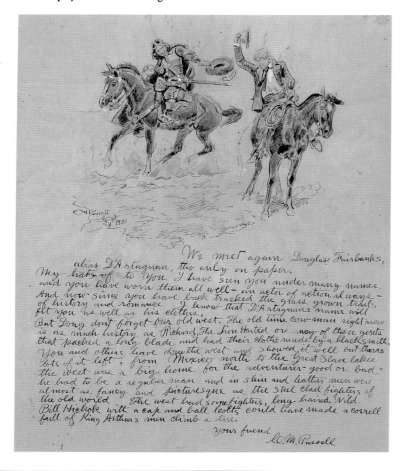

One of Charlie Russell's illustrated letters, this one to Douglas Fairbanks, Jr.

(top) "The Jerkline," oil painting by C.M. Russell. (C.M. Russell Museum)
(bottom) "He Aimed and the Snake was Shattered," pen and ink drawing by C.M. Russell.
(C.M. Russell Museum)

"Flying Lead and Splinters," ink wash by C.M. Russell. (C.M. Russell Museum)

Russell was a humorous, light-hearted man but he was saddened by the changes and injustices he saw during the rapid development of the West. (C.M. Russell Museum)

small electrical power substations. But there is no denying the fact that these are weapons of annihilation, controlled around the clock by personnel of the 341st Strategic Missile Wing based in Great Falls. A major influence on the Great Falls economy, Malmstrom Air Force Base operates an aerial refueling mission as well as the missile program.

■ FORT BENTON

An earlier military installation, **Fort Benton** is now a peaceful community loaded with history and small-town charm. Lewis and Clark camped at this site, less than an hour downriver from Great Falls, in June of 1805. Because of the trouble they and other early travelers encountered with waterfalls upriver, Fort Benton became

the head of commercial navigation on the great river route of the West. Fort Benton came to be known as the "birthplace of Montana" after the first steamboat from St. Louis arrived in 1859. Within a year, it was also a terminus on the Mullan Road, which linked the Missouri to the Columbia River and the Pacific Northwest. Other wagon roads soon radiated from this river port like spokes from a hub, and by the mid-1860s, thousands of miners were passing through town en route to the gold camps of southwestern Montana. It is said that two-and-a-half tons of gold dust were shipped downriver from Fort Benton in 1866, and that between 1872 and 1882, 445,000 buffalo robes made the same trip. By the same token, tons of supplies and equipment destined for Montana's gold camps were freighted

Logo on a steam-powered tractor at Mehmke's Antique Farm Machinery Museum, near Great Falls.

OPEN HOUSE ON THE PRAIRIE

*T*he Air Force personnel who look after the missiles in Montana are stationed at Malmstrom Air Force Base, just outside of Great Falls. The public information officers there answer questions by mail about the Minuteman system with a vague line drawing of a missile in a silo. To callers who wish to chat about the missile installations, they reply in the most general terms. Then, in the summer, the base holds an open house for anybody who wants to come, and officers and enlisted men show their visitors around and tell them just about anything they want to know. This event, called Big Sky Days, is usually on a weekend in July. One year, along with about twenty-nine thousand other people, I went. At the gate, an Air Force guy in a short-sleeve blue uniform shirt was directing traffic. Nearby he had parked a Chevy Blazer with the doors open, so he could listen to the radio. "Standing in the Light," by Fleetwood Mac, was playing. Malmstrom is mostly runway. The thousands of cars parked together took up only a little piece of it. In the distance, heat shimmers rose where it seemed to disappear around the curve of the earth.

Big Sky Days was the kind of summer event where people in shorts walk around dazed and asquint. Long lines waited to go up into the camouflage-painted B-52. In a big hangar, Air Force wives and local groups ran booths selling "Rambo Hotdogs" and "Commie Busters" T-shirts. At one booth, kids could get their faces painted camouflage. By the end of the day, about half the kids had. An M-60 tank in the middle of the hangar drew kids by the hundreds. It was like the most popular rock at monkey island. Members of Air Force security in mesh flak jackets and black berets, with automatic rifles across their backs, helped kids climb on and off. By the hangar doors, pilots in flight suits walked up to each other and put their heads together. Then, after a moment, they threw back their heads and laughed big openmouth pilot laughs.

—Ian Frazier, *Great Plains,* 1989

upriver and dumped on the landing at Fort Benton, then hauled overland by ox and mule teams.

Fort Benton today is a mature, law-abiding town of about 1,600, its ambience a far cry from the lynchings and gunfights that marked its renegade youth. Paved, tree-lined streets have replaced mud- and manure-caked wagon roads. Sleek canoes and motor boats glide where sternwheel steamers once chugged into port. Neat rows of wood-frame residential housing now stand where Indian trading houses, a brewery, an adobe fort, and at least a dozen saloons once sprawled along the river. Fort Benton's preservation-minded residents have rescued their past and now share it with visitors at their riverfront park, historic landmark district, Lewis and Clark Memorial, and museums focusing on agriculture and the upper Missouri River.

■ EXPLORING THE MISSOURI RIVER

Just as it did more than a century ago, Fort Benton still serves as an important starting point for river travel. Not only can you enjoy scenic boat tours right from town, but more adventurous explorers can float the **Upper Missouri National Wild and Scenic River,** which stretches 150 miles (240 km) downriver from Fort Benton

Drawn by C Sohon.   Bowen &Co. lith. Philada.

FORT BENTON;_HEAD OF STEAM NAVIGATION ON THE MISSOURI RIVER.

By the mid-1860s, thousands of miners were traveling by riverboat from St. Louis to Fort Benton en route to the gold camps of southwestern Montana. (Bancroft Library, University of California at Berkeley)

to Fort Peck Lake. The Bureau of Land Management maintains a visitor center in Fort Benton to orient floaters to the only major portion of the 2,300-mile-long (3,700-km) Missouri that has been preserved in its natural, freeflowing state.

As it courses through a lunar landscape of eroding breaks and badlands, sagebrush and sandstone formations, this turbid stretch of river moves relentlessly forward, yet reaches back in time. What it does not offer in white-knuckle rapids and icy, fresh water, the Missouri more than compensates with historic drama and its own isolated beauty.

Once the domain of Blackfeet, Assiniboine, and Cree Indians, the Missouri was a moving stage on which many of the major players in Montana history made their first appearance. Lewis and Clark marveled at the "seens of visionary inchantment" they viewed in the scenic White Cliffs area. Prince Maximilian, Albert Bierstadt, Karl Bodmer, and other European explorers and artists weren't far behind. Anxious for a look at the New World's exotic frontier, they sought a romantic view of the American West and recorded it in priceless illustrations and paintings of the landscape, wildlife, and native cultures they encountered as they made their way upriver. Indians and fur traders swapped beaver pelts for beads and whiskey at riverside trading posts. Near the end of their ill-fated, three-month march to Canada, Chief Joseph and his band of Nez Perce crossed this stretch of river en route to the destination they never reached. Steamboats puffed upriver, supplying a steady market for fuel supplied by "woodhawks" along the river. Cattlemen turned their herds out to graze the river's rough edges, a formidable landscape that came in handy for cattle rustlers and outlaws. Homesteaders found this country too harsh to cultivate but not before they built the weathered shacks that remain as evidence of their optimism.

For all the action this river has seen, it is hauntingly quiet now, the perfect tonic for anyone wishing to escape the babel of humanity. But for an occasional chorus of Canada geese or the distant song of coyotes calling, the isolated breaks of the Missouri are silent and refreshingly lonesome. Despite the disappearance of some of its earlier residents, like the grizzly bear, wolf, and buffalo, the Missouri still provides refuge for a diverse bunch of mammals, birds, amphibians, reptiles, and fish.

Rattlesnakes are among the strangers you might encounter here, so be prepared to rely on yourself because you are miles—on river and bad roads—from medical help. Essential gear, besides food and camping equipment, includes hiking boots, rain jackets, plenty of fresh water, and all manner of sunscreens: lotion, long

(following pages) "Indian Village" C.M. Russell Museum

sleeves, wide brims, and sunglasses. A canoe trip on the Missouri can last from a day to a week, the longer the better. Popular launching spots, besides Fort Benton, are Coal Banks Landing and Judith Landing. Lewis and Clark Cruises (see "Tours" in "PRACTICAL INFORMATION" for specifics) provides boat tours down the Missouri from Fort Benton.

While the river below Fort Benton is a national treasure, preserved for its historic and scenic values, the Missouri above Great Falls is prized as one of Montana's great trout streams. Fed by mountain headwaters and regulated by four dams, the upper river supports sizeable populations of catchable rainbows and browns. No slouch as a scenic river, this stretch is also popular with rafters and canoeists as it makes its way through canyons, past mountains, and onto open plains. Diverse habitats, ranging from bottomlands and backwater sloughs to dense forests and short-grass prairies, provide sanctuary for a variety of wildlife, including waterfowl, raptors, and upland game, deer, elk, smaller mammals, and furbearers.

■ CENTRAL MONTANA MOUNTAINS

To the east are the plains, rivers, and isolated mountain ranges of central Montana. Not as famous as southwestern Montana's Madison and Gallatin, the streams that meander through central Montana are uncrowded and fun to fish. Not as postcard-perfect as the high-rise peaks to the northwest, the mountains are smaller, more manageable, and easily reached.

Two of the most uncommonly beautiful river valleys in all of Montana carry the deceptively ordinary names of the Smith and the Judith. Both rivers rise in the mountains of central Montana and find their separate ways to the Missouri. Born in the Castle Mountains east of White Sulphur Springs, the **Smith River** winds beneath imposing limestone walls and through remote, largely private sheep and cattle ranching country between the Little Belt and Big Belt mountain ranges. Because of its isolation and limited public access, the Smith is a floater's river. Overcrowding has become a problem in recent years, necessitating the state fish and wildlife agency to regulate the number of people on the river.

In contrast, the **Judith River**, farther east, is surrounded by national forest lands and not so stand-offish. Accessible by improved gravel roads, this is a valley for leisurely driving, biking, hiking, or horseback riding. Not as big a river as the

Smith, the Judith and its mountain-fed tributaries support smallish trout. What they lack in sporting appeal, however, is compensated by the surrounding beauty of lush meadows and limestone canyons.

Up the road, the tiny outpost of **Utica** carries a sizeable reputation as one of the liveliest towns of the open-cattle-range era, when cowboys from throughout the grass-rich Judith Basin came to town to spend their week's earnings on Saturday night. This area has also enjoyed on-again-off-again eminence as one of the world's few producers of gem-quality sapphires. Valued worldwide for their clarity and deep blue color, sapphires have been mined from Yogo Gulch, in the Little Belt Mountains southwest of Utica, since 1896. Over the years, this lode has produced $10 million worth of gemstones. Synthetic sapphires have crowded the market and devalued the real thing, but rich veins of sapphire-bearing clay still exist in the gulch, making it a popular spot for rockhounds.

Some of the serious money in central Montana's development came from gold and silver. While the gold rush of the 1860s and the silver strikes of the eighties were concentrated in the highly mineralized mountains of southwestern Montana, the boarded skeletons of saloons and assay offices in the Castle, Judith, and Little Belt mountains confirm a fever of epidemic proportions. Fortunes were fabulous but fleeting in the mining camps of Castle, Maiden, Kendall, and Hughesville. Delayed rail service and distant smelting facilities, combined with a panic on the silver market, caused the more isolated camps of central Montana to collapse nearly as quickly as they sprang to life.

A few homes and outbuildings are all that remain of the silver mining center of **Castle,** once a 14-saloon town in the Castle Mountains southeast of White Sulphur Springs. In the Judith Mountains, northeast of Lewistown, there is even less evidence of **Maiden,** where an estimated $18 million in gold was produced before a fire leveled the town in 1905. Another mining camp in the Judiths was overestimated in nearly every respect, including its name. Mining operations never amounted to much in **Gilt Edge,** but legend has it that Calamity Jane was a frequent guest of its jailhouse. Nearby **Kendall,** in the low-lying Moccasin Mountains north of Lewistown, was a more serious venture. At the turn of the century, it boasted a two-story hotel, opera house, two churches, a mercantile, four stagecoach lines, and several saloons. Kendall became a ghost in 1912, when a branch line of the Milwaukee Road (a partly electrified railroad that spanned central Montana) sidestepped it to establish the town of Hilger nearby. Many of Kendall's buildings collapsed and others were moved to area ranches. In the Little Belts, several small camps rose briefly to prominence, including Hughesville, Barker, Lehigh, Monarch, and Neihart. Once the trade center of this mining district, **Neihart** remains a small but active jumping off place for year-round recreation in the surrounding mountains.

An icicle-lined cave with a frozen waterfall is one of the attractions that draws explorers on hot summer days to the **Big Snowy Mountains,** less than an hour's drive from Lewistown. Lake fishing, hiking trails, more caves and waterfalls, fossils, camping, picnic grounds, and stunning, 360-degree views lure visitors. **Big Spring Creek,** which offers some of Montana's finest trout fishing and best drinking water, originates in these mountains. About seven miles (11 km) south of Lewistown, where the creek emerges from one of the largest freshwater springs in the United States, visitors to the Big Springs Trout Hatchery can see where many of Montana's famed trout get their start. Unlike the wild, self-propagating trout that dwell in Montana's rivers, these hatchery trout will be planted in freshwater lakes and reservoirs. Annual output of up to three million trout and kokanee salmon accounts for a sizeable proportion of the state's total production.

To the south are the **Crazy Mountains,** supposedly named after a westering woman who became deranged and wandered the area alone after everyone else in her family was killed during a Blackfeet Indian raid. Today these mountains are known simply as the Crazies. This small but magnificent range is a favorite of hikers, horsemen, and hunters. Soaring peaks, alpine lakes, cascading streams, and sweeping views make the Crazies one of Montana's most spectacular alpine areas. To the Crow Indians these were sacred peaks, a place to summon spirits. Later travelers sought landmarks to measure their progress, and few were more dramatic than the Crazy Mountains, rising 7,000 feet (2,130 m) above the plains, 11,000 feet (3,360 m) above sea level.

■ ROCKY MOUNTAIN FRONT

Along the western edge of the heartland, travelers find another clearly defined transition point. Here, the plains pour out of the mountains, rolling east of U.S. Route 89/87 as far as the eye can see. The vertical wall of the Rocky Mountains rises abruptly to the west. This is the Rocky Mountain Front, a visual feast cooked

Castle is one of dozens of ghost towns that haunt the mountains and hillsides of central and western Montana.

up about a hundred million years ago in a superheated, over-pressurized, underground kitchen. Today's apparent calm belies the intense forces still at work beneath this transition zone. Earthquakes rumble frequently through western Montana, indicating that these mountains are still on the move.

Rocked by human conflict, the visible landscape is equally dynamic. What appears to be a land of quiet beauty has become a battle zone, where developers and conservationists, ranchers and wildlife advocates square off almost daily over the issues of oil and gas exploration, logging, wilderness protection, and grizzly bear habitat. Oil and gas deposits are believed to lie beneath the overthrust belt that was created when huge slabs of rock formations slid over one another. While conservationists, including Blackfeet Indian traditionalists, fight to preserve these pristine lands, the oil industry wants to explore their potential for commercial drilling.

One of the Front's most controversial residents, the grizzly bear, has stirred debate over another complex issue that raises a fundamental question: Whose land is this, anyway: the wildlife populations that were here first, or the human community that came later? The grizzly's leading defender, the late A. B. Guthrie, Jr., was a celebrated resident of the Front until his death in 1991. Pulitzer Prize-winning author of *The Way West, The Big Sky,* and several other novels about the early development of the West, Guthrie described the grizzly as "a living, snorting incarnation of the wilderness and grandeur of America." His allegiance to the bear was a sore point with his rancher-neighbors, most of whom run their cattle and sheep on the fringe of prime grizzly habitat.

Recognizing the importance of the Rocky Mountain Front to this and other wildlife and plants, The Nature Conservancy has preserved 18,000 acres of prairies, wetlands, foothills, and forests along the east slope of the Rockies, a lowland extension of the adjacent Bob Marshall Wilderness. The Conservancy's **Pine Butte Swamp** is the grizzly's last prairie stronghold, a place where the threatened beast and other wildlife can migrate freely between mountains and plains. Here, the bears come each spring to feed and raise their young in a lush lowland while snow still covers the high country. This merger of diverse habitats is home to more some of Montana's rarest native plants and animals, plus a rich prehistory that includes the nesting sites of dinosaurs, a buffalo jump, and a portion of the Great North Trail, used by Asiatic peoples migrating across the land bridge to North America more than 10,000 years ago. Visitors to Pine Butte Swamp, less than 30 miles (48 km) west of Choteau, can explore the preserve on their own or participate in week-long natural history tours and workshops that feature the area's plants, animals, geology, and paleontology. (See "Guest Ranches" in "PRACTICAL INFORMATION" for lodging at Pine Butte.)

From cattle and sheep to wheat and barley, plains to alpine peaks, the Central Heartland embodies the physical diversity of Montana. An agricultural giant, it is but a pinpoint on America's demographic map. The heartland was built on the backs of farmers and small-town folks who still celebrate the rural lifestyle at county fairs, church suppers, and community dance halls. But their way of life is threatened, their future as uncertain as the grizzly's. As more and more Americans desert the farm, central Montana supports fewer and fewer residents. Yet, it remains the kind of place most people would love to call home.

(following pages) Rising 7,000 feet (2,130 m) above the plains of central Montana, the Crazy Mountains were a landmark for early travelers, and a sacred place for Crow Indians.

YELLOWSTONE COUNTRY

IF YELLOWSTONE PARK WERE SIMPLY A PIECE OF REAL ESTATE defined by the legal boundaries that established it as the world's first national park in 1872, Montana would hardly be justified in claiming it as a major attraction. Barely overlapping Montana's southern border, the park's 2.2-million-acre expanse lies almost entirely in Wyoming's northwest corner. But Yellowstone is more than the largish square it occupies on both states' highway maps. It is the centerpiece of one of the nation's most intact ecosystems, the so-called **Greater Yellowstone Ecosystem,** which shapes the landscape and penetrates the mindset of three states—Wyoming, as well as Montana and Idaho. An immense wilderness plateau, it straddles the Continental Divide radiating an aura of elemental power.

Rising in the mountains of Yellowstone's backcountry, icy creeks gather size and strength as they surge north, providing Montana with some of the world's finest trout streams. Elk, grizzly bears, buffalo, geese, swans, and other Yellowstone residents migrate freely in and out of the park, making Montana a second home. It is conceivable that even the park's thermal waterworks gurgle north through underground plumbing to create the random hot springs that dot southwestern Montana. Indeed, the forests and wildernesses, pristine waters, wildlife refuges, and roadless areas that surround the park, together with the park itself, constitute some 14 million acres of wild country within the Northern Rockies. Montana's claim on Yellowstone Country extends north from the park roughly to Bozeman, Livingston, and Big Timber on Interstate 90. To the west, it stretches to the Madison River and beyond to the Gravelly Range and the Tobacco Root Mountains; to the east, it reaches to Red Lodge, at the base of the 12,000-foot-high (3,650-m) Beartooth Plateau.

Given the nature of the landscape, Yellowstone Country is as close to heaven as most outdoor lovers will get in this life. Sacred sites range from the Grand Canyon of the Yellowstone to 12,799-foot-high (3,901-m) Granite Peak (Montana's apex), from the trout-rich Madison River to feather-friendly Red Rock Lakes, a wildlife sanctuary for the trumpeter swan. Most residents devote their leisure time to fishing and hunting, hiking, biking, climbing, camping, horseback riding, and in winter, skiing and snowmobiling. Even driving is a pleasure when the road follows a sparkling river and promises glimpses of golden eagles, elk, and bighorn sheep along the way.

Four scenic highways—the Beartooth, along with the Paradise, Gallatin, and Madison valley routes—provide access from south-central Montana into Wyoming's Yellowstone National Park. All four are destinations in their own right. Three flank great rivers, and one, the Beartooth Highway, has been stealing hearts and testing flatlanders' acrophobia since its completion in 1936.

■ BEARTOOTH HIGHWAY

The **Beartooth Highway** (U.S. Route 212) is an engineering triumph. Ascending the glacier-carved walls of Rock Creek Canyon south of Red Lodge, it teeters up switchbacks and hairpin curves with names like "Mae West" and "Frozen Man," delivering travelers from one heart-in-the-throat view to the next until it levels off at about 11,000 feet (3,350 m) on the Beartooth Plateau. Snow-white peaks and plateaus, alpine lakes, elk, moose, lupine, buttercups, and daisies are all part of the view from the top of the world. First-time visitors are literally breathless by the time they reach the rarefied air on top. After catching their breath and stabilizing their knees, most put the Beartooth Highway near the top of their most-loved-trips list. CBS news correspondent Charles Kuralt once described it as "the most beautiful roadway in America."

The highway is generally open from late May to mid-October, but snow can come at any time to this high country. While marmots celebrate summer by sunning themselves on newly exposed rockslides, visitors play in snowfields by the side of the road, and Olympic-class skiers descend snow-encrusted headwalls as part of their training at the Red Lodge International Ski Race Camp. Give yourself at least three hours to drive the 68-mile-long (109-km) Beartooth Highway between Red Lodge and Yellowstone's northeast entrance. This is a drive to be relished, not rushed.

Born as a coal-mining camp, **Red Lodge** grew on the backs and brawn of European immigrants. Today, this spirited mountain village relies on agriculture, recreation, and tourism for its economic well-being, but it has never lost sight of its proletarian roots. Ethnic distinctions have been diluted here as elsewhere in Montana, but neighborhoods still wear names like Finn Town, Little Italy, and "Hi Bug"—a schoolyard tag invented by kids to describe where the English-speaking upper class lived. Every August, the international stew that simmered here is served up at Red Lodge's nine-day-long Festival of Nations.

Sitting at the base of the skyscraper Beartooth Range, Red Lodge can count on a good six to seven months of snow, making it one of the state's top ski and winter sports areas. A dumping of six feet (two meters) of snow in April is not uncommon. While the rest of Montana is rejoicing in green grass and crocus, hardcore skiers are stretching the season at **Red Lodge Mountain,** one of the Northern Rockies' premier spring skiing areas. (See "WINTER RECREATION" for specifics.) When the snow finally retreats, Red Lodge embraces summer the way someone with a terminal illness clings to each day of life. This is a season of celebrations, ranging from the **Peaks to Prairie Relay** and the uphill-all-the-way **Beartooth Run** to the **Red Lodge Music Festival, Home of Champions Rodeo,** and the **Festival of Nations.**

■ ABSAROKA-BEARTOOTH WILDERNESS

The Absaroka-Beartooth Wilderness is to hikers what Yellowstone National Park is to motorists. Just as adjoining Yellowstone Park was envisioned more than a

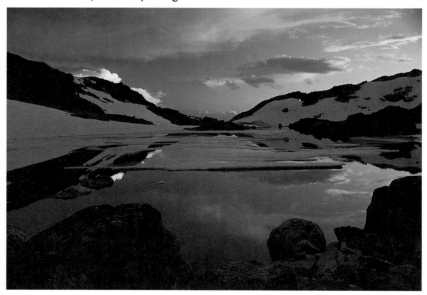

Rough Lake is one of nearly 1,000 lakes that dot the alpine plateaus of the Absaroka-Beartooth Wilderness in south-central Montana.

Wildflowers embroider the plains and the mountains in a patchwork of color. Pictured here (clockwise from top left) are false lupine, fairy slipper, blue bonnet, and shooting stars.

century ago as a national pleasuring ground for the masses, the Absaroka-Beartooth Wilderness is the legacy of visionary conservationists who recognized the value of keeping this heavenly plateau forever wild. Remote and rugged, this alpine wilderness encompasses the lower 48's largest single expanse of land above 10,000 feet (3,050 m). Indeed, 28 peaks, all within the Beartooth Range, rise to 12,000 feet (3,660 m) or higher. At their base, mammoth boulders and icy lakes are strewn across the landscape like giant fistfuls of confetti. The less rugged, more rounded mountains of the Absaroka Range form the western half of a backcountry playground that covers nearly a million acres within two national forests in south-central Montana.

Snow can come at any time to this high country, making it one of Montana's least hospitable destinations. Yet, backpackers arrive like pilgrims at this high ground, making it one of the most heavily used wildernesses in America. About 700 miles (1,120 km) of trails take visitors seemingly to the top of the world. Many of the lakes are stocked with trout, mostly cutthroat and brookies, but also prized golden trout and arctic grayling. Rocky cliffs and remote river drainages shelter some of the Northern Rockies' most distinguished residents, including bighorn sheep, mountain goats, elk, bear, and moose. Prolific wildflowers defy one of Montana's harshest climates with audacious blossoms of phlox, orchids, and lilies during a spring season that lasts all summer.

July and August are the most reliable months for dry weather, but a trip into the Absaroka-Beartooth Wilderness is never to be entered into lightly. The Beartooths stir up their own weather, and violent storms frequently pound the plateau as if Zeus himself were hurling thunderbolts from Granite Peak. This is not to say that wilderness visitors invariably encounter snow, sleet, hail, rain, wind, or hypothermia in the wilderness. But they had better be prepared for all of the above, as well as the blinding purity of sunlight at more than two miles (three km) above sea level.

■ PARADISE VALLEY

For some travelers, particularly those from the East and Midwest, the Beartooth Highway is too much, too soon. A devious service station owner in Billings used to delight in directing Yellowstone Park-bound tourists up the Beartooth, insisting it was the only way to get to the park from Billings. Most went on their way and were never heard from again, but a few made a point of returning to Billings to blister their informant for sending them on a journey that unnerved them from the moment they rounded their first switchback. Especially when they realized there was an alternate route to the park, another 100 miles (160 km) west of the Beartooth turnoff.

For those who prefer their mountains from a distance, U.S. Route 89 through Paradise Valley delivers stunning alpine scenery. The road itself follows a well-mannered riverside route between Livingston and the north entrance to Yellowstone National Park at Gardiner. To the east lies the imposing face of the Absarokas; to the west, the foothills of the Gallatins. Gouging out the broad valley between these two ranges is the **Yellowstone River,** one of Montana's finest fishing and floating rivers.

Encircled by mountains, Paradise Valley has a way of lifting your eyes upward, which seems a good enough explanation for the origin of its name. Horace Albright, once superintendent of Yellowstone Park and later the head of the National Park Service, said of the valley, "If that area were in any other state, it would have been a national park." Area ranchers would never put up with such a foolish notion, but even the most vocal opponents of land-use planning now wish the valley had been protected from free market economics in 1981 when the late publisher Malcolm Forbes sold his 12,000-acre ranch along the north edge of Yellowstone Park to the Church Universal and Triumphant (CUT). A highly controversial cult-like church that claims a worldwide membership of anywhere between 30,000 and 150,000, CUT transferred its headquarters from southern California to Park County, Montana, when it bought the ranch, and has been enlarging the property and altering the landscape ever since. Housing developments, mobile home parks, farming and ranching operations, even a massive, underground complex of fallout shelters occupy 30,000 church-owned acres at the south end of the valley, with additional holdings in Livingston and nearby Gallatin and Yellowstone counties.

Whether due to its scenic appeal, its isolation, or more likely, its fly-fishing, the valley has attracted another unusual crowd in recent years, this one from the celebrated world of arts, letters, and motion pictures. Over the years, fame's exiles, including writers Tom McGuane, William Hjortsberg, Tim Cahill, and Richard Brautigan, artist Russell Chatham, movie director Sam Peckinpaugh, and actors Peter Fonda, Margot Kidder, Warren Oates, and Jeff Bridges have all sought refuge in the Paradise Valley. They come and go, but some, like Chatham

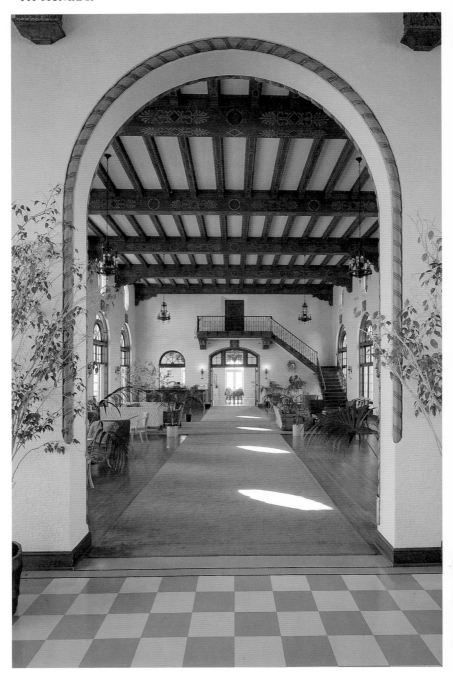

and Cahill, have stayed, and others, like McGuane, have abandoned Paradise Valley for even more remote properties.

About an hour north of Yellowstone Park, the small city of **Livingston** was once a principal operations center for the Northern Pacific Railroad. With hundreds of workers employed by the NP's extensive machine shops, Livingston's dependence on the railroad made it vulnerable to every national recession that came along. In the early 1980s, the railroad, then under the ownership of Burlington Northern, consolidated its operations and laid off well over half the workers at the Livingston shops. But the real blow came in 1986, when BN abandoned the shops altogether. A new business, Montana Rail Link, bought BN's southern Montana line. Another new company, Livingston Rebuild Center, refurbished the BN facilities and now employs up to 150 mechanics, machinists, and painters to rebuild locomotives, railcars, and other heavy equipment from throughout the United States and Canada. Once boss of the Livingston economy, the rail industry now shares the reins with recreation and tourism.

The ornate Livingston passenger depot, built at the turn of the century, proclaimed the Northern Pacific's prominence as the "Yellowstone Park Line" and Livingston as the "Original Entrance to Yellowstone Park." Now a museum and exhibition hall, the **Depot Center** anchors Livingston's downtown historic district, characterized by the elaborate brickwork and cornices on turn-of-the-century commercial and residential buildings that once housed the town's founders, its blue-collar workers, and a busy red-light district.

Across from the depot, on West Park Street, is another Livingston landmark, **Dan Bailey's Fly Shop.** A must-see attraction for fly-fishermen, the shop was opened in 1938 by one of the sport's founding fathers, Dan Bailey. Bailey's sells everything from $400 graphite fly rods to 75-cent scraps of dyed rabbit fur, and does a sizable mail-order business. This is one of the world's largest wholesalers of fishing tackle. Bailey's employs about two dozen fly tiers on a piecework basis to produce more than half a million trout flies a year. Thousands of anglers and amateur tiers visit the shop to watch as these professionals turn out royal wulffs, blue-winged olives, and other intricate patterns with remarkable speed and precision. Livingston's scenic location and its prominence as a fly-fishing destination has inspired an abundance of fine landscape, wildlife, and Western art. This community of 6,700 supports half a dozen art galleries plus small, specialized collections within fly-fishing shops.

The Gallatin Gateway Inn, south of Bozeman, was built in 1927 as a hotel and railway depot for visitors en route to Yellowstone Park.

■ GALLATIN CANYON

The Yellowstone River is but one of dozens of renowned rivers in south-central and southwestern Montana that draw anglers from around the world. Another is the Gallatin, which flows right off the cover of *Field & Stream*. Born in the northwest corner of Yellowstone Park, the Gallatin dodges boulders and scours tree-lined banks as it rushes down mountains and through canyons to meet the Missouri at Three Forks. Along the way, it furnishes habitat for fish and wildlife, rapids for rafters, riffles and pools for anglers, and refuge for campers, picnickers, and foot danglers. From Bozeman to Yellowstone Park, it shares the Gallatin Canyon with U.S. Route 191, a narrow, twisting highway that ushers motorists to the splendid Spanish Peaks area of the Lee Metcalf Wilderness, Cottonwood Canyon, Hyalite Canyon, and the Palisades Falls National Recreation Trail. Dozens of campgrounds and picnic areas and hundreds of miles of trails cater to outdoor enthusiasts. Accommodations along the route include Montana's most complete, all-season, destination resort at **Big Sky**, plus cabins, guest ranches, fishing and hunting lodges, and even an elegantly restored railroad hotel (see "Accommodations" in "PRACTICAL INFORMATION" for specifics). In winter, there are enough slopes, lifts, trails, lodges, and restaurants along this route to keep downhill and cross-country skiers and snowmobilers happy for a week, if not the entire season.

■ BOZEMAN

Gallatin Canyon is peopled at each end by two contrasting communities, both wholly devoted to outdoor recreation. At the north end, Bozeman has enough other interests to stand on its own as a regional trade center and the home of **Montana State University.** But underlying this academic and cultural façade is a sports-crazy town that lives for the ski season and longs for opening day on nearby trout streams. A city of under 25,000, Bozeman is jammed with mountain bikes, kayaks, ski racks, and car-top carriers, and has more than its share of sporting goods shops, guides and outfitters, outdoor writers and photographers, subscribers of *Outside Magazine,* and devotees of Patagonia equipment and clothing. With its proximity to Yellowstone National Park, Bridger Bowl and Big Sky ski areas, hiking, climbing, and fishing, it is no mere coincidence that Patagonia has relocated its mail-order division to Bozeman.

Influenced, perhaps, by its magnificent setting, Bozeman cares about its appearance and presents an appealing face to visitors. Bookstores, art galleries, a bakery, coffee house, and half a dozen memorable restaurants are reason enough to spend a day in downtown Bozeman, which has withstood the threat of outlying shopping malls better than most Montana cities. And visitors return every year for festive events like the **Taste of Bozeman,** when Main Street is closed to traffic so that all those good restaurants can serve up their specialties to hundreds of guests outdoors, banquet-style.

Bozeman's top attraction is the newly expanded **Museum of the Rockies,** the town's 1989 centennial gift to Montana. Famous in paleontological circles as the home of dinosaur guru Jack Horner, the museum greets visitors with life-like, robotic re-creations of a *Triceratops* family, roaring and rooting around an interior fern garden. Although Horner's presence casts an aura of paleontological primacy over the institution, the Museum of the Rockies is more than a testing ground for new thinking on a growing collection of timeworn bones. With the ambitious goal of explaining the Northern Rocky Mountain region over the past 80 million

The annual Bobcat-Grizzly football game between Montana State University and the University of Montana dates back to 1897.

years, the museum gives nearly equal time and space to prehistoric peoples, the birth of the Rockies, the impact of man on the region, and Plains Indian art, history, and culture. It also attempts to teach us about our place in the universe with its digital Taylor Planetarium, the only one of its kind in the Northern Rockies that is open to the public.

A LOVE STORY

I was at the Top Hat having a drink with Little Troy Burnham, talking about the deer season, when a woman who had been sitting at the front of the bar got up and came over to us. I had seen this woman other times in other bars in town. She would be there in the afternoons around three, and then sometimes late at night when I would be cruising back. She danced with some men from the air base, and sat drinking and talking late. I suppose she left with someone finally. She wasn't a bad looking woman at all. Blond, with wide, dark eyes set out, wide hips, and dark eyebrows. She could've been thirty-four years old, although she could've been forty-four or twenty-four, because she was drinking steady, and steady drink can do both to you, especially to women. But I had thought the first time I saw her: Here's one on the way down. A miner's wife drifted up from Butte, or a rancher's daughter just run off suddenly, which can happen. Or worse. And I hadn't been tempted. Trouble comes cheap and leaves expensive is a way of thinking about that.

"Do you suppose you could give me a light," the woman said to us. She was standing at our table. Nola was her name. Nola Foster. I had heard that around. She wasn't drunk. It was four o'clock in the afternoon, and no one was there but Troy Burnham and me.

"If you'll tell me a love story, I'll do anything in the world for you," Troy said. It was what he always said to women. He'd do anything in the world for something. Troy sits in a wheelchair due to a smoke jumper's injury, and can't do very much. We had been friends since high school and before. He was always short, and I was tall. But Troy had been an excellent wrestler and won awards in Montana, and I had done little of that, some boxing once was all. We had been living in the same apartments on Ryman Street, though Troy lived there permanently and drove a Checker cab to earn a living, and I was hoping to pass on to something better. "I *would* like a little love story," Troy said, and called for whatever Nola Foster was drinking.

"Nola, Troy. Troy, Nola," I said, and lit her cigarette.

"Have we met?" Nola said, taking a seat and glancing at me.

"At the East Gate. Some time ago," I said.

"That's a very nice bar," she said in a cool way. "But I hear it's changed hands."

"I'm glad to make your acquaintance," Troy said, grinning and adjusting his glasses. "Now let's hear that love story." He pulled up close to the table so that his head and his big shoulders were above the tabletop. Troy's injury had caused him not to have any hips left. There is something there, but not hips. He needs bars and a special seat in his cab. He is both frail and strong at once, though in most ways he gets on like everybody else.

"I *was* in love," Nola said quietly as the bartender set her drink down and she took a sip. "And now I'm not."

"That's a short love story," I said.

—Richard Ford, *Rock Springs,* 1987

■ WEST YELLOWSTONE

Ninety miles (144 km) south of Bozeman, **West Yellowstone** *is* a city of visitors. Well over one million people enter the park each year through this small town of 900 year-round residents, making it the busiest of the park's five gateways. In July and August, at the height of the season, "West" looks like a tourist trap, but give it a chance and it will grow on you, especially if you came to fish. Listen to the conversation as you stroll down Madison or Firehole or Gibbon avenues, and you will know why the streets are named after some of the world's best-known trout streams, all located within 30 minutes of town. West Yellowstone is to serious anglers what Carnegie Hall and the Metropolitan Opera are to music lovers. Headquarters for the International Federation of Fly Fishers, it has top billing on every angler's dream list of places to go and things to do.

Not far from town, dead trees poke through the surface of **Quake Lake,** an eerie reminder of the mega-jolt that toppled half a mountain into the Madison River canyon on the night of August 17, 1959. The landslide dammed a river, created a lake, and buried 28 campers in an unmarked grave. About 250 vacationers were trapped overnight in the canyon when whole sections of U.S. Route 287 cracked like eggshells and dropped into existing Hebgen Lake. Registering 7.1 on the Richter scale, the earthquake was one of the strongest in U.S. history and

YELLOWSTONE NATIONAL PARK

Wyoming's Yellowstone National Park is the magnet that pulls most visitors into south-central Montana, where three of the park's five entrances are located. America's largest national park outside of Alaska, Yellowstone has been drawing curiosity seekers from throughout the world ever since mountain man John Colter reported tales of hissing geysers, burbling mud pots, and pools of boiling paint to an unbelieving public in 1810. For many years, this mysterious place was known simply as "Colter's Hell." In his journal of American travel notes, Rudyard Kipling described it as "a howling wilderness of three thousand square miles, full of all imaginable freaks of a fiery nature."

Several short, self-guiding trails introduce visitors to headline attractions, like the Grand Canyon of the Yellowstone and Upper Geyser Basin, which encompasses the world's greatest cluster of geysers, including Old Faithful. A longer but lovely introductory trail is the three-mile (five-km) climb to the top of Mount Washburn, between Tower and Canyon. From the summit, visitors enjoy panoramic views of Yellowstone Canyon, Hayden Valley, Yellowstone Lake, and on clear days, the Tetons, Absarokas, and Gallatins. Hikers can also view the mosaic burn pattern created by the historic fires of 1988. More than a third of the park's 2.2-million-acre landscape was altered by the fires, with more than 790,000 acres of forest blackened to one degree or another. But meadows and forest understory have bounded back, creating prodigious wildflower displays and increased forage and habitat for wildlife.

For those who want to know more about fire ecology, bears, geysers, or the many other features that make Yellowstone one of America's greatest outdoor classrooms, the **Yellowstone Institute** offers more than 80 field courses each year (see "Useful Addresses" in "PRACTICAL INFORMATION"). The Institute is housed at the historic Buffalo Ranch in the Lamar Valley, near the park's northeast gate.

AVOIDING THE CROWDS

Close to three million people now visit the park each year. During the peak months of summer, traffic crawls along the park's Grand Loop Road and grinds to a standstill every time a bison or bull elk is sighted within camera range. There are a couple of ways to beat the crowds, however. One is to visit the park during the off-season. In September, hormone-crazed bull elk entertain visitors with their

Midway Geyser Basin's Grand Prismatic Spring is one of more than 10,000 thermal features in Yellowstone National Park.

macho antics at the outset of breeding season. In spring, at the other end of the cycle, a drive through Yellowstone is like visiting a wildlife nursery. Satisfied bison and elk moms suckle their wobbly calves in roadside meadows, while Canada geese drill downy, yellow goslings on paddle and splash missions in a watery wilderness.

A welcome hush settles over Yellowstone as it fills up with snow in winter. If the park's spouting geysers and fumaroles seem eerie in summer, they are unearthly in winter. Frosty bison move in and out of view as clouds of mist and steam roll through, transforming the powerful beasts into shaggy ghosts. Snow whites-out the roads and confines travel to skis, snowshoes, snowmobiles, and guided snowcoach tours.

Yellowstone watchers fear the winter season may be too popular for the good of the wildlife that top the list of reasons why people visit. They warn that the park's bison and elk don't need the added impact of snarling snowmobile engines and backcountry interlopers on top of the rigors of winter. It's hard not to love this park to death, even in the off-season when visitation is markedly down.

INTO THE BACKCOUNTRY

The best way to avoid peak-season congestion is to abandon your car for day hikes or extended hiking and horseback trips through Yellowstone's spacious backcountry. The park has more than a thousand miles of backcountry trails to acquaint visitors with its many moods and curiosities. The privileged few who use them are gifted with sights never seen from a Winnebago: the secret eruptions of the remote Shoshone Geyser Basin, the terraced waterfalls and wilderness jacuzzis of the "Cascade Corner," the chance view of a golden-tipped grizzly sow steering her cubs across Hayden Valley, the unexpected burps and splats of unnamed mud pots.

Yellowstone's backcountry is bear country. There are an estimated 700 bears in and around the park, including about 200 grizzlies. While few people actually see *Ursus horribilis,* the great bear ranges throughout the park. Hikers should generally avoid traveling alone, and should always check trail conditions and bear sightings before heading out. Given the National Park Service's aggressive efforts to reduce bear-human conflicts, it is difficult to avoid these precautions. Brochures, leaflets, and fliers litter the park.

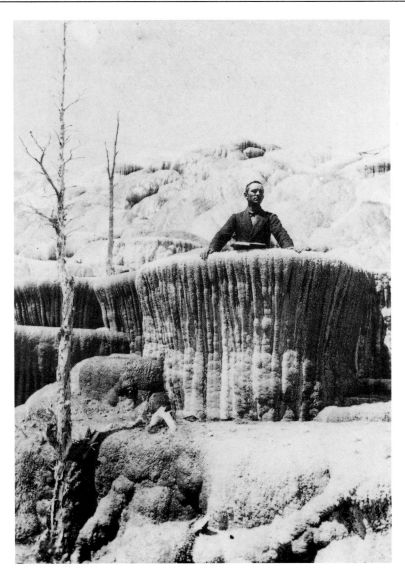

Preaching at Pulpit Terrace in the Mammoth Hot Springs area of Yellowstone Park. (Montana Historical Society)

shook an eight-state region. People across Montana were startled from their sleep, but the heaviest damage was at this site, where the U.S. Forest Service maintains a memorial visitor center and vista point.

The vast majority of tourists visit the West Yellowstone area during the summer, but fall and winter are becoming increasingly popular. With the growing popularity of snowmobiling and cross-country skiing, Yellowstone Park and the town of West Yellowstone have become one of the Northern Rockies' hottest winter destinations. Billing itself as "the snowmobile capital of the world," West Yellowstone goes all out for power sledders, who use the town as a base camp to explore not only Yellowstone Park but hundreds of miles of trails on national forest lands outside the park. There's plenty of room for cross-country skiers, who also flock to West Yellowstone and the park. An excellent public trail system, right in town, provides early winter training for the U.S. Nordic and Biathlon teams.

■ MADISON RIVER VALLEY

Flanked on the east by the soaring peaks of the Madison Range, this drive offers skyward views of Montana's second-highest mountain range and the broad, alluvial plains that fan out from its base to create one of the state's most handsome valleys. Heavy timbers frame entrances to ranches that lie at the end of long, gravel roads. The names etched into these gates—Bar Seven, Longhorn, Jumping Horse—are clues to one of the major occupations that drive the economy of the valley. But the real evidence is a landscape dotted with cattle and sheep as far as the eye can see. Year after year, Madison County ranks among Montana's top cattle- and sheep-producing counties. And year after year, the **Madison River** draws more nonresident anglers to its banks than any other trout stream in Montana. Originating in Yellowstone Park, the river follows U.S. Route 287 for about 60 miles (100 km) from West Yellowstone to Ennis, then leaves the highway before joining the Gallatin and Jefferson rivers at Three Forks to form the Missouri.

Ranching and fishing converge in the small community of **Ennis,** where well-heeled anglers meet high-heeled cowboys over beers in watering holes like the Longbranch and Silver Dollar. Over the years, fly shops and art galleries have replaced farm and ranch supply stores, but the atmosphere in Ennis remains distinctly Western. At no time is the valley's love affair with livestock more apparent than during rodeo weekend, when the population of Ennis swells to accommodate contestants and spectators at one of Montana's most popular Fourth of July rodeos. An attractive purse, a sure crowd, and a wild horse race make Ennis one of the top rodeos for professional cowboys and cowgirls working the summer circuit, as well as for local ranch hands. When the dust has settled and the professionals have moved on to the next arena, spectators turn their attention to the many nearby attractions that make Ennis such a popular base camp for summer visitors.

■ HISTORICAL DETOURS

Two of Montana's liveliest ghost towns, Virginia City and Nevada City, lie just 15 miles (24 km) west of Ennis, on Montana State Highway 287. An 1863 gold strike brought thousands of prospectors to the area and secured Virginia City's place in history as Montana's second territorial capital. (See "Ghost Towns" in "SOUTHWEST MONTANA" for more about this area.)

Most Montana communities support a historic home or museum like the Headwaters Heritage Museum in Three Forks.

Three state parks north of Ennis reach back even further in history. Just outside the aptly named community of Three Forks, three of southwestern Montana's great rivers—the Jefferson, the Madison, and the Gallatin—join to form the Missouri River. The site was an important crossroads for several Indian tribes. The Lewis and Clark expedition also camped here in July 1805, nearly 2,500 miles (4,000 km) above their starting point near St. Louis, where the Missouri feeds into the Mississippi. In his journal, Meriwether Lewis said he and his co-captain, William Clark, agreed to name the forks after President Thomas Jefferson, "the author of our enterprize," Secretary of the Treasury Albert Gallatin, and Secretary of State James Madison. They proceeded westward along the Jefferson, certain, as were most early explorers, that the Missouri headwaters would take them to the Pacific Ocean. The history of the area is preserved in a beautiful setting at **Missouri Headwaters State Park,** a popular spot for camping, picnicking, hiking, fishing, and floating.

For 2,000 years before the arrival of guns and horses, Indians killed the buffalo they needed for food, clothing, shelter, and tools by stampeding them en masse over cliffs. Not far from the Missouri Headwaters, **Madison Buffalo Jump State Park** preserves one of these early killing grounds. Layers of bones and remnants of primitive tools mark these slaughtering sites, where Indian parties often spent several days gutting carcasses, removing hides, and drying meat.

Montana's first and best-known state park preserves one of the largest limestone caverns in the Northwest, less than 20 miles (32 km) west of Three Forks on Montana State Highway 2. **Lewis and Clark Caverns** began forming more than 300 million years ago. Sediments at the bottom of a shallow inland sea hardened into limestone and were eventually exposed to air as the sea drained away and the nearby Tobacco Root Mountains were uplifted. As groundwater penetrated and dissolved fractured limestone, a network of channels began forming. Today, these channels and caves are punctuated by stalactites, stalagmites, columns, and crystals. Visitors can explore the caves on guided tours during the summer. The park also has a visitor center, café and gift shop, campground, picnic area, and nature trail.

■ ROADS LESS TRAVELED

For those who seek a more intimate, less developed view of this landscape, several rugged roads wind tentatively through the wild country that borders Yellowstone

Park. Starting as ordinary, two-lane highways, they taper off first to gravel, then dirt. Some wind up at trailheads that designate foot and horse traffic only. These memorable trips make few demands in proportion to the pleasures they yield. A flexible itinerary and a tolerance for bumpy, dusty roads are a small price to pay for a chance view of a golden eagle feeding by the side of the road or mountain goats perched on rocky outcrops overhead. For extended visits, most travelers are self-sustained. There are some private cabins and guest ranches, however, in addition to a number of public campgrounds.

The remote **Centennial Valley,** just west of the park, is an essential trip for photographers, birders, and wildlife watchers. The valley is bordered on the south by a wall of mountains that approach the 10,000-foot (3,050-m) level. The rugged Centennials catch heavy snows that replenish the lakes and marshes of 42,000-acre **Red Rock Lakes National Wildlife Refuge,** which provides sanctuary for the trumpeter swan. This vast wetland sustains a multitude of other birds and animals. Because of its location halfway between West Yellowstone and Monida on a dirt and gravel road, passage is slow and subject to weather conditions. The best time to visit is between May and September when the road is generally dry. Recently designated a national scenic backroad by the BLM, the Centennial Valley Road has its own built-in speed bumps to ensure that motorists take it slow.

North of the park, **Columbus** is the starting point for a cluster of secondary routes into the Beartooth Range along the Stillwater and Rosebud drainages. Though long dependent on farming and ranching, this Yellowstone River community is enjoying an economic revival tied to mining and manufacturing. The Stillwater Mining Company, located at the edge of the Absaroka-Beartooth Wilderness near Nye, is the nation's only producer of platinum-palladium metals, used widely in industry and technology. Columbus is also the home of Montana Silversmiths, the world's largest manufacturer of Western-style silver products, including belt buckles, jewelry, and saddle and bridle trim.

The last outpost of any size before heading into the mountains is **Absarokee,** 15 miles (24 km) south of Columbus on Montana State Highway 78. The small town bears an Indian name that originally was used to identify the Crow tribe. Once part of the Crows' vast homeland, Absarokee was on the Crow Reservation until the reservation was reduced to its current size and location near Hardin. The historic **Bozeman Trail** also crossed through this southern portion of Stillwater County. In 1862, founder John Bozeman envisioned the route as a shortcut from

eastern Wyoming, through Indian territory, and on to the gold fields of Virginia City. Despite its ease of travel and abundance of water, grass, and game, the trail was abandoned in 1868 due to persistent attacks by the Sioux. Today, travelers can retrace a portion of the trail on short wagon-train vacations (see "Tours" in "PRACTICAL INFORMATION"). Visitors can enjoy another Western tradition, still very much alive in Montana, at either of two lively rodeos held in Absarokee each summer. In early June, the Northern Rodeo Association kicks off its season here, and in July, seasoned contestants from throughout the area entertain a spirited crowd at the **Old Timers' Rodeo.**

Absarokee is the jumping-off point for deeper exploration of Beartooth country on different routes, each constituting a variation on the theme of grandeur. Follow East Rosebud Creek 14 miles (23 km) to the tiny settlement of Roscoe, then another 12 miles (19 km) on gravel to East Rosebud Lake, which marks the beginning of one of the Beartooth's most spectacular canyons. A short hike up East Rosebud Creek reveals a Yosemite landscape with an El Capitan-like upthrust at nearly every bend in the trail. An extended hike or horseback ride on the same trail takes conditioned explorers over the top of the boulder-strewn, lake-studded Beartooth Plateau before dropping down to Cooke City, at the northeast corner of Yellowstone National Park.

A 20-mile (32-km) road follows West Rosebud Creek from tiny Fishtail to a hydroelectric plant below Mystic Lake. Early in the century, the Montana Power Company chose the site to build its 300-foot-long (90-m) concrete dam and power plant in these highest of all Montana mountains because of its vertical drop and massive snowfall. Considered an engineering feat at the time of its construction, such a proposal today would generate far more controversy than electricity. Hikers and horsemen en route to the Absaroka-Beartooth Wilderness begin their journey with a three-mile (five-km) ramble up to Mystic Lake, itself a popular fishing spot.

A 40-mile (64-km) journey along the Stillwater River packs plenty of scenic views, camping, and stream fishing in the heart of Beartooth country. The route also leads to the the nation's richest deposits of platinum, palladium, and related metals, and the Stillwater Mining Company's highly automated mining operation near Nye.

Beartooth country is a skyscraper wilderness of granite peaks, boulder-strewn plateaus, and alpine lakes.

■ BOULDER RIVER

The 1964 Wilderness Act, passed to preserve the pristine qualities of certain natural areas forever, defines wilderness as "an area where the earth and its community of life are untrammeled by man, where man himself is a visitor who does not remain." The act prohibits motorized travel within wilderness boundaries, but people who shun hiking and horseback riding can still surround themselves with wilderness on the **Boulder River Road.**

Reaching some 50 miles (80 km) south of Big Timber to the abandoned mining town of Independence, this partially paved road fingers its way into the Absaroka-Beartooth Wilderness along a non-wilderness corridor. As a result, travelers are enveloped on three sides by "capital W" wilderness for about a third of the distance. For the entire distance, they are encircled by sublime views of rivers and peaks, canyons and gorges, and meadows and hay fields where sheep mingle with elk and deer. Eagles and hawks soar overhead, while rainbow trout flash in rivers and streams below.

"They don't make land like that anymore," said NBC newsman Tom Brokaw in an interview after purchasing a ranch on the nearby West Fork of the Boulder. "Montana is special in the world. I come over a rise there and I feel like I'm in Tibet." Other celebrities attracted to the exotic frontier of the Boulder Valley include Brooke Shields, Michael Keaton, novelist Tom McGuane, and Robert Haas, chairman of Levi Strauss & Co. They come for the unspoiled beauty and the unhurried lifestyle. Here, they come and go without a fuss, even in nearby **Big Timber,** a small Western town of about 1,600 where the real stars are the cowboy poets who convene at the high school gymnasium every August to croon their lonely ballads and recite their latest rhymes of the range. Heaping servings of Western lore and a good time to boot make the two-day **Montana Cowboy Poetry Gathering** a gut-buster for anyone with a hankering for a taste of the West.

The cosmopolitan views of visiting anglers and hikers, combined with those of the valley's new luminaries, are tempered by the rock-hard, conservative politics of Sweet Grass County and the mores and folkways of ranchers who have raised sheep and run cows here for over a century. The sociology of Big Timber is nearly as engaging as the landscape that surrounds it.

Horse and wagon trips add history and adventure to a Montana vacation.

SOUTHWEST MONTANA

FEWER THAN 60 YEARS AFTER LEWIS AND CLARK ENTERED the unmapped wilderness of what is now Montana, miners and merchants were beating a path across the mountains and deserts of California, Colorado, and Idaho to reach its southwestern gold fields. News of gold strikes on Grasshopper Creek in 1862 and Alder Gulch the following year traveled fast. By the mid-1860s, Montana had nearly 30,000 permanent, non-Indian settlers, where five years earlier there had been none. Another strike in 1864, this one on Last Chance Gulch, established Helena as the "Queen City of the Rockies" and southwest Montana as the progenitor of the state's most enduring nickname, the Treasure State.

In the 1860s at the height of the gold rush in Montana, the strikes were so rich it was said that a prospector could shake a dollar's worth of dust from an uprooted sagebrush. In five years, the digs at Alder Gulch (now Virginia City) produced $30–$40 million worth of gold; Last Chance Gulch produced an estimated $19 million in just four years. By 1866, Montana was second only to California as a gold producer. But the gold played out, and so did silver. Then in 1882, the fortuitous discovery of a thick vein of copper beneath the undistinguished gold camp of Butte ushered in the greatest era of all in Montana mining history and immortalized Butte as "the richest hill on earth."

Right behind the miners came the stockmen who supplied Montana's mining camps with fresh meat. The valleys were as rich in grass as the mountains were in precious metals. While the plains of eastern Montana fattened hundreds of thousands of cattle for the export market during the state's great open range cattle era of the 1870s and '80s, Montana's early mining camps provided a ready market for pioneer stockmen. Those who mastered the basics of building a herd and selling in the Deer Lodge and Beaverhead valleys emerged as leaders of Montana's developing livestock industry.

Computerized livestock breeding programs and technology-driven mining operations are still the bones and sinew of this corner of the state. But its spirit resides in the weathered ghost towns, Victorian mansions, and carriage houses that bespeak the bonanza years of Montana's colorful mining frontier. Much of Montana's political and economic history was written in this part of the state, and it is easily revisited in galleries, museums, mansions, and miners' union halls. Where

COPPER MONEY

*W*hen the late Senator Robert LaFollette listed [William A.] Clark as one of one hundred men who owned America, and cited fourteen great corporations in his hands to prove it, he neglected to recite a more revealing fact. Differing from the other ninety-nine "owners of America," Clark stood alone, unique, in the fact that of all the great enterprises with which he was connected, not one share of stock nor bond issue by any one of them was either listed or quoted or could be bought on any stock exchange in the United States.

William A. Clark, "copper king."
(Montana Historical Society)

WILLIAM ANDREWS CLARK
PIONEER PROSPECTOR AND MINER
MERCHANT BANKER RAILROAD BUILDER
BENEFACTOR OF CHILDREN AND PHILANTHROPIST
THIS MEMORIAL IS ERECTED BY
THE SOCIETY OF MONTANA AND OTHER FRIENDS
AS A TRIBUTE TO HIS GREAT ACHIEVEMENTS
AND TO PERPETUATE HIS MEMORY

Inscription from bas-relief in capitol rotunda in Helena

—C. B. Glasscock,
The War of the Copper Kings: Builders of Butte and Wolves of Wall Street, 1935

SOUTHWEST CORNER AND BITTERROOT COUNTRY

S. P. = STATE PARK
N. W. R. = NATIONAL WILDLIFE REFUGE

25mi
25km
0
0

—N—

TO IDAHO FALLS

TO YELLOWSTONE NAT'L PARK

ENNIS
VIRGINIA CITY
MADISON R.
NEVADA CITY
ALDER
MTNS.
RANGE
GRAVELLY RANGE
SNOWCREST RANGE
RED ROCK LAKES N.W.R.
CENTENNIAL MTNS.
CENTENNIAL VALLEY RD.
DILLON
BEAVERHEAD R.
BANNACK S.P.
CLARK CANYON RESERVOIR
TENDOY MTNS.
WISE RIVER - POLARIS RD.
JACKSON
SALMON
MONTANA
IDAHO
CONTINENTAL DIVIDE
287
287
41
15
93

prospectors once mined these hills and panned these streams for the sparkling "color" that meant instant prosperity, visitors today mine the area not just for its history but also for its natural beauty and recreational opportunities—its trout streams and forested mountains. Georgetown Lake, the Anaconda-Pintler Wilderness, the Big Hole River, and Gates of the Mountains are just some of the getaways that make this part of the state so attractive to sightseers and sportsmen.

Most of the region's small cities grew from primitive mining camps after the discovery of gold placers and silver lodes, as well as rich deposits of copper, lead, and zinc. The two largest are Helena and Butte.

■ HELENA

Helena's early fortunes were made of gold. The city's main street is still named **Last Chance Gulch**, a permanent memorial to four discouraged prospectors who declared this unlikely spot to be their "last chance" after following strike after played-out strike around the West. It turned out to be their best chance when, in 1864, they discovered the first of several gold deposits that catapulted Helena into second place, right behind Alder Gulch, as Montana's leading gold producer. Within 10 years, tents and crude log cabins had given way to mansions, mercantiles, and hundreds of small businesses. By 1888, an estimated 50 millionaires lived here, making it the richest city per capita in the United States. Strategically located on early travel routes and at the center of Montana's mining district, Helena's survival was assured. In 1875, it became Montana's third territorial capital (after Bannack and Virginia City, the sites of Montana's first two major gold strikes). Then, in 1894, it became the permanent state capital in a runoff election against Anaconda, after a $3 million campaign financed by rival copper barons Marcus Daly and William A. Clark.

Much of Helena's early history has been preserved in its architecture, both downtown and in adjacent residential neighborhoods. The extravagant jumble of Baroque, Gothic, Italianate, and Romanesque designs reflects the exuberance of Helena's Victorian period. Arched windows, ornate pillars and masonry patterns, sculpted metal, carved faces, flowers, and lion heads are all visible on the massive stone buildings that anchor Helena's historic Last Chance Gulch. While fires, earthquakes, demolition, and decay have leveled many of Helena's historic

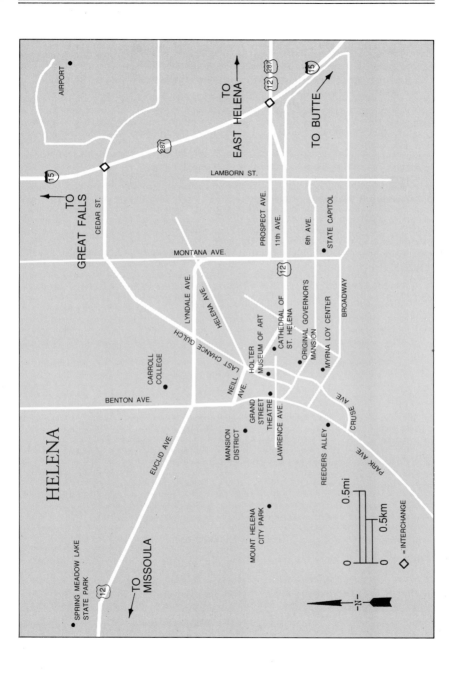

HELENA

TO GREAT FALLS

TO MISSOULA

TO EAST HELENA

TO BUTTE

AIRPORT

SPRING MEADOW LAKE STATE PARK

CEDAR ST.

LAMBORN ST.

MONTANA AVE.

BENTON AVE.

EUCLID AVE.

CARROLL COLLEGE

LYNDALE AVE.

LAST CHANCE GULCH

HELENA AVE.

NEILL AVE.

PROSPECT AVE.

11th AVE.

6th AVE.

STATE CAPITOL

BROADWAY

CATHEDRAL OF ST. HELENA

ORIGINAL GOVERNOR'S MANSION

MYRNA LOY CENTER

HOLTER MUSEUM OF ART

GRAND STREET THEATRE

LAWRENCE AVE.

MANSION DISTRICT

REEDERS ALLEY

CRUSE AVE.

PARK AVE.

MOUNT HELENA CITY PARK

0.5mi

0.5km

0

0

◇ = INTERCHANGE

N

buildings, nearly a hundred still stand as reminders of the city's golden era. The growth of Helena can be traced from the gulch eastward as downtown fixtures like the original Governor's Mansion and the territorial and original State Capitol (now the Lewis and Clark County Courthouse) were abandoned for more modern buildings on the east side of town.

The century-old mansions of Helena's venerable west-side neighborhoods flaunt an opulent mix of styles and designs that combine parquet floors, Tiffany windows, tile fireplaces, handcrafted woodwork of oak and cherry, gracious, high-ceilinged rooms, spacious front porches, gazebos, and carriage houses. The **original Governor's Mansion**, (304 North Ewing), built as a private residence in 1888 by entrepreneur William Chessman, is open to the public for tours. The nearby Sanders mansion, built by politician and vigilante Wilbur Fisk Sanders in 1875, is now a gracious bed and breakfast inn. (See "Accommodations" in "PRACTICAL INFORMATION" for specifics.)

Towering above all these secular monuments to the earthly treasures of an earlier period is the magnificent **Cathedral of St. Helena.** Modeled after the Votive Cathedral of the Sacred Heart in Vienna, it boasts stained-glass windows from

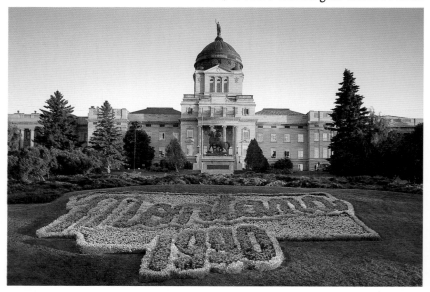

The State Capitol in Helena is crowned with a copper dome.

The cathedral of St. Helena lends European dignity to the capital's skyline.

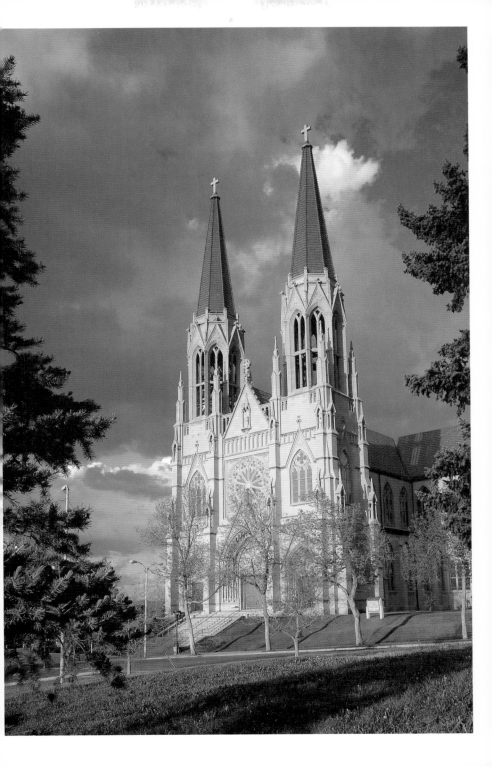

Bavaria, a white marble altar from Italy, and twin spires crowned with gilded crosses that face east and west to catch the first and last light of day. Rising 230 feet (70 m) above the tree-lined streets of Helena—as if to compete with the surrounding peaks of the Rocky Mountains—the cathedral lends European dignity to the city's skyline.

History and the arts are a source of pride to Helena residents. Many are involved in efforts to restore downtown buildings and neighborhood mansions, one of which even transformed their abandoned, turn-of-the-century jail into the **Myrna Loy Center**, a performing arts and film center. Helena is home to the **Archie Bray Foundation**, an internationally recognized center for the ceramic arts; the **Holter Museum of Art** and its annual **Rendezvous of Western Art**; and **Grandstreet Theatre**, a lively school and stage for the dramatic arts. The **Montana Historical Society**, 225 North Roberts, houses two museums—the Montana Homeland Historical Museum and the smaller F. Jay Haynes Museum, which depicts frontier photography. Also here are two art galleries, one of which features the works of C. M. Russell, along with a fine archives and historical library.

While the city's early growth was financed by gold dust and nuggets, Helena now owes its existence to the less tangible but self-perpetuating occupation of politics. Much of the business of state government is conducted beneath the dome of the **State Capitol**, but state offices are located in buildings throughout town. Crowned in copper, the capitol serves as a reminder that while gold shines brighter, the reddish-brown ore coming out of Butte, beginning in the 1880s, was the dominant star in Montana's mining and political history.

■ BUTTE

The discovery of rich copper ores in Butte coincided with the introduction of the electric light bulb and telephone on the world market, and the rest, as they say, is history. Large mining interests turned to Butte, and between 1882 and 1890, copper production increased from nine million to 130 million pounds; Butte's population tripled. The population peaked right around World War I with an estimated 20,000 miners and 100,000 residents, making it one of the West's largest inland cities. Once Montana's largest city, Butte now ranks fourth, with about 33,000 residents.

This mile-high mining town is known affectionately as "Butte, America," because the valley in which it lies was lost in a frontier twilight zone between the Louisiana Purchase and Oregon Territory, and never legally procured as part of either chunk of real estate. A true melting pot, it drew thousands of foreign-born immigrants in search of a living wage. They clustered together in ethnic neighborhoods that still bear the names of Corktown, Dublin Gulch, Finntown, Chinatown, and Little Italy. Some of these enclaves were literally devoured by the huge open-pit mine that began replacing underground mining operations in 1955, but Butte, more than any other city or town in Montana, has retained its ethnic character. While the Irish dominate Butte in body and spirit, there are still distinct pockets of Finns, Slavs, and Italians, and remnant populations of many other nationalities.

Whether due to its ethnic roots, its labor heritage, or both, Butte is a rough town with a tender heart. Surrounded by gallow frames, mine spoils, ore dumps, and mine shafts, and perched on the edge of the defunct, mile-wide Berkeley Pit, Butte stands uncontested as Montana's most unattractive city. It has been described in the national press as "the ugliest city in America." Behind its bleak, pock-marked face, however, shine the smiling eyes and indomitable spirit of its

The Wah Chong Tai Co. thrived in Butte's turn-of-the-century melting pot. (Montana Historical Society)

*Improved technology and market conditions for precious metals have created a resurgence in mining.
This open-pit gold mine (top) is south of Helena. These gold bricks (above) are not as pure as they look;
they will be further processed outside the state. (opposite) Molten gold.*

residents. People are the power behind Butte and they have been ever since they muscled the ore and fought the labor wars that made Butte the most militant union town in the nation.

Butte was all business when it went to work, but when the shift changed, Butte knew how to have fun. Hundreds of saloons and gambling parlors stayed open around the clock to serve three shifts of miners. This was a town that never shut down and never gave up. Market fluctuations, changes in mining technology, overseas production, and depletion of high-grade ores all inflicted near-fatal blows to the economy of Butte over the years. What everyone but Butte interpreted as the final blow came in 1983, when the Atlantic Richfield Company (ARCO) announced the suspension of all mining operations in Butte. Mining in Butte will never be what it was during the nation's industrial era, but small-scale copper mining has made a comeback, and Butte has diversified its economy with a sound mix of businesses built on mining, energy and environmental research, along with public utilities, education, and medical services.

For most of its existence, Butte was a company town, held captive by global markets and corporate policies beyond its control. Forced to take control of its destiny when it was abandoned by ARCO, Butte now stands as a role model for other Montana towns singing the American heartland blues. While Butte had the vision to contemplate life after copper, it never lost sight of its rich ethnic-labor heritage and mining history. The entire city is a living museum, with real-life exhibits in the card room of the M&M bar and café, the tightly packed miners' shanties that cling to steep hillsides, uptown mansions that memorialize the copper kings, Irish wakes that celebrate the lives of the departed, Christmas Eve at the Serbian Church, St. Urho's Day at the Helsinki Bar, and St. Patrick's Day in every bar and on every sidewalk.

Visitors can familiarize themselves with Butte's mining heritage on walking tours of uptown Butte, driving tours of underground mine sites, guided trolley tours of the city, and at the **World Museum of Mining**, the **Mineral Museum** on the campus of **Montana Tech**, the **Copper King Mansion**, the **Arts Chateau,** and the visitor center at the **Berkeley Pit,** for many years the nation's largest truck-operated open-pit copper mine. The **Butte Chamber of Commerce** at 2950 Harrison Ave. has info on all these options. Two other attractions stand as monuments to the characteristic determination of "Buttians" to beat the odds: a 90-foot (27-m), 51-ton lighted statue of **Our Lady of the Rockies** that overlooks Butte from atop the Continental Divide; and the multi-million-dollar **U.S. High Altitude Sports Center,** which grew out of Butte's speedskating tradition and serves as a training facility and competition skating rink for Olympic-class athletes.

On first impression, Butte offers little more than a tarnished landscape and the services that are bound to appear at the junction of two interstate highways. But venture past the convenience stores and fast-food joints clustered at the exit ramps and poke around uptown Butte. Drop into **Gamer's Confectionery,** where customers operate the cash register and make their own change, or any of the neighborhood bars. A warm reception is guaranteed, and it won't be long before "yous guys" see the heart of gold that beats behind the homely facade of the city built on copper.

■ ANACONDA

About 25 miles (40 km) west of Butte is another small city that owes its existence to copper. Indeed, **Anaconda** would be known today as "Copperopolis" if its founder, Marcus Daly, had had his way. Hand-picked by Daly as the site of a giant reduction works to process the ores coming from his Anaconda mine in Butte, Anaconda became a classic company town whose fortunes were tied directly to those of Daly's mining operations. When the mines were producing, life was good in Anaconda, and Marcus Daly was its patron saint. Besides providing good jobs for hundreds of smelter workers, he endowed his beloved Anaconda with a trolley line, an amusement park, a magnificent hotel, and a racetrack. (Only the amusement park is still in operation.) At one time, the 585-foot-high (180-m) smelter stack was the tallest in North America; the plant had the world's largest smelting capacity. By the end of World War II, the Anaconda Copper Mining Company (ACM), which had absorbed the interests of Daly and the other early copper barons of Butte, had also acquired copper mines in Chile and Mexico, becoming the world's largest producer of copper.

ACM lost its monolithic stature in the worldwide copper industry in 1970, when a Marxist government rose to power in Chile and nationalized all of that nation's copper mines. Trouble in Latin America coincided with the domestic challenge of meeting new air pollution standards, and the company began divesting itself of its Montana properties, one by one. In 1977, ACM merged with the

Atlantic Richfield Company, and in 1980, the company suspended its smelting operations in Anaconda and Great Falls indefinitely. For the first time in its existence, the company town of Anaconda was without a company.

While still unsure of its future, Anaconda has a firm grip on the significance of its role in Montana history. It is said that seven truckloads of printed material from the Anaconda Reduction Works are preserved by the local historical society, along with maps, photographs, and memorabilia of Anaconda's early ethnic groups and social organizations. For those who prefer their history condensed, try a historic walking tour (see the chamber of commerce), or head to the museum and art gallery. Anaconda's elaborate **Washoe Theater** is an art deco classic, and its **Hearst Free Library,** donated to the city by newspaper eminence Phoebe Hearst (whose husband helped finance Daly's mining ventures), is yet another reminder of the outside money that influenced the development of southwestern Montana. **Washoe Park,** a gift of Daly to the city, is still Anaconda's favorite playground with its ball fields, flower gardens, picnic areas, swimming pool, and state fish hatchery.

Anaconda's Washoe Theatre is an art deco classic.

Nearby **Lost Creek State Park** is one of the best-kept secrets in the state parks system. Spectacular limestone cliffs and granite formations, waterfalls, mountain goats, and bighorn sheep make this a worthwhile sidetrip for anyone visiting Anaconda.

■ STOCKGROWERS' TOWNS

Southwestern Montana has two other mid-sized communities, both firmly rooted in the livestock industry. Deer Lodge, 25 miles (40 km) north of Anaconda, and Dillon, about 80 miles (130 km) south, lie along major rivers flowing through broad mountain valleys. Just as the mountains around Butte and Helena yielded rich deposits of copper and gold, these valleys provided the grass and water that launched Montana's cattle industry.

Canadian trapper and mountain man Johnny Grant was the first to make a go of ranching in the Deer Lodge Valley, and he is sometimes acknowledged as the founder of the industry in Montana. By 1863, only 10 years after acquiring a few rundown cows, he was running 4,000 head and nearly as many horses on his Deer Lodge property and supplying most of the beef for the mining camps of Bannack and Virginia City. Grant sold his spread in 1866 to a German immigrant, Conrad Kohrs, who built it into one of the most prosperous cattle ranches in the West. As headquarters for an empire that covered more than a million acres of grazing land in the western United States and Canada, Kohrs' operation was one of few that survived the brutal winter of 1886-87.

Today, the **Grant-Kohrs Ranch** is preserved on the outskirts of **Deer Lodge** as a National Historic Site. Visitors can poke around in the early barns and outbuildings, or tour the original ranch house, once regarded the finest in the Territory. Cattle still graze here and draft horses are still used to work the land, making this the next best thing to a working ranch for visitors who desire to know more about ranching without getting their cowboy boots dirty. Plan to stay awhile in Deer Lodge, especially if you enjoy history, because the **Old Montana Prison**, the **Montana Law Enforcement Museum**, the **Towe Ford Museum**, and the **Powell County Museum** are all located in the same block downtown.

For a larger view of the livestock industry, you can't do better than a drive through the scenic **Big Hole Basin** in the heart of the region. Watered by the

This antique Ford (top) is one of 90 on display at the Towe Ford Museum in Deer Lodge. (bottom) The Towe collection covers the period from 1903 to the 1960s, and includes Henry Ford's personal Lincoln camper.

meandering Big Hole River, the hay grows wild in this high mountain valley, contributing heavily to Beaverhead County's standing as the top cattle and hay producer in the state. Mountain valleys were "holes" to the early trappers and mountain men, and this was one of the biggest in the area, so the name stuck. Known today as the "valley of 10,000 haystacks," the Big Hole looks like an agrarian landscape from the past, with haystacks piled high as houses throughout the valley's 50-mile (80-km) length and 15-mile (24-km) width. Cutting a cleaner profile than the haystacks are the 30-foot-high (nine-meter) beaverslides that are used to stack the hay. The derrick-like, wooden structures were devised by two Big Hole ranchers in 1907.

The trade center for Big Hole and Beaverhead valley ranchers is **Dillon,** which got its start as a railroad town on the route to mineral-rich Butte. The stately homes of early merchants and stockmen still preside over Dillon's older, tree-lined neighborhoods. Once Montana's largest wool shipping point, Dillon is better known today as the home of **Western Montana College,** which specializes in improving rural education and serves as a branch campus of the University of Montana. Dillon is also a base camp for recreation in the surrounding Beaverhead National Forest, the nearby Beaverhead and Big Hole rivers, Clark Canyon

Taking a break during one of several wagon train rides that rolled across Montana in 1989, the statehood centennial.

Reservoir, and the Wise River-Polaris scenic byway. Dillon's **Labor Day Rodeo,** locally billed as "Montana's Biggest Weekend," ranks among the state's best rodeos with its dances, rodeo performances, a wild horse race, parade, and barbecue.

■ GHOST TOWNS

For every gold camp that survived, there are dozens that went bust when the diggin's played out. The century-old drama of prospectors, road agents, vigilantes, harlots, and abandoned wives and children is etched in the weathered frames of cabins, saloons, hotels, and assay offices that once lined the folds and gulches of these mountain valleys. A few ghost towns, especially Bannack and Virginia City, have been preserved, their stories intact. Most, however, are blown-down, rusted-out relics whose stories can only be imagined by the visitors who seek them out.

For beginning students of ghost town lore, **Bannack** is an illustrated primer on Montana's gold mining history. The site of Montana's first major gold rush, Bannack erupted when hundreds of prospectors flocked to a strike on nearby Grasshopper Creek in 1862. Within a year, the population had swollen to 3,000, and in 1864 Bannack became Montana's first Territorial capital. Eventually the gold played out and so did Bannack, but not before a sizable community had been established. Gunfights and hangings once shattered the silence of this remote valley, while more peaceable citizens crowded the saloons, dance halls, miner's court, church, and school. Today, Bannack is a quiet park, managed by the state for its historic value. A walking tour and visitor center familiarize visitors with the social and structural fabric of this 1860s' gold rush town. In late July, Bannack celebrates its history with a weekend of frontier crafts and food, music, buggy rides, gold panning, a black powder rifle shoot, and frontier church service. **Bannack Days** is the biggest weekend of the year in this otherwise lonely outpost. The park is located west of Dillon, off Montana State Highway 278.

Visitors can still stroll the boardwalks of one of the West's richest and most colorful mining districts, about 60 miles (100 km) east of Dillon, on Montana State Highway 287. **Virginia City** and **Nevada City** lie within a mile of one another along Alder Gulch. News of an 1863 gold strike here spread like knapweed, and within a year several thousand prospectors had crowded into makeshift camps along the gulch. The most enduring of these overnight mining camps was Virginia

MINERS AND MAYHEM

*O*f the settlements in Alder Gulch, Virginia City was the principal, though Nevada, two miles below, at one time was of nearly equal size and population. A stranger from the Eastern States entering the gulch for the first time, two or three months after its discovery, would be inspired by the scene and its associations with reflections of the most strange and novel character. This human hive, numbering at least ten thousand people, was the product of ninety days. Into it were crowded all the elements of a rough and active civilization. Thousands of cabins and tents and brush wakiups, thrown together in the roughest form, and scattered at random along the banks, and in the nooks of the hills, were seen on every hand. Every foot of the gulch, under the active manipulations of the miners, was undergoing displacement, and it was already disfigured by huge heaps of gravel, which had been passed through the sluices, and rifled of their glittering contents. In the gulch itself all was activity. Some were removing the superincumbent earth to reach the pay-dirt, others who had accomplished that were gathering up the clay and gravel upon the surface of the bed-rock, while by others still it was thrown into the sluice boxes. This exhibition of mining industry was twelve miles long. Gold was abundant, and every possible devise was employed by the gamblers, the treaders, the vile men and women that had come with the miners to the locality, to obtain it. Nearly every third cabin in the towns was a saloon where vile whiskey was peddled out for fifty cents a drink in gold dust. Many of these places were filled with gambling tables and gamblers, and the miner who was bold enough to enter one of them with his day's earnings in his pocket seldom left until thoroughly fleeced. Hurdy-gurdy dance-houses were numerous, and there were plenty of camp beauties to patronize them. There too, the successful miner, lured by siren smiles, after an evening spent in dancing and carousing at his expense, steeped with liquor, would empty his purse into the lap of his charmer for an hour of license in her arms. Not a day or night passed which did not yield its full fruition of fights, quarrels, wounds, or murders. The crack of the revolver was often heard above the merry notes of the violin. Street fights were frequent, and as no one knew when or where they would occur, every one was on his guard against a random shot. Sunday was always a gala day. The miners then left their work and gathered about the public places in the towns. The stores were all open, the auctioneers specially eloquent on every corner in praise of their wares. Thousands of people crowded

the thoroughfares, ready to rush in any direction of promised excitement. Horse-racing was among the most favored amusements. Prize rings were formed, and brawny men engaged at fisticuffs until their sight was lost and their bodies pommelled to a jelly, while hundreds of on-lookers cheered the victor. Hacks rattled to and fro between the several towns, freighted with drunken and rowdy humanity of both sexes. Citizens of acknowledged respectability often walked, more often perhaps rode side by side on horseback, with noted courtesans in open day through the crowded streets, and seemingly suffered no harm in reputation. Pistols flashed, bowie-knives flourished, and braggart oaths filled the air, as often as men's passions triumphed over their reason. This was indeed the reign of unbridled license, and men who at first regarded it with disgust and terror, by constant exposure soon learned to become part of it, and forget that they had ever been aught else. All classes of society were represented at this general exhibition. Judges, lawyers, doctors, even clergymen could not claim exemption. Culture and religion afforded feeble protection, where allurement and indulgence ruled the hour.
—Nathaniel Pitt Langford,
Vigilante Days and Ways,
1890

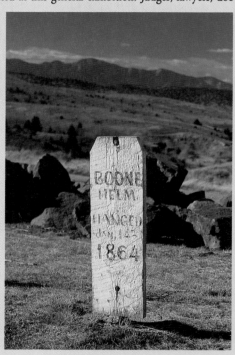

Road agent's grave at Boot Hill cemetery in Virginia City.

This weathered façade (top) is one of several restored buildings from Montana's gold rush days at Virginia City. (above) Mining memorabilia on display at the World Museum of Mining in Butte.

City, which mushroomed into a commercial hub of 10,000 and served as Montana's second Territorial capital from 1865 to 1875. In one year, $10 million in gold nuggets was panned from the streams that feed into the gulch, and since the initial strike, an estimated $70 million has been taken from the area. Thanks to the painstaking restoration efforts of a Montana ranch family headed by the late Charles and Sue Bovey, visitors can drop coins into a nickelodeon, photograph a two-story outhouse, and browse through shops, buildings, merchandise, and memorabilia that are true to the era. One of Montana's foremost summer theater troupes, the **Virginia City Players,** performs nineteenth century melodrama every night during the summer at the Virginia City Opera House.

Less developed but equally diverting are the 1870s' gold camp of **Garnet,** north of Drummond; the 1880s' silver boomtown of **Granite,** near Philipsburg; the 1870s mining camp of **Elkhorn,** near Boulder, which produced both gold and silver; and **Marysville,** north of Helena, home of the fabulous Drumlummon mine, which yielded $16 million in gold and silver. Dozens of other ghost towns haunt the mountains of southwestern Montana. The **Ghost Town Hall of Fame,** at Fairmont Hot Springs east of Anaconda, displays photos and narrative descriptions of many of them. You can buy comprehensive guides to Montana's ghost towns at many bookstores around the state.

■ OUTDOOR RECREATION

The abiding treasures of this region are not the gold placers, silver lodes, and copper veins whose value is determined by a fickle metals' market. In an increasingly crowded and polluted world, this mining district's trump card may well be its rivers and lakes, its vast, untrammeled wilderness and roadless areas, its unpeopled space, and natural beauty. Small cities and towns that once drew prospectors and immigrant laborers now attract retirees, sportsmen, and refugees from urban America.

The centerpiece of the region's natural attractions is a superlative trout fishery nurtured by the headwaters of the Missouri River. Ever since August 22, 1805, when Meriwether Lewis noted in his journal that his party had landed "528 good fish, most of them large trout," the **Beaverhead River** has become famous for its "porkchops," chunky browns and rainbows that tip the scales at four-plus pounds (two kg) each. Indeed, the upper Beaverhead produces more trophy-size trout per mile than any other stream in the state.

More accessible and easier to fish, the **Big Hole** draws more anglers each year than the Beaverhead. Many come in June to fish the Big Hole's famed salmonfly hatch, which triggers Montana's most celebrated trout feeding binge. Others come for the opportunity to catch rare, river-dwelling arctic grayling, thought to be extinct everywhere in the lower 48 states except for the upper Big Hole drainage. Rising as a trickle in the Beaverhead Mountains, the Big Hole flows through wild hay meadows, skirts the north end of the Pioneer Mountains in a grand, graceful arc, and plunges through a canyon before merging with the Beaverhead at Twin Bridges to become the Jefferson River.

Beyond the veinous network of rivers and streams that surge through its valleys, the region is studded with lakes and reservoirs. One of the most scenic is **Georgetown Lake,** actually a reservoir built in 1901 by the Anaconda Company to ensure a lasting water supply for its smelting operation in nearby Anaconda. Shimmering beneath the 10,000-foot-high (3,050-m) peaks of the Anaconda Range, Georgetown Lake is one of Montana's most popular boating and fishing spots, with reliable yields of rainbow trout and kokanee salmon. To the south, near Dillon, **Clark Canyon Reservoir** is an excellent rainbow trout fishery with plenty of camping and boat-launching facilities. To the north, near Helena, three dams on the Missouri have created a chain of recreation opportunities on Canyon Ferry, Hauser, and Holter lakes. Stretching 25 miles (40 km) from the valley east of Helena to Townsend, **Canyon Ferry Lake** draws people from throughout the state to fish its stocked waters, sail and surf its wind-chopped surface, and play on its sandy beaches.

The river below Canyon Ferry Dam has become an important fall feeding ground for bald eagles. Here, just 20 minutes away from the state capital, hundreds of eagles gather around Thanksgiving to feast on spawning kokanee. Hundreds of wildlife watchers also gather to view the magnificent birds with seven-foot (two-meter) wingspans as they cruise the thermals above the same river where, in 1805, Meriwether Lewis noted that "the Bald Eagle are more abundant than I ever observed them in any Part of the country." Lewis and Clark left their imprint just a few miles downriver where the Missouri flows through a narrow passage flanked by what Lewis described as "the most remarkable clifts that we have yet seen." Because these cliffs first appeared as if they would block the expedition's passage, then seemed to open as the explorers got closer, Lewis named this scenic gorge the Gates of the Rocky Mountains. Visitors today can see the same illusion on commercial boat tours departing from the **Gates of the Mountains** boat landing on Holter Lake.

Nearby **Gates of the Mountains Wilderness** is one of Montana's smallest and least visited wilderness areas. Most people are content to view a fraction of the wilderness from the tour boats that glide past it (see "Tours" in PRACTICAL INFORMATION"). For those willing to don hiking boots and a backpack, the "Gates" offer a truly primitive experience within the same distinctive limestone formations and cliffs that can be seen from the river. Canyons, coulees, and gorges invite deeper exploration. A popular hunting area, they provide a home to sizable populations of elk, bighorn sheep, mountain goats, and mule deer. The adjacent **Beartooth Game Management Area** furnishes winter range for the area's large elk herd. Another small, easily accessible recreation area is the **Humbug Spires Primitive Area,** south of Butte. Erratic limestone rock formations, located just off Interstate 15, draw hikers, rock climbers, and geologic sightseers.

Southwestern Montana's foremost wilderness area is the lofty Anaconda-Pintler, straddling the Continental Divide southwest of Butte and Anaconda. Much larger than the Gates of the Mountains or the Humbug Spires, the **Anaconda-Pintler Wilderness** receives surprisingly moderate use. This is high country characterized by alpine meadows, lakes, windswept ridges, and several peaks above 10,000 feet (3,050 m). Nearly all of the land is above 7,000 feet (2,134 m), meaning that snow can come at any time and remains on the ground for more than half the year. There are nearly 300 miles (480 km) of trails in this wilderness, including 45 miles (72 km) of the Continental Divide National Scenic Trail. The Anaconda-Pintler encompasses several lakes and streams, including headwaters of nationally renowned **Rock Creek,** an exceptional trout stream that flows north approximately 70 miles (110 km) to its confluence with the Clark Fork, en route to the Pacific Ocean. Many of the lakes and streams in the wilderness area hold cutthroat and rainbow trout, while mountain goats, elk, moose, deer, bear, and mountain lion occupy the higher ground.

■ SCENIC BYWAYS

People need not climb these mountains nor fish these rivers to catch their spirit. Just being in their presence, surrounded by their majesty and grace, is enough for most visitors to the Northern Rockies. Two scenic roads penetrate the region, providing lavish views as well as access to hiking trails and trout streams, campgrounds, ghost towns, and other historic sites. Montana State Highway 1, known as the **Pintler Scenic Route,** is an inviting alternative to Interstate 90 between Missoula and Butte. For 60 miles (100 km), it parallels sparkling streams, climbs mountain passes, skirts the shores of Georgetown Lake, and visits the towns of Anaconda and Philipsburg, all beneath the towering backdrop of the Anaconda Range. When combined with Interstate 90, it forms a loop that takes in the community of Deer Lodge.

For a closer look at this Northern Rockies landscape, the **Wise River-Polaris National Forest Scenic Byway** bisects a half-million acres of peaks, lakes, and headwaters in the Pioneer Mountains. For half its 30-mile (48-km) length, this mostly unpaved road follows the Wise River, then crosses a divide and emerges from the Beaverhead National Forest near Dillon. Along the way, it delivers motorists to a variety of scenic, historic, and cultural gems, including the ghost town of **Coolidge,** which served as a base camp in the 1920s for miners working the nearby Elkhorn silver mine; 1930s-era campgrounds constructed by the Civilian Conservation Corps; prehistoric Indian sites; and a New Ager's mecca called **Crystal Park,** where small quartz crystals and amethysts are commonly found. Campgrounds, hiking trails, trout streams, and abundant wildlife can stretch what appears on the map to be a short jaunt into an extended tour.

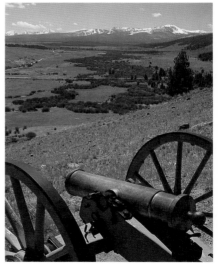

Nez Perce Indians captured the Army's howitzer on this ridge overlooking the Big Hole Battlefield during the 1877 Battle of the Big Hole.

Upon reaching Montana State Highway 278 at the south end of the Wise River-Polaris Road, Bannack State Park and Clark Canyon Reservoir are but a few miles to the south. **Big Hole Battlefield National Monument,** site of an 1877 battle between the U.S. Army and Chief Joseph's Nez Perce Indians, lies to the northwest. This was one of four major battles along the Nez Perce's flight to Canada. (See "Hi-Line: Montana's Northern Tier," for more on this trek.) While the Nez Perce escaped the army here and technically won the Battle of the Big Hole, their numbers and morale were seriously diminished. A visitor center at the Big Hole Battlefield, 12 miles (19 km) west of Wisdom on Highway 43, explains the significance of the Nez Perce Indian War. Walking trails take visitors to the camp site where soldiers surprised the sleeping Nez Perce, a wooded area where Col. John Gibbon and members of the Seventh Infantry were besieged by warriors for 36 hours, and the ridge where Indians captured the army's howitzer and a pack mule carrying 2,000 rounds of rifle ammunition.

■ PROSPECTING FOR SAPPHIRES

While the early visitors to this part of the state were fortune seekers lured by talk of fabulous gold strikes, many of today's visitors are rockhounds, drawn to one of the few places where modern prospectors can dig for sapphires. These brilliant gemstones are found in a rainbow of colors. The most common is green-blue, while blue is the best known and ruby one of the most highly prized. At commercial sapphire mines, visitors can screen "paydirt" from buckets or purchase bags of gravel to sift at home. Some of the mines also have custom gem-cutting shops on site. Most sapphire hunters spend a day or two at the mines for the fun of it, gathering gemstones that range from one-half to 10 carats. But it's easy to get hooked on these treasure hunts, knowing that sapphires as large as 150 carats have been found, then sold for thousands of dollars. Three of these mines line the Missouri River northeast of Helena—the **Spokane Bar, Cleatus** and **El Dorado** mines. Another large deposit lies along Rock Creek, southwest of Philipsburg. Once mined commercially by the St. Louis-based American Gem Mining Syndicate, today's **Gem Mountain Sapphire Mine** is open to rockhounds and recreational prospectors.

BITTERROOT COUNTRY

Wherever mountains are, there exist people to whom mountains are where life should be lived. To millions more they are a fascination, an exhilaration, a challenge, a solace; but when a man tries to state why, he finds himself using the impotent abstractions. Like magnificence. Like solitude. Like self-humility. Like freedom and beauty. Or he goes the other way and speaks of fresh air and fishing, of bighorn and bear. None of these suffices, and together they don't explain. Maybe we can't improve on the simple statement that mountains are mountains.

—A. B. Guthrie, Jr., *Big Sky, Fair Land,* 1988

THE BITTERROOT VALLEY TAKES ITS NAME FROM THE RIVER that flows its entire length, the mountain range that forms its dominant western wall, and the diminutive flower that grows wild among its forests of ponderosa pine. This distinctive valley, which resembles a snout on the face of western Montana, appears isolated from the rest of the state but is central to its history.

As early as 1500, Flathead Indians are said to have lived here, having drifted east with other Salish-speaking tribes from the Columbia River country of the Pacific Northwest. They moved freely across the Continental Divide to hunt buffalo until around 1700, when the arrival of Shoshone and Blackfeet Indians east of the divide forced them back to the western valleys. By the time Lewis and Clark came upon them in 1805, they had established the Bitterroot Valley as their central homeland.

In the 1830s, curious about reports of "Black Robes" who could speak to the Great Spirit, the Flatheads sent delegates east to St. Louis to request that a Catholic mission be established in their valley. In September 1841, the Jesuits founded **St. Mary's Mission,** the first church in the Northwest, in what is now the community of **Stevensville.** By Christmas of that year, more than 700 Indians had been baptized. But the original church did not last beyond its first decade. It faced a number of problems, including scarce funds, continual threats from hostile Blackfeet Indians, and growing disenchantment among the Flatheads. In 1850, the mission closed and the property was sold to Major John Owen, who transformed it into a lively trading post he named **Fort Owen.**

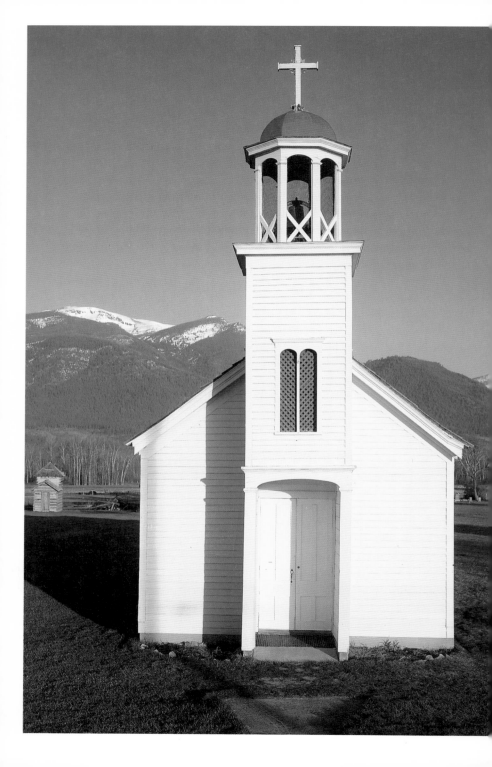

Never a military base, Fort Owen flourished as the commercial hub of Bitterroot Valley. Owen himself had resigned his position as a licensed trader with the U.S. Army to go independent. At Fort Owen, he built on the grain and livestock operations begun by the Jesuits of St. Mary's and soon became a major supplier to nearby gold camps. Fort Owen was also a popular gathering spot for adventurers, trappers, new settlers, and several Indian tribes. Here, travelers were welcome, parties and feasts were frequent, and Indians and whites were friends. Married to a Shoshone, Owen was sympathetic to the growing problems of the natives and became the agent of the Flathead Nation, a position he later resigned out of disgust with the federal Indian Bureau's indifference and neglect. Fort Owen served as Flathead Agency Headquarters until 1860, when the headquarters was moved to its existing location in the Jocko River Valley, north of Missoula. A remnant of this once humming "bastion of civilization" in the remote wilderness of the Northwest has been preserved in Stevensville as **Fort Owen State Park.** Set on the banks of the Bitterroot River, surrounded by the lush pasturelands that supported Fort Owen's livestock, the dimly lighted East Barracks is about all that remains of the enterprise.

Less than half a mile (one km) away is the mission, reconstructed in 1866 by an Italian Jesuit, Father Anthony Ravalli. St. Mary's remained an Indian mission until 1891, when the last band of Flatheads in the Bitterroot were forced to move north. A prominent Stevensville landmark, it memorializes not only the longstanding friendship between the Flathead Indians and the Catholic church, but also the importance of this valley to the peopling of Montana. In terms of permanent settlement, the Bitterroot Valley is where it all began.

■ THE VALLEY TODAY

To reach both St. Mary's and Fort Owen, travelers must leave U.S. Route 93 and cross the Bitterroot River to reach the East Side Highway (State Highway 203/ 269). This secondary route stretches about 30 miles (50 km) through the valley's interior, between Florence and Hamilton, and provides a leisurely alternative to its major north-south artery. With views of the low-lying Sapphire Mountains to the east and the canyons and peaks of the Bitterroot Range to the west, visitors will understand the magnetic pull this valley has had on visitors ever since the Flathead

St. Mary's Mission was established by Jesuit priests in 1841 at the request of Flathead Indians; they'd heard about "Black Robes" who could speak to the Great Spirit. The present church was built in 1866.

Indians were first attracted by its mild climate. Stretching nearly 100 miles (160 km) south of Missoula to the Idaho border, the valley lies in the protective rain shadow of the Bitterroot Mountains, whose 8,000- to 10,000-foot (2,440- to 3,050-m) summits wring eastbound moisture from the Pacific out of the air before it reaches the valley. Logging and livestock are the traditional pillars of the Bitterroot economy, with a growing number of cottage and service industries that reflect the valley's appeal as a retirement community and refuge for urban emigrés. From gardening and beekeeping to horse breeding and log home construction, anything goes in this valley of scattered housing and small ranches.

"Outsiders" have been discovering the Bitterroot ever since mining industrialist Marcus Daly traveled through the valley in 1864 searching for a mining friend, George Hearst, who was feared lost in Canada. Later in his career he remembered the valley's natural beauty and climate, not to mention its thick stands of timber, which he needed for his mine tunnels and smelter works in Butte and Anaconda. In 1888–89, he and his agents began acquiring land for timber as well as for Daly's personal use. He built a 28,000-acre estate on the outskirts of Hamilton that became his summer residence and stock farm. He called it "Riverside," and added a covered and heated horse track for his beloved race horses. After the copper king's death, the **Daly Mansion** was remodeled extensively by his wife, and is now open

Early logging was done with horses. (Montana Historical Society)

to the public during the summer. A beautiful, tree-lined driveway leads to the three-story, 42-room Georgian Revival residence with its 24 bedrooms and 15 bathrooms.

The legacy of Daly's logging and milling operations may well be the log home manufacturing industry that now dominates the valley's economy. Nearly two dozen log home companies are headquartered here. The assembly yards where logs are peeled and notched, then shipped as kit log homes to buyers throughout the world, can be seen just off U.S. Route 93 throughout the valley.

■ HAMILTON

Another major employer in the valley is the medical research industry, which grew from turn-of-the-century efforts to conquer the deadly Rocky Mountain spotted fever, carried by the wood ticks so prevalent in the foothills of the Bitterroots and other Western mountains. Dr. Howard T. Ricketts, one of many fine scientists drawn to the valley to take up the challenge, discovered the link between infected

The logging and sawmill industry today is highly mechanized. (Montana Historical Society)

ticks and spotted fever in 1906. He is remembered by the name "rickettsia," given to the tiny organisms responsible for typhus, spotted fever, and related illnesses. Later scientists developed a successful vaccine against spotted fever, which is still produced at **Hamilton's Rocky Mountain Laboratories,** built in 1928 by the U.S. Public Health Service and now an arm of the National Institutes of Health. In addition to producing the vaccine, which is shipped all over the world, the laboratories conduct basic and applied research in immunologic, allergic, and infectious diseases. A private, spin-off business, Ribi ImmunoChem Research, Inc., markets veterinary pharmaceuticals and conducts cancer research. Begun by a former member of the Rocky Mountain Laboratories staff, the Hamilton company is one of 14 Montana businesses traded publicly on the stock market.

The small but diverse community of Hamilton is a crossroads of scientific and technical workers, U.S. Forest Service personnel, and the valley's more traditional loggers and ranchers. As county seat of Ravalli County, it is also the government and commercial center for the valley's 25,000 residents. It has a substantial retirement population consisting largely of former visitors who were permanently attracted by the area's climate, rural lifestyle, and outdoor recreation. Prized assets are the Bitterroot River, which flows right through town, and Blodgett Canyon, a magnificent gorge through the Bitterroot Range just 20 minutes away.

Another nearby natural treasure is the **Lee Metcalf National Wildlife Refuge,** outside of Stevensville. Named after the late U.S. Senator Lee Metcalf, a native son and conservation giant, the refuge is an island of serenity in the midst of the rambling development of the Bitterroot Valley. It protects 2,800 acres of marshes, meadows, river bottoms, and uplands that sustain more than 200 different kinds of birds, notably blue herons, osprey, and a multitude of ducks, swans, and geese. White-tailed deer are also abundant. A county road accessible from the East Side Highway bisects the lower half of the refuge, and a seasonal hiking trail with observation blinds is open mid-July to mid-September.

■ THE MOUNTAINS

The enduring appeal of the Bitterroot lies in the dramatic skyline etched by Trapper Peak, El Capitan, and the other summits and spires that run the entire length of the Bitterroot Range. The crest of this glacially sculpted range forms the jagged border separating Montana from Idaho. The two states share not only one of the most rugged massifs in the Northern Rockies but also one of the largest federally protected wilderness areas in the lower 48. The 1.3-million-acre **Selway-Bitterroot Wilderness** straddles the border, providing refuge for abundant elk and other wildlife. At first the sheer granite faces of these mountains appear cold and forbidding, but it won't be long before you feel the pull of their valleys and saddles, canyons and crests. Distinctive, U-shaped chasms cut east-west across the range, opening cool, pine-covered avenues of exploration along trout streams fed by icy lakes in the wilderness interior. Several secondary roads lead from U.S. Route 93 to trailheads at the mouths of these canyons.

When the Bitterroots are continually stealing the show, it is easy to overlook the valley's eastern rim, formed by the gentler ridges and folds of the Sapphire Mountains. Easy to reach and well worth the effort, the Sapphires' high meadows and basins shelter elk, moose, bears, mountain lion, bighorn sheep, and mountain goats, as well as a number of smaller mammals and birds. A good trail system awaits hikers, but most visitors prefer driving the Skalkaho Pass Road, which climbs the east face of the range on Montana State Highway 38, west of Hamilton, crosses Skalkaho Pass at 7,260 feet (2,210 m), then drops into Rock Creek Valley and Georgetown Lake near Anaconda. This popular back road for summer loiterers is closed in winter.

At the north end of the Bitterroot Valley, U.S. Route 12 takes motorists over the historic Lolo Trail into Idaho. This was a busy route, used by the Flathead and Nez Perce, and later by non-Indian explorers beginning with Lewis and Clark in 1805. After following the Bitterroot River in September of that year, their expedition camped at a place they named Travellers Rest, near the junction of U.S. Routes 93 and 12 at Lolo. Shortly, they reached Lolo Pass on what is now the Montana-Idaho border, and began the most difficult leg of their westward journey. Hampered by deep snow, bad weather, and a scarcity of wild game, their progress was slow but they managed to reach the Pacific by November. The following July, on their return trip east, they camped again at Travellers Rest, and it was here that they split the outfit into two groups for further exploration of the Yellowstone, Marias, and Missouri rivers. Well over a quarter of the expedition's entire 8,000-mile (12,800-km) journey was spent here in Montana. The U.S. Forest Service

(following pages) Lolo Peak, south of Missoula, is one of many distinctive landmarks along the Bitterroot Range.

maintains a visitor center at Lolo Pass that explains the significance of the Lolo Trail in the opening of the West. The history of the area was also illustrated by early Montana painter Edgar S. Paxson in several of the murals that adorn the walls of the Missoula County Courthouse in the valley's gateway city.

■ MISSOULA

Presiding over the north end of the valley is Montana's cultural superstar and third-largest city. Best known as home to the **University of Montana,** Missoula is a yeasty brew of students and independent small businesspeople, professors, truckers, foresters, artists, and writers. The common denominator of this often factious community is a lifestyle revered by all. "One of the most sophisticated small cities in America" . . . "One of the top 10 universities for education and recreation" . . . "One of the top 10 bicycling cities in the United States": these are some of the badges of distinction Missoula wears, awarded over the years by national magazines and rating guides. At the head of five scenic valleys and the junction of three great rivers, Missoula has no shortage of recreational opportunities. Here is a city of 43,000 residents with more than 140 restaurants, all within minutes of a wilderness trailhead. Here is western Montana's commercial, industrial, educational, and transportation hub, with a trout stream flowing through the center of town.

Loggers, foresters, railroaders, and merchants may have put this town on the map, but it is Missoula's writers, artists, and dramatists who keep it there. Past literary lights include critic Leslie Fiedler, the late poet Richard Hugo, and Western novelist Dorothy Johnson. Still shining brightly are novelists James Welch and James Crumley, essayist and novelist William Kittredge, writer and filmmaker Annick Smith, nonfiction writer Bryan Di Salvatore, and poet Patricia Goedicke. Many are the products of the university's 70-year-old creative writing program, which awards MFA degrees to a select group of graduate students from throughout the nation.

Readings and writing seminars are regular fare in and around Missoula. So are the live performances and exhibits of dozens of performing artists, musicians, dancers, painters, sculptors, potters, and crafters. Missoula is the home of the **Montana Repertory Theatre**—a first-rate regional touring company; the **Missoula**

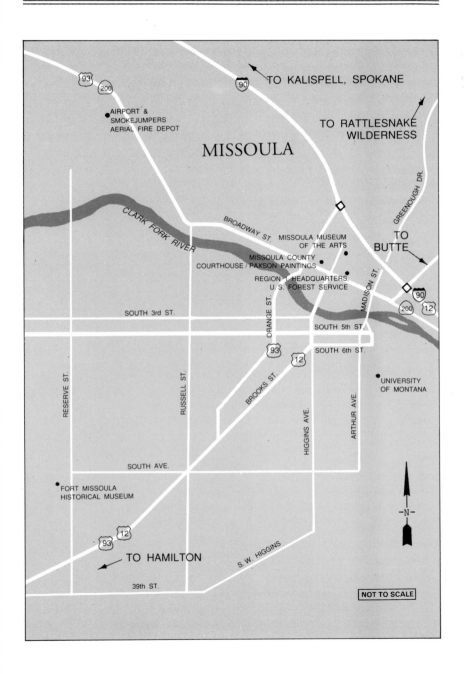

Children's Theatre—largest touring children's theater in America; the **String Orchestra of the Rockies;** the **Garden City Ballet Company;** and a number of other university and community-based music and drama groups. Each spring, the world's top wildlife films are screened and judged at the week-long **International Wildlife Film Festival.**

The **Historical Museum at Fort Missoula** provides a glimpse of the area's history, while more than half a dozen art galleries and the **Missoula Museum of the Arts** exhibit works of local and regional artists. Those who call Missoula home but market their work widely outside the state include sculptor Rudy Autio (and his wife, Lela), a painter and fabric art designer; poster artist Monte Dolack; and painter Kendahl Jan Jubb. Western and wildlife art, the staple of most Montana galleries, is underplayed in Missoula, where contemporary art is refreshingly "in." A former resident novelist accurately described Missoula as "a forgiving, liberal town in a conservative state."

'Dirty Murphy' plays events in several of Montana's cities.

Missoula is also a town—perhaps the only one in Montana—where day in and day out the mike is on and the curtain is up. There is always something happening on the cultural front. Which is not to say that a new stage production or   concert would preempt a fall hunting trip, or sell out as quickly as a Lady Griz basketball game or the annual Bobcat-Grizzly football game (one of the nation's oldest inter-collegiate rivalries, reenacted alternately on the UM campus in Missoula and the MSU campus in Bozeman). Even though many eastern Montanans discount it as "that liberal college town" on the state's western fringe, Missoula is still in Montana. And Montana priorities are firmly in place here.

■ MISSOULA OUTDOORS

The **Rocky Mountain Elk Foundation,** one of the nation's fastest-growing wildlife conservation organizations, is based in Missoula, as is **Bikecentennial,** America's bike-touring headquarters. Cartop carriers are always in place, ready to receive the bikes, skis, kayaks, and rafts that are the essential gear of a Missoulian. Surrounded

A steam railroad engine is one of many artifacts and displays at Fort Missoula's historical museum.

JEANNETTE RANKIN: ACTIVIST FOR PEACE

As the home of Montana's leading liberal arts university, Missoula attracts and nurtures political activists. But the city's most famous pacifist pre-dates the university, and even statehood. Born in 1880 on a ranch outside of Missoula, Jeannette Rankin became the first woman elected to the U.S. House of Representatives and the only member of Congress to vote against U.S. entry into both world wars. A progressive Republican, Rankin came to the peace movement through her involvement in the campaign for woman suffrage. As she worked on a variety of issues to benefit women and children, she became convinced that the quest for peace also belonged in the suffrage movement.

Rankin launched her political career in 1911, when she urged the Montana Legislature to grant women the right to vote. In 1916, she won her first campaign for Congress on a platform calling for woman suffrage, protective legislation for children, prohibition, and peace. After casting her first antiwar vote in April, 1917—five days after being introduced in Congress as its first female member—

Jeannette Rankin speaking in Washington, D.C., before proceeding to the Capitol to be installed as the first woman member of Congress, 1917. (Montana Historical Society)

she said, "I have always felt that there was more significance in the fact that the first woman who was ever asked what she thought about war said NO and I believe that the first vote I had was the most significant vote and a most significant act on the part of women, because women are going to have to stop war."

On that vote, she had the support of 56 other members of Congress. Twenty-four years later, after her re-election to Congress, Rankin stood alone in her opposition to war. On December 8, 1941, the day after Pearl Harbor, she cast the lone vote against U.S. entry into World War II. Asked to justify her unpopular position, she replied, "A just nation never votes unanimously for war." It was her political undoing. Defeated in her 1942 reelection bid, Rankin carried on her crusade through public appearances and antiwar statements. In 1968, the Vietnam War coalesced a group of women who marched on Washington under the banner of the Jeannette Rankin Brigade. In 1972, a year before her death, Ralph Nader noted, "If aging is the erosion of one's ideals, then Jeannette Rankin is young forever."

Statues of Montana's most outspoken feminist and pacifist stand today in both the U.S. Capitol and the State Capitol in Helena. Her ideals still inspire activists at Missoula's Jeannette Rankin Peace Resource Center.

by national forests, mountains, and rivers, locals either inherit or quickly acquire a love of woods and water. Those who lack the time or ability to hike, hunt, bike, fish, or float can enjoy Missoula's addictive environment at one of Montana's most attractive urban parks, which stretches along the Clark Fork River as it passes through downtown Missoula on its way to the Pacific Ocean. Almost as convenient as the park is the **Rattlesnake National Recreation Area and Wilderness**, a 61,000-acre preserve of hiking trails, rocky peaks, and lake-filled basins that lies literally in Missoula's backyard, just a mile north of town.

As Northern Region headquarters for the U.S. Forest Service, Missoula has always been tied to the wood-products industry and the forestry profession. One of the university's strongest programs is its forestry school, which supplies the agency with many of its professionals. Missoula is also the home of the **Smokejumper Training Center and Aerial Fire Depot**, the oldest and largest of its kind in the nation. Stationed west of town near the airport, this is one of the U.S. Forest Service's nerve centers during the summer firefighting season, generally July through mid-September. Visitors can tour the center during the summer and view the action as retardant-filled planes squat for refueling and smokejumpers fuss with their parachutes and wait for the call that will signal their next mission. Photographs, murals, and videos further illustrate the highly technical business of fighting fires from the sky, and the unusual history of firefighting.

■ THE UNIVERSITY INFLUENCE

With an enrollment of about 10,000, the university is Montana's leading liberal arts school. In addition to its College of Arts and Sciences, it maintains seven professional schools of business, education, fine arts, forestry, journalism, law, and pharmacy and allied health sciences. The university also conducts significant research at the UM Biological Station on Flathead Lake, the Lubrecht Experimental Forest, and the Bureau of Business and Economic Research.

Besides the cultural, sports, and entertainment benefits supplied by the university, UM delivers a built-in clientele to the city's constellation of bookstores, music stores, art galleries, restaurants, and food markets. Downtown Missoula has risen to the challenge of shopping malls, franchises, and fast-food restaurants by creating an appealing commercial district, complete with its inviting riverfront park and a farmers market that confirms its standing as Montana's "Garden City." Downtown Missoula is a place where people still practice the leisurely art of browsing as they drift from coffeeshop to bookstore to bakery, gathering up fresh herbs and spices, croissants, and imported cheeses along the way. Except for a few days in winter, when warm air aloft creates a temperature inversion and traps smog and wood smoke in the valley, Missoula's urban environment is as inviting as its natural setting.

In 1987, the Confederated Salish and Kootenai Tribes of the Flathead Indian Reservation staged a vigil on the University of Montana campus against erosion of treaty rights.

THE FLATHEAD
WESTERN WILDERNESS

IF MONTANA HAS A DESTINATION RESORT AREA, THIS IS IT. Bordered by wilderness, encircled by mountains, watered generously by lakes and rivers, and soothed by a Pacific Northwest climate, the Flathead Valley makes its living hosting visitors. Art galleries, championship golf courses, resorts, sailing, skiing, and whitewater rafting are the industry of the Flathead. The raw materials are Flathead Lake and a stockpile of nationally protected recreational resources: Glacier National Park; the adjacent Bob Marshall Wilderness; the National Bison Range; Jewel Basin Hiking Area; Mission Mountains Wilderness, and Flathead National Wild and Scenic River. Add The Big Mountain ski resort and a chain of lakes called the Seeley Swan, and you have a year-round playground of immense proportions.

Summer is the high season here. Visitors cluster on beaches and mingle at resorts, marinas, and yacht clubs. They clog the parking lots and gift shops at Glacier Park. Local businesses cater to a growing nonresident market with fine wines and the cuisine of schooled chefs. But come September, after the crowds have subsided, residents take back their beloved Flathead and preoccupy themselves with the same concerns of other Montanans: squeezing in as many fishing trips as possible before hunting season begins and making ends meet in an area that supports few large employers. Outside of the tourism and forest industries, an aluminum plant at Columbia Falls, and public-sector employment, residents find work on family farms and ranches or in their own creative genius.

The rural lifestyle and natural beauty of the Flathead Valley have drawn a disproportionately large number of Western and contemporary painters, sculptors, ceramicists, and craftworkers to the area. Their work can be seen in studios and galleries and at art fairs throughout the valley, particularly in the Bigfork and Kalispell areas.

What little land is not textured by mountains and managed by the federal government as national forest is cultivated in crops peculiar to the climate and soil of the Flathead Valley, like peppermint, Christmas trees, cherries, and champagne grapes. Assuming it comes at the right time of year, the generous moisture that falls west of the Continental Divide also produces profitable yields of barley, wheat, oats, hay, and seed potatoes.

■ FLATHEAD LAKE

The heart of Flathead Valley lies in a shimmering expanse of water that cultivates both an economy and a lifestyle that are unique in Montana. Stretching nearly 30 miles (48 km) from Bigfork and Somers on the north to Polson on the south, Flathead Lake is the West's largest natural, freshwater lake. Its commanding presence governs not only the climate of this northern valley but also the disposition of all who dwell here. Until recently, Flathead Lake was perhaps most famous for its cherry orchards. The moderating influence of the lake creates a micro-climate conducive to the commercial production of some of the nation's plumpest, sweetest cherries.

Until 1989, mile upon mile of orchards formed a fragrant boulevard of blossoms along the lake's east shore each spring, followed by summer's festive harvest. But that year, orchardists around the lake were reminded that they are no different from other farmers and ranchers in Montana who have learned they cannot trust the weather. On February 1, a brutal, once-in-50-years cold snap sent temperatures plummeting 53 degrees (11°C) in 24 hours, flash-freezing trees and destroying the valley's cherry industry. Some growers have replanted their orchards, but it will be several years before they are producing at pre-1989 levels. Other growers are experimenting with apples, pears, peaches, and apricots. But the crop that is getting the most attention is the vineyard on the west shore of the lake near Dayton.

A recent addition to the producers whose exotic crops distinguish the Flathead Valley from the grain and livestock mainstays of central and eastern Montana, **Mission Mountain Winery** grows pinot noir grapes that are bottled as a pale, ruby champagne. The pinots thrive on the Flathead's long, hot days and cool nights, but to survive in Montana, their vines must be buried in soil over the winter. Mission Mountain also bottles a white riesling, chardonnay, muscat canelli, and Johannisberg riesling, using grapes that are grown in the Yakima Valley of Washington. The tasting room south of Dayton off U.S. Route 93, is open daily from early May to late October.

Flathead Lake supports Montana's largest sailing community, as well as sizeable fleets of motor craft and charter fishing boats. The lake is a favorite among fishermen who enjoy the needle-in-the-haystack approach to fishing,—that is, searching out large trout in deep lakes. Flathead is unrivaled in Montana as a prime fishery

for trophy Mackinaw, or lake trout. Because of the lake's size and depth, fishing on Flathead takes on the appearance of an ocean expedition. Serious anglers arm themselves with steel line and saltwater rods, and probe this inland sea at depths of 130 feet (40 m) from large boats fitted for downriggers. For visitors who would like to try their luck at catching a 20-pound (nine-kg) Mac, there are several guides on the lake, plus boat rentals, tackle shops, and marinas in lakeshore communities.

Visitors who don't need to fish to enjoy a beautiful lake can choose from several boat tours (see "Tours" in "PRACTICAL INFORMATION"). In addition to several private campgrounds and resorts, there are six state parks with camping facilities and boat launches around the lake. A seventh state park, **Wildhorse Island,** sprawls across the southwest arm of Flathead Lake. Accessible only by boat, the island shelters about a hundred bighorn sheep, along with a variety of other mammals and birds. Positioned within the boundaries of the Flathead Indian Reservation, the island was once used by Salish and Kootenai Indians as a hiding place for their horses when they were threatened by Blackfeet horse-raiding parties. Horses that were never retrieved gave the island its name.

■ KALISPELL

With roughly 12,000 residents, the city of Kalispell is as urban as it gets in this valley. Founded in 1891 along the main line of the Great Northern Railway, Kalispell has served northwestern Montana as a transport and trade center ever since. Its patriarch, Charles Conrad, was a pioneer entrepreneur who arrived in Montana on a Missouri River steamboat after losing his Virginia plantation during the Civil War. He rebuilt his fortune in the freighting business at Fort Benton, then moved to the Flathead Valley. In forming the Kalispell Townsite Company, he reserved 72 acres for himself and built a three-story, 23-room, Norman-style mansion, said to be the best example of luxurious, turn-of-the-century architecture in the Pacific Northwest. The mansion (on Woodland Avenue between 3rd and 4th streets) remained in the Conrad family until it was given to the city in 1975, and is open daily, from mid-May to mid-October, for guided tours.

Several other historic homes grace the tree-lined residential neighborhoods of "old" Kalispell. Beyond these dignified roots, Kalispell has branched and sprawled into a typical small city that serves the surrounding valley with a revitalized

The heart of Flathead Valley lies in the shimmering expanse of Flathead Lake, largest natural freshwater lake in the West.

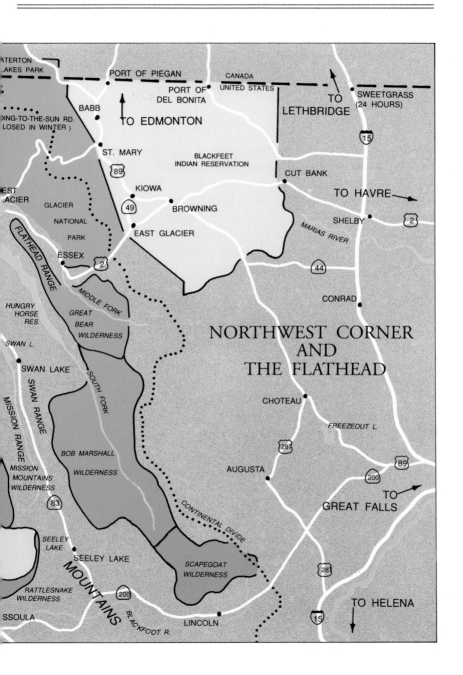

downtown commercial district, convention facilities, a community college, airport, and numerous restaurants, motels, and art galleries.

■ WHITEFISH

While Kalispell serves the functional needs of the valley, some of the Flathead's smaller communities are better examples of the distinctive lifestyle enjoyed by area residents. To the north is the sports-loving town of Whitefish, which sits on the shore of Whitefish Lake, just minutes from Montana's largest ski resort, **The Big Mountain** (see "WINTER RECREATION" for specifics). In summer, its 4,400 residents celebrate their place on Earth with canoe races, regattas, and Olympic-style summer games; in winter, they host one of Montana's most festive winter carnivals.

■ COLUMBIA FALLS AND POLEBRIDGE

The timber products industry and the Columbia Falls Aluminum Plant are the major employers in nearby Columbia Falls. Nearly as important as the paychecks they provide are the recreational benefits of living within minutes of Glacier Park, the North Fork of the Flathead River, 34-mile-long (55-km) Hungry Horse Reservoir, and the Great Bear and Bob Marshall wilderness areas.

One of the most distinctive communities in this region is Polebridge, halfway up the gravel road that lines the western edge of Glacier Park. Consisting of a historic general store known by its patrons as the Polebridge Merc, along with a hostel, café, saloon, and ranger station, Polebridge is the social center of the scattered North Fork community. Deep in logging country, where roads are outfitted with signs proclaiming "this family is supported by timber dollars," the independent thinkers of Polebridge are among Montana's most outspoken proponents of wilderness protection. Typical of the Polebridge spirit is the sign outside the Northern Lights Café announcing "this business is supported by people from all walks of life." If you need to make a phone call or intercept a message from the outside world while exploring the remote reaches of the North Fork of the Flathead, this is the place to do it. The Merc has the only public telephone in these parts, and it's a busy one.

■ BIGFORK

Less than 60 miles (100 km) south, but light years away, is the picture-perfect village of **Bigfork,** overlooking Flathead Lake from a sheltered bay at the mouth of the Swan River. Influenced by the climate of the Pacific Northwest, winters are long and gray here and elsewhere in the Flathead Valley. But when the sun comes out of hibernation, Bigfork blossoms like the potted geraniums and petunias that line its main street and the sweet peas that grow wild in the draws and gullies at its outskirts.

With a year-round population of less than 1,000, Bigfork swells in summer to accommodate the many visitors who come to enjoy its art galleries, live theater, sidewalk cafés, restaurants, resorts, golf courses, and genteel ambiance. Well known as one of Montana's leading fine arts communities, Bigfork is also a growing center for the performing arts. A new, million-dollar theater houses the town's popular **Bigfork Summer Playhouse** and a fledgling springtime event, the **Gathering at Bigfork,** draws some of the nation's leading playwrights to conduct workshops and readings, and to premier new works. It is no wonder that urban refugees from San Francisco, Los Angeles, and elsewhere have settled in the so-called "village by the bay." Bright red barns stand out against the towering blue mountains of the Swan Range; cows graze on steep hillsides; neat rows of junior Scotch pine stretch for miles at Christmas-tree farms throughout the valley. Bigfork is the good life, Montana-style.

■ POLSON

At the opposite end of Flathead Lake, **Polson** is a community of about 3,000 that reaches back to 1840, making it the first settlement on the lake. It is fitting that the community was named after pioneer rancher David Polson, who was also a fine fiddler. Every summer, in late July, Polson hosts the state's biggest fiddling contest when members of the Montana Oldtime Fiddlers Association come to town. All of Polson is a stage, as contestants—ranging in age from six to 90—tune up at various campsites around town. Formal competition takes place inside the middle-school gymnasium. Other attractions, besides the lake and the water-based lifestyle it supports, are the nearby Flathead River and one of the valley's oldest and loveliest lakeshore golf courses.

■ FLATHEAD INDIAN RESERVATION

Polson is the largest city on the 1.2-million-acre **Flathead Indian Reservation,** which takes in the southern half of Flathead Lake and stretches south nearly to Missoula. This is the only Indian reservation in Montana west of the Continental Divide. Unlike the Plains Indians who inhabit Montana's six other reservations, the Salish and Kootenai tribes of the Flathead Reservation are the descendants of a coastal culture. Together, the tribes are known as the Flathead Indians, a name that carried over to many of the land forms in the area despite its disputed origin. Some say that Lewis and Clark gave the Flatheads their name, but there is no evidence that these Indians ever adopted the practice of flattening their children's heads as some of the coastal tribes farther west are believed to have done. Before the arrival of non-native explorers, the Flathead moved freely throughout the Bitterroot and Flathead valleys, with frequent forays east of the Rockies to hunt buffalo.

Intrigued by early stories of Christianity that drifted West with some visiting Iroquois Indians in the 1830s, the Flatheads sent east for "Black Robes," thus bringing Roman Catholicism to Montana. One of the most historic monuments to the church's early development is the mission at St. Ignatius. Set against the magnificent backdrop of the Mission Range, the **St. Ignatius Mission** was established in 1854 by the Jesuits after they abandoned their original mission in the Bitterroot Valley. The new mission began as a simple wooden chapel, cabin, blacksmith, and carpentry shop. The imposing brick church that stands today was built a century ago and includes a number of spectacular murals depicting biblical history, painted by Brother Joseph Carignano. It is the oldest continuously operating mission in Montana and remains one of the Flathead Valley's most prominent landmarks.

In 1855, the Flatheads signed what came to be known as the Hellgate Treaty, which established the current reservation in the Jocko River Valley, north of Missoula. The treaty also promised a reservation in the Bitterroot Valley, but growing pressure from white settlers forced its residents onto the Jocko reservation in 1891. Loss of aboriginal lands in the Bitterroot Valley did not signal the end of encroachment by the U.S. government. In 1887, Congress passed legislation allowing the federal government to partition tribal holdings into 80- and 160-acre parcels. The effect was to destroy the Indians' communal way of life and force them to become individual farmers. With the natives each allotted their piece of

POWWOWS

Powwow is a time of pageantry and celebration on Montana's seven Indian reservations, and there is nothing quite like it in the state's dominant white culture. For three to five days, tribal members abandon the day-to-day challenge of reservation life and come together for renewal and reunion. They perform traditional ceremonies and compete in dancing and games. They race prized horses and parade in beautifully beaded buckskins and feathered headdresses. They call on spirits, give gifts, and look to tribal elders to keep ancient stories alive. Through it all, they fortify the bonds that tie Indian families and clans so closely together.

Non-Indian visitors are welcome as spectators, but don't expect these events to conform to the schedules and comforts of the American middle class. Leave your own cultural trappings behind and go to powwow with the expectation of enriching your understanding of the West by learning about its native culture. Some of Montana's best-known powwows are included in the list of events in "PRACTICAL INFORMATION."

Powwow is a time of celebration and renewal of spirit for Montana's Indian tribes. (photo by Douglas O'Looney)

land, remaining lands were deemed "surplus," and opened to non-native settlers. In the case of the Flathead Reservation, the Allotment Act was especially damaging to the Indians' land base because of the reservation's agricultural potential. Under the act, just over half of the land was opened to homesteading. As a result, the Flathead Reservation has a much larger non-Indian population than Montana's other reservations; in fact, the Salish and Kootenai Indians who live here are a minority within their own reservation. Of the nearly 20,000 people living on the reservation, fewer than one-fifth are enrolled members of the tribe. Because of the loss of so much of their land to homesteaders, the Salish and Kootenai tribes have been aggressive in controlling ownership of their remaining tribal lands, which include a rich body of timber and agricultural lands. In addition, they receive sizeable rent payments from the Montana Power Company for the operation of Kerr Dam near Polson. Of all seven Montana Indian reservations, the Flathead is wealthiest in terms of natural resources.

Bordered on the east by the imperial Mission Range and watered by Flathead Lake, the Flathead and Jocko rivers, the reservation is also rich in scenic and recreational assets, including the nation's first tribally established and managed wilderness. The **Mission Mountains Tribal Wilderness** is an 89,500-acre tract of airy peaks and alpine lakes that provide Flathead Indians with an important link to their ancestral heritage. It adjoins another 74,000-acre parcel managed by the Flathead National Forest as the **Mission Mountains Wilderness.** While these rugged lands are managed cooperatively, there are differences in management practices. Hunting in the tribal wilderness is reserved for tribal members only, and each summer a 12,000-acre portion of the tribal wilderness near 9,820-foot (3,000-m) McDonald Peak is closed to protect an estimated 25 grizzly bears that come to feed on cyclical swarms of ladybugs and cutworm moths. To help finance management of the wilderness, the tribe sells use permits to non-tribal members for a small fee. Permittees are entitled to hike, fish, and camp on tribal wilderness lands. No special permits are required for these activities on the federally designated wilderness, which lies east of the crest of the Mission Range.

The Flathead Reservation also encompasses an important piece of Western Americana—the National Bison Range—as well the Ninepipe and Pablo national waterfowl refuges. Established in 1908 with the progeny of bison that survived the mass extermination of buffalo from the plains in the previous century, the **National Bison Range** now supports a sizeable herd of 400 to 500 bison on 19,000 acres

of natural grassland. Visitors can expect to see bison, as well as pron͜g
deer, and bighorn sheep along an auto tour route that takes in sweeping views of
the Mission Range. Newborn bison calves steal the show here in spring; in early
October, visitors can witness the drama of an authentic buffalo roundup, when
cowboy rangers thin the herd. Range headquarters are at Moiese, west of U.S.
Route 93, at the south end of the reservation.

Less dramatic but no less significant is the **Ninepipe National Wildlife Refuge**
between St. Ignatius and Ronan. Hundreds of glacial potholes and a large reservoir
sustain more than 180 species of birds in this watery environment. Cormorants,
herons, gulls, shorebirds, bald eagles, and pheasants round out the roster of birds,
primarily waterfowl, that nest and rest here. A few miles north, between Pablo and
Polson, the **Pablo National Wildlife Refuge** provides additional wetlands. Spring
migration peaks from late March to early May, and fall populations approach
200,000 birds.

■ GLACIER NATIONAL PARK

The entire Glacier Park/Bob Marshall/Seeley Swan wild realm covers about three
million, largely unpopulated acres of adjoining public lands, an area roughly the
size of Connecticut. The undisputed centerpiece is **Glacier National Park,** which
crowns the North American continent with 1,500 square miles (3,885 sq. km) of
exquisite ice-carved terrain. Here, serrated ridges and horn-shaped peaks reign over
a jumble of turquoise lakes, waterfalls, cascades, river valleys, hanging gardens, and
alpine meadows. Born of geologic and glacial violence, this random landscape
couldn't be more perfect had it been designed and executed by Michelangelo. Like
the ocean, its sheer scope has a way of putting humanity in its place. People are
merely visitors here, unable to meet the rigors of a severe northern climate.

Harsh as it is in winter, Glacier Park is on its best behavior during the summer
months. Each year, nearly two million pilgrims journey to this place still held sacred by Blackfeet Indians, whose reservation forms the park's eastern border. Travelers come from throughout the world to hike its trails, drive its magnificent
Going-to-the-Sun highway—the park's magnificent east-west route—or simply to
drink in the pristine beauty of one of America's largest intact wild areas. Visitors
commonly see mountain goats from roadside turnouts, and need take only a short

hike to see bighorn sheep, white-tailed ptarmigan, and many of the other birds and mammals that live here. More than a thousand species of plants, many of them hardy alpine wildflowers, embroider the park in dazzling primary colors and pastels as they follow spring up the mountains all summer long.

With more than 750 miles (1,200 km) of trails in Glacier, there are at least five lifetimes of memorable hikes in this national park. They range from day hikes into hidden lakes and living glaciers to extended treks across snowfields and cloud-covered mountain passes. Two of the most popular trails lead hikers to Sperry and Granite Park chalets, two backcountry lodges that take the worry out of sleeping in bear country (see "Accommodations" in PRACTICAL INFORMATION"). The landscape of Glacier will leave a lasting imprint on the minds and in the hearts of visitors who absorb its vistas in a way that only hiking allows.

The 52-mile-long (83-km) **Going-to-the-Sun** road quickens the hearts of motorists as it climbs more than 3,000 feet (914 m) from lush, lake-lined valley floors on either side of the park to its windswept summit at Logan Pass on the Continental Divide. Along the way, it sidesteps gushing waterfalls, winds through glaciated

One of Glacier Park's most popular views is St. Mary's Lake and Wild Goose Island.

THE CONTINENTAL DIVIDE

Known among the West's native peoples as the "backbone of the world," the Continental Divide runs along the crests of the Rocky Mountains from Canada to Mexico, literally dividing the waters of the North American continent. In Montana, it zigzags across the Rockies, entering the state from the north at Glacier National Park and exiting in Yellowstone National Park on the state's southern border. Waters running west of the Great Divide feed the Columbia River and drain into the Pacific Ocean; waters flowing east fill the Missouri-Mississippi Basin and drain into the Gulf of Mexico. And from one point in Montana—Glacier Park's Triple Divide Peak—water also flows north to Hudson Bay, making Montana the only state that replenishes three oceans.

While the image of the Continental Divide suggests a distinct, knife-like ridge that neatly splits the Atlantic and the Pacific, the topography varies greatly. On prominent peaks and ridges you can actually see the waters of two oceans dividing at your feet, but at other places along the divide it is hard to even pinpoint the ridge as it meanders across broad plateaus. Sometimes obvious, sometimes obscure, the Continental Divide is Montana's single most important topographical feature. More importantly, it is the birthplace of the nation's waterways.

HIKING THE DIVIDE

The **Continental Divide National Scenic Trail** was established by Congress in 1968, making this lofty spine accessible to hikers, horseback riders, and in some cases, motorized travelers. Roughly 800 miles (1,300-km) of the entire 3,100-mile-long (5,000-km) trail lie along or near the ridgetops of Montana's Rocky Mountains. Passing through some of North America's most scenic backcountry, the trail crosses Glacier and Yellowstone national parks, in addition to 10 national forests with designated wilderness areas, including the Bob Marshall, Great Bear, Scapegoat, and Anaconda Pintler. Historic attractions along the trail include several ghost towns and two mountain passes crossed by Lewis and Clark on their 1804–06 search for an inland water route to the Pacific Ocean. In southwestern Montana, the trail passes high above Big Hole National Battlefield, site of the 1877 clash between the U.S. Army and the Nez Perce Indians, and Red Rock Lakes National Wildlife Refuge, a national sanctuary for trumpeter swans.

The trail has yet to be fully constructed and marked in Montana. Temporary routes have been established pending completion of the final route. Anyone considering a Continental Divide trek should contact the U.S. Forest Service before setting out. (See "Useful Addresses" in "PRACTICAL INFORMATION" for Forest Service addresses and phone numbers.)

valleys, and traverses an imposing, knife-like ridge called the Garden Wall before topping out at just over 6,600 feet (2,012 m) above sea level. Begun in 1916 and completed in 1932, the "Sun" road is an engineering masterpiece that deserves the attention of unhurried motorists.

In direct competition with the Canadian Pacific Railway, which was promoting Banff National Park in Alberta, and the Northern Pacific in Yellowstone National Park, the Great Northern Railway marketed Glacier as the "Switzerland of America," and built hotels and chalets to fulfill the slogan's image. The vaulted ceilings, heavy beams, and pillars of Glacier Park Lodge and Many Glacier Hotel evince the exuberance of an earlier era. Other lodges, cabins, and campgrounds are located throughout the park and are generally open from June to Labor Day, with some remaining open until mid- or late-September. There are additional rooms and campgrounds outside the park. See "Accommodations" in "PRACTICAL INFORMATION" for specifics, or contact Glacier National Park for a complete listing of lodging options.

Adjoining Glacier on the north is Canada's **Waterton Lakes National Park.** In 1932, the governments of Canada and the United States established the world's first international park—**Glacier-Waterton International Peace Park**—to commemorate the friendship and good will between the two nations. Smaller than

Many of Glacier's historic chalets no longer exist. However, the park still has two hike-in chalets in addition to its lodges, inns, and campgrounds. (courtesy, Montana Historical Society)

Glacier, Waterton boasts the same magnificent scenery, activities, and services. The primary route between the two parks is Chief Mountain International Highway along the extreme northeast edge of Glacier. Both the Chief Mountain and Going-to-the-Sun highways are closed to winter travel.

■ BOB MARSHALL COUNTRY

Glacier shares its southern border with a kindred spirit named Bob Marshall. This massive wildlife sanctuary and roadless retreat actually consists of three federally designated wilderness areas: the **Great Bear, Bob Marshall,** and **Scapegoat.** The entire 1.5-million-acre expanse is known as Bob Marshall Country in memory of the young forester whose vision of preservation sparked the wilderness movement more than 50 years ago. Known affectionately by its many friends and visitors simply as the Bob, this is one of America's oldest, largest, and best-known preserves, regarded among foresters and conservationists as the "flagship" of the nation's wilderness fleet.

Encompassing entire river drainages and mountain ranges, 2,400 square miles (6,215 sq. km) in all, Bob Marshall Country embodies the spirit of the Wilderness Act of 1964. It is truly a place "where man himself is a visitor who does not remain." Rather, this is the domain of some of North America's largest, most majestic big-game animals. Together with Glacier National Park, the Bob forms a critically important wildlife corridor for the once-dominant, now-threatened grizzly bear. An estimated 250 to 350 of the great bears roam freely throughout this Northern Rockies refuge. Bighorn sheep graze the eastern slopes of the wilderness, while mountain goats take to higher ground, along the mountain crests. Several elk herds, with animals numbering in the thousands, make the Bob a hallowed place for hunters. More than 50 outfitters work the Bob, guiding clients on fall hunts as well as summer horsepack trips.

The Bob appeals equally to land lovers and water bugs. Besides hiking, hunting, and horseback riding, there are rapids to be ridden and pools to be probed for cutthroat trout. The South and Middle forks of the Flathead River penetrate the core of the Bob. Together with the North Fork, which flows along the western edge of Glacier National Park, they form the nation's longest wild and scenic river system. The Middle Fork promises some of the most challenging whitewater in

(previous pages) Looking toward Glacier's snow-capped Mt. Grinnell from Granite Park Chalet.

Montana, with rapids made immortal by names like "Jaws" and "Screamin' Right-Hand Turn." Several rafting companies in the Flathead offer guided trips ranging from half-day whitewater trips and evening dinner floats to extended camp-float, fly-fishing, and combination horsepack/float trips on wilderness rivers.

A trip to the Bob can be a life-changing experience. Because of its sheer size, you can hike or ride horseback for miles and for days, exploring new country each day and living by your wits with a fishing rod, a map, and a compass. At night, you can explore the mysteries of the universe beneath a starry sky and wonder, with friends around a campfire, what it's all about.

■ SEELEY SWAN VALLEY

Lying immediately west of the Bob is an informal wilderness known as the **Seeley Swan Valley.** Flanked by the imposing walls and peaks of the Mission and Swan mountain ranges, this densely forested valley stretches 90 miles (145 km) from Clearwater Junction at the intersection of Montana state highways 200 and 83, into the heart of the Flathead Valley at Bigfork. Montana State Highway 83, the so-called **Seeley Swan Highway,** is a scenic alternative to the Flathead's more heavily traveled U.S. Route 93.

Along the floor of the Seeley Swan, the Clearwater and Swan rivers link a chain of lakes that mirror snow-capped peaks and thick stands of larch, fir, aspen, and birch. When the valley fills up with snow and the lakes glaze over with ice, the boaters, campers, and canoeists of summer give way to ice fishermen, snowmobilers, and cross-country skiers. Year-round, this quiet land of mountains and rivers and forest-clad lakes provides sanctuary for a diversity of wildlife ranging from the elusive loon to the grizzly bear. White-tailed deer are so abundant they pose a hazard to motorists traveling Montana State Highway 83 in early morning and at dusk.

The water corridors around Seeley Lake sustain the largest population of nesting common loons in the Western lower 48 states. Loons and a lot more can be seen on the Clearwater Chain-of-Lakes driving tour, which extends about 18 miles (29 km) from Salmon Lake to Rainy Lake at the south end of Montana State Highway 83. Have the binoculars ready because there are several designated viewing areas just off the highway at Salmon, Seeley, Alva, and Rainy lakes. North of Seeley Lake, the Clearwater Canoe Trail is an easy, four-mile (six-km) float through an outdoor auditorium specializing in loon music.

(following pages) The Flathead River and Swan Range represent some of the finest scenery of
northwest Montana.

Outside the small communities of Seeley Lake, Condon, and Swan Lake, the valley consists almost entirely of public land. Campgrounds, motels, and rustic resorts dot the larger lakes of the Seeley Swan. Miles of trails take day hikers to picnics beside waterfalls, and backcountry travelers to remote wilderness destinations in the Missions and the Bob Marshall.

■ JEWEL BASIN

The **Jewel Basin** is just that—a pocket of lakes for hikers only. Visitors limited by time or apprehension about backcountry travel can enjoy a condensed wilderness experience in this special management area of the Flathead National Forest between Kalispell and Hungry Horse Dam. Thirty-five miles (56 km) of trails connect most of the area's 27 alpine lakes, putting them within a two- to three-hour hike of the parking lot. The view from 7,528-foot-high (2,295-m) Mount Aeneus has been described as one of the best 360-degree panoramas in western Montana, with sweeping vistas of Glacier Park, the peaks of the Bob Marshall Wilderness, the Swan and the Mission ranges, as well as the lake-studded interior of the Jewel Basin. Most of the lakes are concentrated on the west side of the basin and hold the promise of pan-size cutthroat and rainbow trout.

Prime time in the Jewel Basin is the same as it is for other mountain treks in Montana—the window of opportunity from July into September, when last winter's snow is gone and next year's has yet to arrive. Visitors are advised that Montana's seasonal window can be slammed shut any month of the year by sudden storms.

NORTHWEST CORNER

IN ALL RESPECTS BUT ONE, NORTHWESTERN MONTANA is the antithesis of the Big Open. Perhaps more than any two regions, they represent the physical diversity of the state. Unlike the thirsty, windswept plains of eastern Montana, the northwest woods fill up with snow each winter, yielding roughly double the moisture of the Big Open. In Montana, the difference between 13 and 26 inches (33 to 66 cm) is the difference between a ranch economy and a timber economy. Here, the trees grow so thick that there isn't space to graze a cow.

Nearly everyone who explored this region, using the 600-mile-long (960-km) **Kootenai River** as a highway, had something to say about the dense forests that grew here and their potential value to an expanding frontier. But it was David Thompson, the first non-native explorer to chart these woods and waters, who nailed down the one feature northwestern Montana shares with the Big Open. In his journals, he noted that the area's isolation left its timber "without the possibility of being brought to market."

Railroads eventually made it possible to market the timber, but the area's population still lives a world apart from "mainland" Montana. Not really on the way to anywhere, the Northwest Corner is in Montana but not of it. Residents are oriented not so much to Kalispell, the hub of the nearby Flathead Valley, but to Spokane, Washington, a good 150 miles (240 km) from Libby, this region's largest community. Like the Big Open, the Northwest Corner remains a remote and undiscovered destination.

But here the similarity ends. To a rancher from the plains, this region's tall, dense forests are cause for anxiety as they close in around him and block his customary 180-degree view of the sky. But to a native of these parts, the deep, dark woods are like a cozy down comforter. To be in their midst is to be snug and secure. These woods are like no other woods in Montana. They are taller, thicker, and far more diversified than the fir and pine forests that grow east of the Rockies. Like the coastal forests to the west, these woods are a fusion of plant species. Cedar, hemlock, pine, fir, larch, and spruce—15 species of conifers in all—grow side by side above a thick understory of shrubs, ferns, berries, and wildflowers.

■ LOGGING

For most of its recorded history, this area has relied on the cyclical fortunes of the timber industry for its economic well-being. Before the turn of the century, settlers were clearing wooded areas and hauling trees to the Kootenai or one of its tributaries, where they awaited massive spring log drives that sent the harvest downriver to mills in Idaho. The arrival of railroads transformed logging from a local practice into an industry, and shortly thereafter the federal government created the National Forest Reserves, forerunner of today's Forest Service, to manage the resource. Besides providing a ready market for railroad ties and bridge timbers, the railroads revitalized local markets by luring more settlers out West, and they opened national markets. They also provided mills with a steady supply of timber, making milling a profitable, year-round enterprise.

Northwest Montana's first sawmill was built in 1889 near Eureka. Since then, millions of logs have been transformed at local mills into billions of board feet of finished lumber, house logs, plywood, pulp, and paper products. Evidence of the logger's trade is everywhere, from the extensive clearcuts and logging roads that scar hillsides to the giant logging trucks that rumble down narrow mountain roads, and the ubiquitous green signs posted outside homes and businesses proclaiming the owner's allegiance to the timber industry.

There is good reason for all those green signs. This industry is in trouble, not just here but in all the timber-producing states. Over-cutting, compounded by a soft market, national concern for endangered species, and protracted debates over wilderness and forest management practices have created a critical shortage of raw timber. In the mills, technology and mechanization have replaced many of the people who once held the good-paying jobs in the community. Today, the mill at Libby employs roughly half the number of workers it did 10 years ago. While a former editor of Libby's *Western News* proclaimed early in the century that "without question, lumbering is Lincoln County's greatest industry and will continue to be so," the future of northwestern Montana's principal industry is very much in question.

■ MINING

More promising are the ore deposits in the Purcell and Cabinet mountain ranges. Ever since gold was discovered along Libby Creek in 1860, miners have been lured

Wild mountain streams and the deep, dark forests of the state's northwest corner are similar to those found in the high country of Idaho and British Columbia.

by the prospect of major deposits in these mountains. Turn-of-the-century mining camps sprang up near Troy, Libby, and the Yaak River Valley to the north. But this is hardrock country, and for many years mining fell off due to the cost of removing precious metals from the ore bodies in this area. New technology has revived the hardrock industry throughout western Montana, however, and the nation's largest silver mine is now operated by the Asarco Corp. near Troy. More than four million ounces of silver are removed annually from this mine alone, and nearby deposits of both silver and copper have attracted investment in additional mining ventures. Known mineral reserves within the Kootenai National Forest are valued at $5 billion.

■ LIBBY

During much of this century, the Lincoln County seat of **Libby** was a company town that owed its existence to a Wisconsin lumberman, Julius Neils, who purchased an existing mill in Libby in 1910 and eventually transformed it into the largest single lumber enterprise in Montana. In addition to the mill, the J. Neils Lumber Company owned timberlands, logging equipment, and railroads. Later purchased by the St. Regis Paper Company and now owned by Champion International, the mill is still a key component of the Libby-area economy, but it is no longer the only show in town. Many now see mining as the industry that will keep Libby employed at the levels it previously enjoyed under Julius Neils' paternal watch.

Nevertheless, this community of 2,500 is proud of its roots and celebrates its lumberjack culture every July during **Logger Days,** the oldest festival of its kind in Montana. Unlike the eastern Montana rodeo circuit that draws working cowboys and cowgirls, whose lean, suntanned bodies are concealed by cowboy hats, boots, and chaps, Libby Logger Days is an exhibition of biceps, beards, and billed caps. Professional loggers compete for prizes, using chainsaws, crosscut saws, and axes.

Nordicfest, celebrating the community's Scandinavian and northern European heritage, draws thousands of visitors to its food booths, juried craft shows, and musical performances in September. Visitors are also attracted at this time of year to the stunning show of fall color that ignites the wooded landscape. Western larch and aspen are the medium by which monochromatic hillsides become an impressionist's canvas of points and strokes applied in every gradation of color between green and gold. More than any other conifer, the western larch, or tamarack, distinguishes these woods from those east of the Rockies because it sheds its lacy web of needles after their seasonal blaze of color has smoldered and died.

■ BULL RIVER VALLEY

Two of the prime spots to view fall colors are the Bull and Yaak river valleys. The Bull River waters a largely unsettled valley south of Troy. Bordered on both sides by the peaks of the Cabinet Mountains, the **Bull River Valley** encompasses public and private forest lands between U.S. Route 2 and Montana State Highway 200. The Bull River Road (Montana State Highway 56) ushers travelers to backcountry lakes and campgrounds, as well as to a noble grove of giant western red cedars and to Montana's westernmost wilderness. Bighorn Lodge near Noxon has a fine country inn and hunting lodge within Bull River Valley (see "Accommodations" in "PRACTICAL INFORMATION").

The **Ross Creek Cedar Grove,** just west of Bull Lake, preserves 100 acres of old-growth cedars that measure up to eight feet (over two meters) wide and 175 feet (53 m) tall. A short, self-guiding nature trail takes visitors through this outdoor cathedral and explains its history and significance.

On the east side of the road lies the 94,000-acre **Cabinet Mountains Wilderness.** This federally protected wilderness extends along the crest of the Cabinet Mountains, whose peaks appear higher than their actual elevation because they rise from the lowest corner of the state. Within viewing distance of 8,712-foot-high (2,655-m) Snowshoe Peak (the Cabinets' highest summit), the Kootenai River leaves Montana at a mere 1,820 feet (555 m) above sea level. The crest of the Cabinets is plenty high to capture eastbound moisture from the Pacific. Snow lies several feet deep in these mountains, providing more than 100 inches (250 cm) of runoff. The result is a tangle of trees, delicate ferns, and berry bushes. A network of trails penetrates this temperate jungle, taking hikers from the edge of the wilderness to its interior alpine lakes and ridgetops. Visitors come primarily for the fishing, berry-picking, and wildlife watching. A remnant population of grizzly bears inhabits the Cabinets, but more abundant are elk, deer, mountain goats, and bighorn sheep. This long, narrow forest preserve can be reached from Libby and U.S. Route 2 on the east side as well as from the Bull River Road on the west.

■ THE YAAK

The **Yaak River Valley,** to the north, is a wilderness without the capital W. If northwest Montana is remote, then this northwesternmost valley, known among Yaakers simply as the Yaak, is the end of the line. A paved road, north of Troy, follows not only the fall colors but the colorful history of the valley nearly to the Canadian border. Abandoned homesteads, mining camps, logging roads, and clearcuts interrupt but never obscure the transcendent beauty of the Yaak River and the surrounding Purcell Mountains. Besides a few stray grizzly bears, caribou, and the usual complement of elk, deer, moose, mountain lions, and black bears, the Yaak is inhabited by loners, loggers, and a handful of urban migrants who believe they have died and gone to heaven. The social and commercial hub of the valley is the town of **Yaak,** which consists of the Dirty Shame Saloon and the Yaak Mercantile, a one-stop, one-room supply depot that stocks gas, propane, and limited groceries, swaps paperbacks, rents pipe dies and cable pulleys, takes phone messages, and dispenses hunting and fishing information.

Loggers, loners, and lions know that Yaak River country is just this side of heaven.

■ LIBBY DAM

From Yaak, motorists can follow Montana State Highway 508 back to Libby, or continue east along a paved forest road to Dodge Summit, then drop down to giant **Lake Koocanusa** at the base of the Purcells. The lake, whose name is an amalgam of Kootenai, Canada, and USA, was created by the impoundment of the Kootenai River, a major tributary of the Columbia River. The massive project, begun in 1966 and completed in 1973, was carried out under the terms of an international treaty signed by the United States and Canada to achieve flood control, navigation, irrigation, and power generation on the river they share. In addition, the construction of **Libby Dam,** just 20 minutes from the town of Libby, created a brand new recreation area. Stretching 90 miles (145 km) north of the dam, Lake Koocanusa crosses the international border about halfway up the lake. Montana's longest and highest bridge spans the lake near Rexford. Numerous campgrounds, boat ramps, and recreation areas surround the reservoir, while a visitor center, observation deck and lounge can be found at the dam.

Like most dams, this one sparked considerable debate over the loss of wildlife habitat, alteration of streamflow, and erosion of the local tax base due to flooding of productive lands. New recreation and wildlife sites have appeased some of the critics, but many residents still mourn the shackling of a great wild river. On the lighter side, the project revealed insight into the Montana mindset the day former President Gerald Ford came to town to dedicate Libby Dam. Local lore has it that the president's bodyguards were alarmed by all the guns they saw, mounted on gunracks in nearly every pickup in town. Instructed to remove all these firearms, the local sheriff is said to have responded with a laugh that said, "You gotta be kidding." Apparently he satisfied visiting law-enforcement personnel with a quick lesson in local culture, explaining that in Montana, hunting is a religion and guns are a birthright.

■ KOOTENAI COUNTRY

When Montanans are not hunting or fishing, they are likely to be scouting their next hunting or fishing trip. In the Northwest Corner, the possibilities are unlimited, not just for sporting expeditions but simply for enjoying the outdoors. Covering 2.25 million acres—an area nearly three times the size of Rhode Island—the

Kootenai National Forest *is* northwestern Montana. In addition to the Kootenai River, Lake Koocanusa, and the Cabinet Mountains Wilderness, the forest encompasses several smaller rivers, more than 100 lakes, and two special management areas in addition to the Ross Creek Cedars.

The **Northwest Peaks Scenic Area** is a rugged 19,000-acre landscape of high peaks and deep valleys that nearly touches both Canada and Idaho. With few trails and unpredictable weather, it appeals to adventurers seeking a primitive experience. **Ten Lakes Scenic Area,** to the east, is for the rest of us. Sculpted by glaciers, this cavernous valley of high lake basins, streams, waterfalls, forests, and wildflowers has

BIG TROUBLE IN A SMALL TOWN

Since our fish were big enough to deserve a few drinks and quite a bit of talk afterwards, we were late in getting back to Helena. On the way, Paul asked, "Why not stay overnight with me and go down to Wolf Creek in the morning?" He added that he himself had "to be out for the evening," but would be back soon after midnight. I learned later it must have been around two o'clock in the morning when I heard the thing that was ringing, and I ascended through river mists and molecules until I awoke catching the telephone. The telephone had a voice in it, which asked, "Are you Paul's brother?" I asked, "What's wrong?" The voice said, "I want you to see him." Thinking we had poor connections, I banged the phone. "Who are you?" I asked. He said, "I am the desk sergeant who wants you to see your brother."

The checkbook was still in my hand when I reached the jail. The desk sergeant frowned and said, "No, you don't have to post bond for him. He covers the police beat and has friends here. All you have to do is look at him and take him home."

Then he added, "But he'll have to come back. A guy is going to sue him. Maybe two guys are."

Not wanting to see him without a notion of what I might see, I kept repeating, "What's wrong?" When the desk sergeant thought it was time, he told me, "He hit a guy and the guy is missing a couple of teeth and is all cut up." I asked, "What's the second guy suing him for?" "For breaking dishes. Also a table," the sergeant said. "The second guy owns the restaurant. The guy who got hit lit on one of the tables."

By now I was ready to see my brother, but it was becoming clear that the sergeant had called me to the station to have a talk. He said, "We're picking him up too much lately. He's drinking too much." I had already heard more than I wanted.

Maybe one of our ultimate troubles was that I never wanted to hear too much about my brother.

The sergeant finished what he had to say by finally telling me what he really wanted to say. "Besides he's behind in the big stud poker game at Hot Springs. It's not healthy to be behind in the big game at Hot Springs."

"You and your brother think you're tough because you're street fighters. At Hot Springs they don't play any child games like fist fighting. At Hot Springs it's the big stud poker game and all that goes with it."

I was confused from trying to rise suddenly from molecules of sleep to an understanding of what I did not want to understand. I said, "Let's begin again. Why is he here and is he hurt?"

The sergeant said, "He's not hurt, just sick. He drinks too much. At Hot Springs, they don't drink too much." I said to the sergeant, "Let's go on. Why is he here?"

According to the sergeant's report to me, Paul and his girl had gone into Weiss's restaurant for a midnight sandwich—a popular place at midnight since it had booths in the rear where you and your girl could sit and draw the curtains. "The girl," the sergeant said, "was that half-breed Indian girl he goes with. You know the one," he added, as if to implicate me.

Paul and his girl were evidently looking for an empty booth when a guy in a booth they had passed stuck his head out of the curtain and yelled, "Wahoo." Paul hit the head, separating the head from two teeth and knocking the body back on the table, which overturned, cutting the guy and his girl with broken dishes. The sergeant said, "The guy said to me, 'Jesus, all I meant is that it's funny to go out with an Indian. It was just a joke.'"

I said to the sergeant, "It's not very funny," and the sergeant said, "No, not very funny, but it's going to cost your brother a lot of money and time to get out of it. What really isn't funny is that he's behind in the game at Hot Springs. Can't you help him straighten out?"

"I don't know what to do," I confessed to the sergeant.

"I know what you mean," the sergeant confessed to me. Desk sergeants at this time were still Irish. "I have a young brother," he said, "who is a wonderful kid, but he's always in trouble. He's what we call 'Black Irish.'"

"What do you do to help him?" I asked. After a long pause, he said, "I take him fishing."

—Norman Maclean, *A River Runs Through It,* 1976

long been considered a candidate for federal wilderness protection. Hiking and horseback trails crisscross its 15,700-acre interior, with public campgrounds at a couple of trailheads. The best approach is from U.S. Route 93, between Fortine and Eureka. Both of these scenic areas are gorgeous and empty.

While nearly all of northwestern Montana is shaded by trees, it is bordered on the north and south by two open, river-fed valleys that support limited agriculture. On the north, the **Tobacco Valley** takes its name from the crop once cultivated here by Kootenai Indians. **Eureka,** its major community, is now more famous for its Christmas trees. To the south, **Thompson Falls** sits on the Clark Fork River and relies on a mix of logging, mining, agriculture, and recreation. The nearby Noxon and Cabinet Gorge reservoirs draw boatloads of skiers, anglers, and other water bums. Both communities enjoy mild climates in an otherwise cool, wet corner of Montana.

STEINBECK'S MONTANA

I am in love with Montana. For other states I have admiration, respect, recognition, even some affection, but with Montana it is love, and it's difficult to analyze love when you're in it. . . . It seems to me that Montana is a great splash of grandeur. The scale is huge but not overpowering. The land is rich with grass and color, and the mountains are the kind I would create if mountains were ever put on my agenda. Montana seems to me to be what a small boy would think Texas is like from hearing Texans. Here for the first time I heard a definite regional accent unaffected by TV-ese, a slow-paced warm speech. It seemed to me that the frantic bustle of America was not in Montana. Its people did not seem afraid of shadows in a John Birch Society sense. The calm of the mountains and the rolling grasslands had got into the inhabitants. It was hunting season when I drove through the state. The men I talked to seemed to me not moved to a riot of seasonal slaughter but simply to be going out to kill edible meat. Again my attitude may be informed by love, but it seemed to me that the towns were places to live in rather than nervous hives. People had time to pause in their occupations to undertake the passing art of neighborliness.

—John Steinbeck, *Travels with Charley: In Search of America,* 1962

T H E   A R T S

MOST VISITORS ARE SURPRISED BY THE VITALITY AND DIVERSITY of the arts in Montana. Those who expect to see quality Western art will not be disappointed. Montana's Western art museums are among the finest. Those who view contemporary art, literature, and the performing arts as strictly East Coast or urban attractions will be astonished. Consider the evidence and a few outside observations:

- Montana has more professional, non-profit art museums per capita than any other state, and its visual artists receive more fellowships per capita than any other state.
- Montana has nine symphony orchestras, plus the New World Symphony of Miami, which has chosen the resort community of Big Sky as its summer residence.
- A 1989 *Los Angeles Times* story named Montana "the literary capital of the country." A year later, *Sunset* magazine singled out Missoula as foundation for the state's literary tradition, and noted that, "One of the area's 174 softball teams, the Montana Review of Books, . . . once even boasted an outfield responsible for 12 published novels."
- The Yellowstone Art Center's annual art auction has been called "the best non-commercial art auction in the United States."

While these declarations come as a surprise to most non-residents, they make perfect sense to Montana artists and art lovers. Because the state's small rural communities are so widely dispersed, each must look to itself for cultural survival. Sheer distance keeps one community from living off another's culture. It is not unusual to find an art center, symphony, and theater group in towns with fewer than 15,000 residents. Other factors are the relatively low cost of living in Montana compared with that of large urban areas, and a natural environment that feeds the soul.

■ WESTERN ART

The **C. M. Russell Museum Complex** in Great Falls boasts the world's most complete collection of Charles M. Russell's original oils, watercolors, bronzes, and illustrated letters in a gallery next door to the cowboy artist's original log-cabin studio.

The museum also exhibits original works by many of Russell's contemporaries. The **Montana Historical Society** in Helena also has an extensive collection of Russell art, as well as a permanent collection of early Western photography by F. Jay Haynes, official turn-of-the-century photographer for the Northern Pacific Railroad and Yellowstone National Park. Large murals depicting the Lewis and Clark expedition and Flathead Indian history, painted by early Western artist Edgar S. Paxson, adorn the foyer of the **Missoula County Courthouse** in Missoula.

The **Museum of the Rockies** in Bozeman has a permanent collection of works by Paxson, Russell, Olaf Seltzer, R. E. DeCamp, and William Standing, and a fine collection of bead and quillwork, clothing, toys, weapons, and ceremonial items used by Plains Indian tribes. The **Museum of the Plains Indian** in Browning also displays a comprehensive collection of Blackfeet Indian artifacts. Original paintings and murals by Charlie Russell and E. S. Paxson appear in the **Montana State Capitol** in Helena. The **Bob Scriver Studio** in Browning features the artist's Western and wildlife sculpture. The **Zemsky-Hines Gallery** in Big Timber presents the work of noted Western artists Jessica Zemsky and Jack Hines, as well as the work

Charlie and Nancy Russell with actor Douglas Fairbanks in Los Angeles. Fairbanks, a great admirer and collector of Russell's work, is dressed for his role as D'Artagnan in the movie "The Three Musketeers."

of other regional artists. Livingston's **Depot Center** shows the works of Charles Russell, Frederic Remington, Edward Borein, Thomas Moran, Karl Bodmer, and others. **Coffrin's Old West Gallery** in Miles City exhibits and sells the prints of L. A. Huffman, who came to Montana Territory as an Army photographer in 1878 and recorded the history of an era dramatized by great buffalo herds, the last of the Indian wars, and the arrival of railroads and ranchers.

■ CONTEMPORARY ART

Although Montana is known for its multitude of Western painters, the state is also blessed with many prominent contemporary artists such as Russell Chatham of Livingston, whose landscapes come alive with the spirit of this spacious land. The **Yellowstone Art Center** in Billings has the most significant contemporary collection in Montana, and its annual art auction is said to be the best of its kind in the nation. The **Montana Historical Society** in Helena houses the Poindexter Gallery, with its important collection of original works by artists of the New York school of modern art, including Willem DeKooning, Franz Kline, and Jackson Pollock. Also in Helena, the **Archie Bray Foundation** is one of the nation's leading centers for ceramic arts, featuring traditional and contemporary pottery, ceramics, and sculpture, including the works of Peter Voulkos, Rudy Autio, David Shaner, Ken Ferguson, Bernard Leach, and Shoji Hamada. **Paris Gibson Square** in Great Falls rotates exhibits in three galleries at its Center for the Contemporary Arts, and conducts classes, seminars, and tours.

Missoula Museum of the Arts features rotating exhibits, gallery talks, an annual art auction. **Hockaday Center for the Arts** in Kalispell has a permanent collection of regional works, plus rotating exhibits in three galleries, tours, and classes for students and adults. **Custer County Art Center** in Miles City is housed in the city's old water works plant, which provides spacious display areas for changing exhibits. **Beall Park Art Center** in Bozeman is a showcase for the city's vital arts community, with its exhibits, workshops, lectures, concerts, and performances. **Holter Museum of Art** in Helena has two spacious galleries for rotating exhibits of Montana and regional artists. **Arts Chateau** in Butte is housed in the old Charles Clark Mansion, where parlors and a second-floor kitchen have been transformed into art galleries, and the rest of the 26-room mansion has retained its elegance as a period museum.

In a state best known for its Western art, Billings' Yellowstone Art Center has built an impressive collection of contemporary art.

■ THE PERFORMING ARTS

The performing arts in Montana run from opera and Shakespeare to recitations by some of the top cowboy poets in the West. Nine Montana communities support symphony orchestras. They range from the state's largest orchestra in Billings (and the only one that pays all of its musicians) to an act of love called the **Prairie Symphonette** in the shrinking northeastern farm town of Scobey (pop. 1,150). In between are orchestras in Bozeman, Missoula, Great Falls, Kalispell, Helena, Butte, and Miles City.

Bozeman has the distinction of sustaining Montana's only opera company, the **Intermountain Opera,** anchored by Metropolitan Opera baritone Pablo Elvira, who lives in Bozeman during the off-season. Bozeman is also the home of **Shakespeare in the Parks,** a professional touring company that performs Shakespearean comedy for audiences in Montana and the region during the summer months. The company grew out of Montana State University's media and theater-arts department.

"Separated Spear Woman in Bird Headdress" by Winold Reiss. (courtesy of C. M. Russell Museum)

Missoula is Montana's other university town and it, too, nurtures an active community of performing artists. Theater groups include the **Montana Repertory Theatre,** a professional touring company based in the university's drama-dance department; the **Missoula Children's Theatre,** which tours nearly 300 communities annually; and the **Missoula Community Theatre,** which performs year-round. In addition to its symphony orchestra and chorale, Missoula is the home of the **String Orchestra of the Rockies,** an ensemble of top musicians that perform throughout the state, and the **Garden City Ballet.**

Three communities have made a specialty of summer theater. The **Bigfork Summer Playhouse,** the **Fort Peck Summer Theatre,** and the **Virginia City Players** draw residents and tourists to rotating schedules of comedy, vaudeville, and Broadway musicals. Other recommended acts are Bozeman's **Montana Ballet** and classical guitarist **Stuart Weber; Great Falls' Symphony, Montana Chorale, Cascade Quartet,** and **Daystar,** an Indian drama-dance company; Helena's **Grandstreet Theatre** and **Aleph Movement Theatre;** Kalispell's **Glacier Orchestra** and **Raphael Christy,** a one-man show featuring the wit and wisdom of Charlie Russell; Polson's **Port Polson Players;** Dillon's **Junior Fiddlers;** Big Sky's **New World Symphony,** and Billings' **Symphony, Chorale, Studio Theater, Actors Theatre Montana,** and **Calamity Jane's Dinner Theater.** The University of Montana, Billings, Bigfork, and Helena have recently completed showcase theaters for the performing arts.

■ THE LITERARY LANDSCAPE

In 1984, half a dozen Montana writers and historians hatched the idea of assembling an anthology of Montana literature as a birthday present to the state on the occasion of its 1989 statehood centennial. The result, four years later, was a five-pound, 1,161-page volume entitled *The Last Best Place,* now in its third printing. Acclaimed coast to coast as a literary milestone, the bestseller secured Montana's standing as an important, if remote, enclave for writers. As one reviewer put it, "There's something about Montana that makes Montanans write and makes other people arrive here with notebook in hand and typewriter in the back seat." Visitors have been recording their images of Montana ever since Lewis and Clark traveled up the Missouri River in 1804. Native peoples had developed a strong oral tradition long before that. Much of the appeal of *The Last Best Place* is in the

CROSSING MONTANA IN THE NINETEENTH CENTURY

Montana's first travel book appeared in 1865, after Captain John Mullan completed a wagon road that stretched more than 600 miles (960 km) across the Northern Rockies. The Mullan Road linked Fort Benton, Montana—the end of the line for Missouri River navigation—with Fort Walla Walla on the Columbia River in Washington. Designed as a military road, it was used far more by pioneers than by soldiers. Some of the admonishments and recommendations that Mullen made in his *Miners and Travelers' Guide to Oregon, Washington, Idaho, Montana, Wyoming and Colorado via the Missouri and Columbia Rivers* offer humorous insight into the human condition, as well as the travel conditions in the last century. He cautioned readers, for example, to govern their animals "as you would a woman, with kindness, affection, and caresses, and you will be repaid by their docility and easy management."

While leaving the gender gap wide open, Captain Mullan deserves some credit for narrowing the transportation gap that separated the northern plains from the Pacific. He also provided useful advice on equipment and supplies, including tips on where to find fresh vegetables along the trail, how many bushels of beans and sides of bacon to bring, and what to do when the wagon breaks down.

"Every article to be used in crossing the plains should be of the best manufacture and strongest material . . . Starting at dawn and camping not later than 2 P.M., I have always found the best plan for marching. . . . Never take anything not absolutely necessary. This is a rule of all experienced voyageurs."

re-telling of these native stories, many of which appear in print for the first time. Side by side traditional myths of Napi, the Ghost Owl, and Lodge-Boy are the contemporary observations of best-selling Montana authors like A. B. Guthrie, Jr., Tom McGuane, James Welch, and Ivan Doig.

The University of Montana's 70-year-old creative writing program, a seductive landscape, the "get-away" factor, and a low-rent lifestyle are often given as the reasons for the state's abundance of writers. Bozeman poet Greg Keeler narrows it down to the basics, "Some of us were born here, and some of us came for the trout." For whatever reason, Montana's writing tradition is firmly entrenched and now grows on its own strength. The university town of Missoula is the unrivaled capital of Montana's statewide literary community, supporting a surprising number of published authors, poets, and playwrights, and somewhere between 15 and 20 bookstores, many of them independent and locally owned. See "PRACTICAL INFORMATION" for a selected bibliography of Montana books and a listing of bookstores.

WINTER RECREATION

ALTHOUGH MONTANA IS GENERALLY VIEWED as a summer destination, winter is an attraction in its own right. The difference between the two seasons is in the way people travel. While summer travel is geared to the open road, the goal in winter is to ditch the car as soon as possible. Snow and ice take the pleasure out of exploring Montana's vast and diverse landscape, so winter travel is generally confined to a single destination. A number of attractive resorts and expanded winter services in nearby Yellowstone National Park make Montana an increasingly popular winter destination.

The mountains of western Montana begin filling up with snow in September and October, and by December the winter season is in full swing. Because of Montana's dry climate, snow piles up as deep, dry powder—perfect for skiing and snowmobiling. Each year, a growing number of skiers abandon the congestion and long lift lines of better-known ski areas in Colorado and Utah for the uncrowded, easygoing, and more affordable atmosphere of Montana's downhill ski areas. There are also a number of cross-country ski resorts within gliding distance of national forest and wilderness trailheads. Montana phone numbers are all area code 406.

■ DOWNHILL SKIING

Montana has 14 downhill areas, ranging from destination resorts to locally popular day-use areas. In the following brief descriptions, daily adult lift ticket rates are designated as: $ = under $20 and $$ = over $20. The largest ski areas are listed first.

The Big Mountain. West of Glacier National Park in northwestern Montana, this destination resort draws heavily on the western Canadian market as well as skiers from the Pacific Northwest who arrive by AMTRAK. The area has 50 marked runs, one quad chairlift, four triple chairs, and one double chair. On-site facilities include a variety of lodging options, several restaurants and bars, ski shop, ski school, day care, and Nordic center; $$. Write: P.O. Box 1400, Whitefish, MT 59937, or phone 862-3511, (800) 858-5439 (U.S.), or (800) 637-7547 (Canada).

Big Sky. About midway between Bozeman and Yellowstone National Park, this is one of Montana's top destination resorts. There are 55 runs on two mountains, two gondolas, two triple chairs, and four double chairs. Facilities include more than

Red Lodge Mountain is famous for its spring skiing. (courtesy, Travel Montana)

1,000 rooms and condominium units, several restaurants, bars and shops, ski shop, day care, and superb cross-country skiing at nearby Lone Mountain Ranch; $$. Write: P.O. Box 1, Big Sky, MT 59716, or phone 995-4211 or (800) 548-4486.

Bridger Bowl. Just minutes north of Bozeman, this is primarily a day-use area with limited lodging on the slope. Lots of powder, challenging runs, and full services in nearby Bozeman make this a popular area for serious skiers. There are 50 runs and five double chairs. Facilities include limited condominium units and private home rentals, day lodge with cafeteria and bar, ski shop, and day care; $$. Write: 15795 Bridger Canyon, Bozeman, MT 59715, or phone 587-2111 or (800) 223-9609.

Red Lodge Mountain. Located outside the friendly Western town of Red Lodge in the Beartooth Mountains of south-central Montana, this is a popular day-use area with lots of intermediate slopes and great spring skiing. As Montana's easternmost ski area, it draws heavily on skiers from the upper Midwest. There are 30 runs, one triple chair, and four double chairs. On-site services include a restaurant and cafeteria, a couple of bars, ski shop, kids' ski program, and gift shop; $$. Full lodging, food, and services are available in nearby Red Lodge. Write: P.O. Box 750, Red Lodge, MT 59068, or phone 446-2610 or (800) 444-8977.

Montana Snowbowl. Just 12 miles (20 km) northwest of Missoula, this is the home of the annual National Gelande Jump Championship. Steep slopes and deep bowls make this day-use area especially popular with advanced skiers. There are 30 runs and two double chairs. On-site facilities include cafeteria, saloon, ski shop, and nursery. Full lodging, food, and services are available in Missoula; $. Write: 1700 Snowbowl Road, Missoula, MT 59802, or phone 549-9777.

Showdown Ski Area. Part of the Kings Hill Winter Sports complex in the Little Belt Mountains of central Montana, this is a popular family area that draws heavily on the Great Falls market. There are 32 runs, one triple chair, and one double chair. On-site facilities include cafeteria, saloon, ski shop and nursery. Fine Nordic skiing and snowmobiling nearby. Limited lodging and food are available in nearby Neihart and White Sulphur Springs, 30 miles (48 km) south; full services in Great Falls, 60 miles (100 km) northwest; $. Write: Box 92, Neihart, MT 59465, or phone 236-5522.

Marshall Ski Area. Not far from Missoula, this is a beginners' and intermediates' day-use area with seven runs and one triple chair, along with night skiing. On-site facilities include day lodge, snack bar, and ski shop. Full services in Missoula, seven miles (11 km) west; $. Write: 5250 Marshall Canyon Road, Missoula, MT 59802, or phone 258-6619.

Discovery Basin. Located near Georgetown Lake and the Anaconda Pintler Wilderness, this is a popular day-use area for skiers in the Butte-Anaconda area. There are 13 runs and two double chair lifts. Facilities include a day lodge with cafeteria, ski shop, and nearby cross-country ski trails. Lodging is available at Fairmont Hot Springs, 32 miles (50 km) east, and in Anaconda, 20 miles (32 km) east, and Butte, 45 miles (72 km) east; $. Write: P.O. Box 221, Anaconda, MT 59711, or phone 563-2184.

Great Divide. About 25 miles (40 km) northwest of Helena near the ghost town of Marysville, this is the capital city's neighborhood ski area. There are 37 runs and two double chairs. Facilities include a day lodge with restaurant and bar, and a ski shop. Full services in Helena; $. Write: Box SKI, Marysville, MT 59640, or phone 449-3746.

Lost Trail Powder Mountain. Straddling the Montana-Idaho border about 90 miles (145 km) south of Missoula, this day-use area is known for its reliable snow and long season. There are 18 runs and two double chairs. Facilities include a day lodge with cafeteria and a ski shop. Limited lodging in Darby and nearby resorts; full services in Hamilton, 45 miles north (72 km), and Salmon, Idaho, 45 miles (72 km) south; $. Write: Box 191, Darby, MT 59829, or phone 821-3211 or 821-3508.

Rocky Mountain Hi. About 30 miles (50 km) west of Choteau on the Rocky Mountain Front, this is a locally popular, family day-use area that includes 25 trails and one double chair. Facilities include a day lodge with cafeteria and bar, ski shop, and day care. Lodging is available in Choteau; $. Write: Box 727, Choteau, MT 59422, or phone 466-2422.

Maverick Mountain. Located in the Pioneer Mountains northwest of Dillon, this is a locally popular day-use area that can be rented by groups for private skiing three days a week. There are 10 trails and one double chair. Facilities include a day lodge with food and beverage service and a ski shop. Limited lodging at nearby resorts; full services in Dillon; $. Write: Polaris, MT 59746, or phone 834-3454.

Two other neighborhood ski areas are **Beef Trail,** near Butte, and **Turner Mountain,** near Libby. Each has two single chairs serving about eight runs.

■ CROSS-COUNTRY SKIING

Montana has several, one-of-a-kind cross-country ski resorts, plus some excellent day-use Nordic centers and trail systems. Here are brief descriptions of the foremost resorts and areas:

Big Mountain Nordic Center. Located at the Big Mountain downhill resort near Whitefish, this has become an international training and racing center for cross-country and biathlon teams. For the public, there are nine miles (15 km) of groomed and tracked trails, plus instruction, rentals, and guided tours of nearby Glacier Park and other backcountry areas. Write: Box 1400, Whitefish, MT 59937, or phone 862-3511, (800) 858-5439 (U.S.), or (800) 637-7547 (Canada).

Bohart Ranch Cross Country Ski Center. Adjacent to Bridger Bowl Ski Area, the center has 18 miles (30 km) of groomed and tracked trails suitable for diagonal stride skiing and skating, plus rentals, lessons, and a warming cabin. There is also a biathlon range for year-round training and competition. Full services in nearby Bozeman. Write: 16621 Bridger Canyon Road, Bozeman, MT 59715, or phone 586-9070.

Skiers can rent a caboose for overnight stays at the Izaak Walton Inn, a popular cross-country ski lodge near Glacier Park.

Cross-country skiing at Lolo Pass, near Missoula.

Holland Lake Lodge. Just off Highway 83 in the Seeley Swan Valley, this comfortable lodge offers 15 miles (25 km) of groomed trails, plus rentals and guided trips. Lodging runs from about $35 per night for two people in the lodge to $60 for up to four in cabins, meals extra. Write: Condon, MT 59826, or phone (800) 648-8859.

Izaak Walton Inn. On U.S. Route 2 between Glacier National Park and the Great Bear Wilderness, this historic railroad inn has been described by *Cross Country Skier* magazine as "the coziest cross-country ski area in the Rockies." More than 18 miles (30 km) of groomed and tracked trails are augmented by a network of backcountry trails. AMTRAK stops at the back door. Rentals, instruction, and tours of Glacier Park are available. A one-week package ranges from $450 to $500 per person, double occupancy. Shorter stays can be arranged. Reservations recommended. Trail system is open to day skiers. Write: Box 653-D, Essex, MT 59916, or phone 888-5700.

Lone Mountain Ranch. Montana's finest Nordic resort, this guest ranch is within skiing distance of the Big Sky downhill ski resort, between Bozeman and Yellowstone National Park. The ranch offers 47 miles (75 km) of groomed and tracked trails for skiers and skaters, plus guided tours into Yellowstone Park, instruction and rentals, sleigh ride dinners, on-the-trail gourmet lunches, excellent food and lodging. Most trips are booked on a week-long, package basis at a per-person rate of around $800, double occupancy. Reservations are required. The trail system is open to day skiers. Write: Box 69, Big Sky, MT 59716, or phone 995-4644.

Nightingale Nordic. About 25 miles (40 km) southwest of Missoula on U.S. Route 12, this Nordic center is owned and operated by the Rossignol family. There are 10 miles (16 km) of groomed and tracked trails for skiers and skaters, plus rentals, instruction, a warming cabin, and food service. Lodging, food, and services are available in nearby Lolo or Missoula. Write: Box 369, Graves Creek Road, Lolo, MT 59847, or phone 273-2415 or 273-0655.

Red Lodge Nordic Ski Area. Just outside of Red Lodge, this trail system offers nine miles (15 km) of groomed trails for skiers and skaters, plus instruction, rentals, a skiathlon course, guided backcountry tours, and shuttle service to nearby Red Lodge Mountain downhill ski area. Full lodging, food, and services in town. Write: Box 283, Red Lodge, MT 59068, or phone 446-3158.

Sundance Lodge. This is a small, remote lodge in the Big Hole Valley of southwestern Montana. Located off Montana State Highway 43 between Wisdom and

Wise River, the lodge offers 15 miles (24 km) of groomed and tracked trails, plus additional trails in the Beaverhead National Forest. Ski rentals available. Lodging runs $40 to $60 per night for two, meals extra. Write: Wise River, MT 59762, or phone 689-3611.

Yellowstone Rendezvous Trail System. The town of West Yellowstone maintains 15 miles (24 km) of groomed and tracked trails that are used for early-season training by the U.S. Nordic and Biathlon teams. The trail system is next door to Yellowstone National Park. Full lodging, food, and services, plus rentals, instruction, and guided tours of the park, in town. Write: West Yellowstone Chamber of Commerce, Box 458, West Yellowstone, MT 59758, or phone 646-7701.

■ GLACIER AND YELLOWSTONE NATIONAL PARKS

Popular summer destinations, the Yellowstone and Glacier dazzle winter visitors with their quiet beauty and abundant wildlife. Of the two, Yellowstone is far more developed for winter visitors, with its many miles of groomed cross-country ski and snowmobile trails, ski and snowmobile rentals, guided ski and snowcoach tours, plus lodging and food service inside the park. Plenty of lodging awaits visitors just outside the park, in West Yellowstone, Gardiner, and Cooke City. No visitor services are open inside Glacier Park during winter, but the Park Service does maintain about a dozen cross-country ski trails. Lodging, food, and services are available just outside the park at West Glacier, East Glacier, and Essex. For more information about winter in the parks, Write: Superintendent, Yellowstone National Park, WY 82190, or phone (307) 344-7381; and Superintendent, Glacier National Park, West Glacier, MT 59936, or phone 888-5441.

■ SNOWMOBILING

Since 1977, when Montana set aside a portion of its gasoline tax for development of snowmobile recreation, nearly 3,000 miles (4,800 km) of trails have been designated for snowmobiling, most of them in national forests. Each year they are marked and groomed through cooperative agreements between local snowmobile clubs, the Montana Department of Fish, Wildlife and Parks, and the U.S. Forest Service. Easily the most popular destination for snowmobilers is **West Yellowstone,** which bills itself as the "snowmobile capital of the world." With 200 miles

(320 km) of groomed trails in Yellowstone Park and another 400 miles (640 km) on surrounding forests, West Yellowstone offers a vast trail system that begins in town, where snowmobilers share city streets with motorists. Snowmobile sales, service, rentals, instruction, and guide service, plus complete lodging and food service, are all available in town. Other locally popular snowmobile areas in Montana are Cooke City, Lolo Pass, Seeley Lake, Lincoln, Kings Hill, Polaris-Wise River, and Georgetown Lake. For more information about snowmobiling, write the Montana Snowmobile Association, Box 3202, Great Falls, MT 59403, or the Montana Department of Fish, Wildlife & Parks, 1420 6th Ave., Helena, MT 59620, or phone 444-2535.

■ GUIDED WINTER TOURS

Big Sky Alpine Guides. For downhill skiers who would like to sample more than one of Montana's ski areas, this company will make all of the arrangements, including transportation and lodging. Design your own tour or choose from one of the company's packages. Write: Box SCHUSS, Marysville, MT 59640, or phone (800) 666-8754.

Off the Beaten Path. This Bozeman-based travel consulting service designs personalized itineraries. You let them know what you're interested in seeing and doing, and they put the trip together using your guidelines. Emphasis is on high-quality facilities and services. Write: 109 East Main, Bozeman, MT 59715, or phone 586-1311.

TW Recreational Services. As the major concessioner in Yellowstone National Park, this company provides guided ski and snowcoach tours of the park, plus ski and snowmobile rentals, lodging, and meals. Write: TW Recreational Services, Inc., Yellowstone National Park, WY 82190, or phone (307) 344-7311.

Yellowstone Alpen Guides. Also based in West Yellowstone, this company provides snowcoach tours of Yellowstone National Park as well as guided ski tours inside and out of the park, skier drop-offs, and charters. Write: Box 518, West Yellowstone, MT 59758, or phone 646-9591.

Yellowstone Tour & Travel. This West Yellowstone company provides guided snowmobile tours of Yellowstone National Park and the surrounding backcountry, plus snowmobile rentals and instruction, and lodging and meal packages. Write: Box 369, West Yellowstone, MT 59758, or phone (800) 221-1151.

Snowmobile police bundle up for business in Yellowstone National Park. (photo by Don Pitcher)

SCENIC ROADS

IN A STATE AS GRAND AND DIVERSE AS MONTANA, nearly every highway has scenic appeal. Depending on your preference for plains or mountains, gravel or blacktop, however, some are more inviting than others. When traveling on backroads through western Montana's forests, it's always a good idea to have a forest map in addition to the state highway map (see "Useful Addresses" in "PRACTICAL INFORMATION" for Forest Service addresses and phone numbers). When driving on eastern Montana's back roads, it's important to keep your eye on weather conditions since even the slightest rain can turn the clay-like soil to gumbo and stop you in your tracks. Unpaved roads should be regarded as seasonal routes, best traveled in summer and early fall. The numbers in front of the following road descriptions are keyed to the Scenic Roads map.

■ EASTERN MONTANA

1) Montana State Highway 200 from Lewistown to Sidney (paved): Take to the open road through the heart of the Big Open. This trip is a meditation on sage and sky; for the sheer love of driving, it can't be beat (270 miles, 430 km).

2) Crooked Creek, Hell Creek, and Pines roads (gravel): These roads provide rugged, all-weather access to giant Fort Peck Lake and the C. M. Russell Wildlife Refuge. These are scenic routes through badlands and breaks, with few people and lots of watchable wildlife. All lead to recreation areas on the lake. Crooked Creek Road runs north from Winnett (about 40 miles, 65 km); Hell Creek Road is north of Jordan (about 30 miles, 48 km), and Pines Road runs southwest from Montana State Highway 24, north of the town of Fort Peck (about 25 miles, 40 km).

3) Makoshika State Park (gravel/unimproved): There are about 10 miles (16 km) of scenic roads in this badlands park, taking visitors to overlooks, vistas, and nature trails. Travelers are advised to check weather and road conditions before proceeding beyond Tower Junction toward Artists Point or the Sand Creek Overlook.

4) U.S. Route 212 between Alzada and Crow Agency (paved): Rough breaks and badlands, ponderosa pine forests, abundant wildlife, rivers that flower the plains, two Indian reservations, and the Custer Battlefield National Monument are all part of the view along southeastern Montana's major east-west artery (165 miles, 265 km).

5) **Route 314 between Busby and Decker** (paved): Red cliffs, wildlife, and the Rosebud Creek breaks are all part of the immediate view, while the Rosebud Mountains rise in the west (about 35 miles, 55 km).

6) **Tongue River Breaks** (gravel): Follow the Tongue River from Ashland to Birney, then down to the Tongue River Reservoir on a road that follows the river (after you pass the Diamond Cross Ranch, be on the lookout for a sign to the Tongue River Dam; follow the sign). You will drive through the austerely beautiful Tongue River Canyon, with views of coulees and breaks, red scoria rock, and weathered pines. Camping, boating, and good fishing for walleye, crappie, and bass at the reservoir (about 45 miles, 70 km).

7) **Ok-A-Beh** and **Bad Pass** roads at Bighorn Canyon National Recreation (paved): Ok-A-Beh, between Fort Smith and the Ok-A-Beh boat ramp, takes motorists through a short-grass prairie with expansive views of the Bighorn Mountains and Bighorn River Valley (11 miles, 18 km). At the south end of the canyon (entered via Lovell, Wyoming), the Bad Pass Road connects Horseshoe Bend and Barry's Landing. The best view of the canyon is along this road at Devil Canyon Overlook (17 miles, 27 km).

■ CENTRAL MONTANA

8) **Rocky Mountain Front** (paved): Follow U.S. Routes 89/287 from Glacier National Park to Wolf Creek. This is a dramatic landscape where the mountains meet the plains (about 140 miles, 225 km).

9) **Interstate 15, between Shelby and Great Falls** (paved): In late summer, precede the harvest through the heart of Montana's Golden Triangle grain-growing region. Rippling waves of grain break over an ocean of ripening wheat fields all around (85 miles, 135 km).

10) **Interstate 15, between Great Falls and Helena** (paved): Follow the Missouri River through Charlie Russell country as the suns sets over Square Butte and paints a picture as brilliant as the ones created by Russell himself. A paved recreation road between Cascade and Wolf Creek provides river access and more leisurely views of the river and the rock sculpture of Wolf Creek Canyon (90 miles, 145 km, total; recreation road is about 35 miles, 55 km).

MONTANA SCENIC ROADS

HAVRE

24   13   16

191

GLASGOW

2

191 / HEARTLAND
TO HI - LINE

BACKROADS TO
FORT PECK LAKE

200   SIDNEY

19

S
200

GLENDIVE

94

LEWISTOWN

MAKOSHIKA BADLANDS

HIGHWAY 200 / THE BIG OPEN

12

MILES CITY

12

59

94

BILLINGS

90

US 212 / CHEYENNE
AND CROW COUNTRY

212

BIGHORN
CANYON

87

ROUTE 314 /
ROSEBUD CREEK BREAKS

TONGUE
RIVER BREAKS

212

90

BEARTOOTH HIGHWAY
(CLOSED IN WINTER)

0   50mi

0   50km

11) **Judith River Valley** (gravel): Follow this back road along the Judith and the South Fork of the Judith through the grass-rich valley where Charlie Russell lived when he first arrived in Montana. This is working cattle and dude-ranch country along the eastern edge of the Little Belt Mountains (about 50 miles, 80 km).

12) **U.S. Route 191 between Big Timber and Malta** (paved): View central Montana's "island" mountain ranges—the Crazies, the Snowies, the Judith Mountains and the Little Rockies—as you drive through the farm and ranch country between Big Timber and Lewistown, and the breaks and badlands of the Missouri River farther north (235 miles, 375 km). Inviting side trips (on mostly unpaved roads) include the ice caves and waterfalls in the Big Snowy Mountains, Judith Mountain ghost towns north of Lewistown, Slippery Ann Wildlife Viewing Area at the western edge of the C. M. Russell National Wildlife Refuge, the historic mining town of Zortman in the Little Rockies, and Mission Canyon at the south end of the Fort Belknap Indian Reservation.

13) **Boulder River Valley south of Big Timber** (pavement/gravel): Follow Route 298 past some of Montana's most beautiful ranches along a corridor that leads to the Absaroka-Beartooth Wilderness. The road turns from pavement to gravel to dirt before ending at a wilderness trailhead, with fishing, camping, and hiking along the way (about 45 miles, 70 km).

14) **Beartooth Highway/U.S. Route 212** (paved): Renowned as one of North America's most beautiful drives, the Beartooth begins at Red Lodge and climbs the glacially carved walls of Rock Creek Canyon en route to Yellowstone National Park. Switchbacks and hairpin turns twist higher and higher until the highway levels off at nearly 11,000 feet (3,360 m). This breathtaking route is generally open from late May to mid-October (68 slow miles, 110 km).

■ WESTERN MONTANA

15) **Yaak River Road** (paved): Route 508, north of Troy, follows the Yaak River through the Kootenai National Forest, with views of the Purcell Mountains. At Yaak, turn south on 508 to get back to Libby (loop is about about 100 miles, 160 km), or continue east on Route 92 to Rexford. There, you can cross Lake Koocanusa to Montana State Highway 37 or travel south on Forest Road 228 along the west side of the lake (loop is about 150 miles, 240 km).

16) Going-to-the-Sun Road (paved): This is Glacier National Park's magnificent east-west highway, starting at either St. Mary or West Glacier and crossing the Continental Divide at Logan Pass. It is normally open from early June into October. Summer crowds and many scenic turnoffs make this a slow trip (55 miles, 88 km).

17) Hungry Horse Loop (gravel): Make a full circuit around 34-mile-long (55-km) Hungry Horse Reservoir, along the west edge of the Great Bear Wilderness. There are plenty of campgrounds, boat launches, trailheads, and great views all the way around (115 miles,185 km; takes about six hours).

18) Flathead Lake Loop (paved): Montana State Highways 35, 82, and U.S. Route 93 form a loop around Flathead Lake, providing scenic views of the lake and the Swan Range, plus access to state parks and campgrounds (about 85 miles, 135 km).

19) Seeley Swan Highway (paved): Montana State Highway 83 follows a chain of lakes through dense forests, with views of the Mission Range and the Swan Range; access to several campgrounds, lakes, hiking trails, and fishing spots (91 miles, 145 km).

20) U.S. Route 93, south of Missoula (paved): This is a busy highway that follows the Bitterroot River and provides magnificent views of the Bitterroot Range and the Sapphire Mountains; the **East Side Highway** (County Road 269), between Florence and Hamilton, is a leisurely alternative, with access to the Lee Metcalf Wildlife Refuge. At the south end of the valley, the secondary **East Fork** and **West Fork** roads provide scenic access to fishing, hiking, and camping.

21) Pintler Scenic Route (paved): Montana State Highway 1, between Drummond and Anaconda, follows Flint Creek to Georgetown Lake, with views of the Flint Creek Range and the Anaconda Pintler Wilderness, and access to fishing, camping, and ghost towns (55 miles, 90 km). Interstate 90, east of Anaconda, forms a loop back to Drummond, via Deer Lodge and the Grant-Kohrs Ranch National Historic Site.

22) Wise River-Polaris Road (pavement/gravel): This is an enjoyable back road through the Pioneer Mountains, recently designated a National Scenic Byway. Besides great views of the East and West Pioneers, it offers access to camping, hiking, and fishing, the ghost town of Coolidge, and a rockhounder's playground called Crystal Park. Most easily traveled in the summer, but also popular with snowmobilers and skiers in the winter (40 miles, 65 km).

Motorists slowly make their way up the scenic Beartooth Highway; poles beside the road are snow markers.

23) Centennial Valley Road (gravel): This is a rough road to paradise, best traveled in summer. It lies west of Yellowstone National Park, between the Centennial Mountains and Red Rock Lakes National Wildlife Refuge. The refuge is home to the rare trumpeter swan and a tremendous diversity of waterfowl, shorebirds, songbirds, and raptors. Elk, moose, antelope and other wildlife species are abundant in the surrounding, sparsely settled valley (about 55 miles, 90 km).

Looking toward Mt. Reynolds from Logan Pass, Glacier Park.

PRACTICAL INFORMATION

■ TRANSPORTATION

Much of Montana's appeal lies in its detachment from urban America, but getting to Montana requires more time and expense than reaching more centrally located destinations. The high cost of transportation is generally offset by the relatively low cost of food, lodging, goods, and services, and by most U.S. standards, Montana is a travel bargain.

BY AIR

Because Montana is so far removed from the nation's major air routes, it is about as expensive to fly from Denver to Montana's capital city of Helena as it is to fly from Los Angeles to New York. Nonetheless, there are plenty of flights in and out of Montana. Four of the nation's major airlines—Northwest, Delta, United, and Continental—serve the principal cities, with commuter lines making connections from smaller towns. Montana's largest commercial airports, ranked in order of passenger boardings, are Billings, Bozeman, Great Falls, Missoula, Helena, Kalispell, and Butte. West Yellowstone has commercial air service in the summer, and the smaller towns of Miles City, Glendive, Sidney, Wolf Point, Glasgow, Havre, and Lewistown are served year-round by commuter flights.

BY CAR

Most of Montana's visitors arrive by car on interstate highways. Two east-west interstate highways (Interstates 90 and 94) converge in Billings, while Butte lies at the junction of Montana's major north-south and east-west routes (Interstates 15 and 90). State highways and secondary roads provide access to Montana's smaller towns and hidden places, while gravel roads reach deep into Montana's vast back-country and open spaces. The deeper they go, the better they get. Visitors should take note that eastern Montana is notorious for a soil condition that turns clay into greasy grabby gumbo and renders travel difficult to impossible after even the slightest rain. It is always a good idea in this part of the state to check on weather and road conditions before leaving the pavement. There are so few people out here that if you get lost or stuck, you may be on your own for quite awhile.

Highway rest areas appear sporadically along the interstates, but there aren't enough of them to satisfy most motorists, especially in winter, when many are closed. The Montana Highway Department does a fine job of maintaining roads in good driving condition year-round. Sudden storms occasionally block highways in winter, but not for long. Nevertheless, smart winter motorists are prepared for the worst. Although few motorists carry all of these items, the ultimate winter sur-vival kit would include snow tires or chains, a shovel and window scraper, flares or a reflector, a blanket or sleeping bag, a first-aid kit, sand, gravel or traction mats, a flashlight with extra batteries, matches, a lighter or candle, paper, non-perishable foods, and a tow chain or rope.

Because distances are long and traffic is light, Montanans are notoriously fast drivers. While the state's highway patrol officers are generally tolerant of Montanans' 70-mph (112-kph) mindset, they have little tolerance for nighttime speeders and none at all for drunk drivers.

BY RAIL

AMTRAK'S *Empire Builder* parallels U.S. Route 2 across northern Montana, en route between St. Paul and Seattle. The passenger train makes daily stops at 11 stations along the Hi-Line. At East and West Glacier, it drops summer visitors off at Glacier National Park, and at Whitefish, it delivers skiers to The Big Mountain winter resort.

BY BUS

Greyhound Lines provides east-west service along Interstates 90 and 94, with stops in all major cities, including Glendive, Miles City, Billings, Livingston, Bozeman, Butte, and Missoula. Greyhound also travels U.S. Route 191 between

Bozeman and Idaho Falls, with a stop in West Yellowstone. Two local bus companies, Rimrock Stages and Intermountain Bus Co., provide passenger service to Anaconda, Dillon, Helena, Great Falls, Kalispell, Havre, Lewistown, Shelby, and Cut Bank. Kaarst Stage of Bozeman provides seasonal service from Bozeman and Livingston to Yellowstone Park, and a Wyoming bus line, Powder River Transportation, travels Interstate 90 south of Billings through Hardin.

■ SEASONS

Montana has two distinct travel seasons and two shoulder seasons. Although winter travel is growing each year, the vast majority of Montana's visitors prefer to explore Montana in the trusted comfort zone of summer. Warm-weather travel reaches its

Sheep wagons are still commonly seen across Montana; this one has been retired to the Sodbusters Museum in Windham.

An old gas pump stands outside the Utica Museum in Central Montana.

peak during July and August, Montana's hottest, driest period. This is Montana's high season: school is out, skies are clear, roads are dry, fishing, hiking, and camping are in full swing, and summer events are back to back. Autumn is Montana's sleeper shoulder season. An initial jolt of cold weather, usually in early September, scares most visitors away. But residents know the best time of year is at hand. Warm, bright days and crisp nights linger into October, even early November. Summer crowds have subsided, aspen and larch kindle Montana's fall colors, the air is exhilarating, and the fishing is prime. The other side of autumn is spring, which is received as a tonic by residents, but is too cool and wet for most visitors. Rivers are high, backroads and trails are still snowed in, and spring storms are frequent.

Montana often makes the national news with record low temperatures from a couple of notorious weather stations near Glacier and Yellowstone national parks. As a result, Montana has an undeserved reputation as an icebox. Unlike many areas of the nation, however, where winter settles in for keeps, Montana's cold spells are frequently interrupted by Chinook winds and mild periods. Its dry climate also makes Montana milder than most Midwestern states. While temperatures can be extreme in Montana, humidity is low, so the weather is never oppressively hot or cold. The coldest sub-zero day in Montana is never as cold as the coldest winter day in Minneapolis or Chicago. And the hottest summer day in Montana is never suffocating like a summer day in Washington, D.C. Humidity rarely reaches 70 percent, and generally ranges between 50 and 65 percent. Average annual rainfall is 15 inches (38 cm), varying from less than 10 inches (25 cm) on the plains to more than 100 inches (250 cm) in the mountains. Average daytime temperatures vary from 28° F (-2° C) in January to 85° F (29° C) in July.

Montana's weather patterns are generally more extreme in the east than they are in the west. Winters are colder and summers are hotter on the plains than they are in the mountains, where a milder, Pacific weather system prevails.

■ ESSENTIALS

Whatever the season, Montana's dress code is informal. Wardrobes run from shorts and slacks in summer to wool pants, flannel shirts, and sweaters in winter. Jeans are always in season and jackets or sweaters are never out of reach. Contrary to modern folklore, not every Montanan wears cowboy boots. Visitors are often amused, however, by the high proportion of Montana businessmen who combine boots and ties.

Most sports practitioners wouldn't leave home without their favorite fly rod, touring bike, or kayak. All of those toys and more can be put to good use in Montana. But if you're traveling far or just getting started, most sporting goods stores around the state will rent the equipment you need to sample the great outdoors. From backpacks to skis, mountain bikes to horses, all can be had on a rental basis.

■ ACCOMMODATIONS

Montana has a variety of lodging choices, covering the price and quality spectrum, but even the finest accommodations are affordable when compared to urban standards. The type of travel experience you seek will determine the type of lodging you need. Those planning an extended road trip will have plenty of motels, hotels, bed and breakfast homes, or campgrounds to choose from. If you plan to visit a single destination, you will want to plan ahead and select a ranch or resort based on its location or the kinds of activities it offers. Advance reservations are advised for lodging inside Glacier and Yellowstone national parks and for most ranches, resorts, and bed and breakfasts. Generally, reservations are not necessary for motels; however, rooms become scarce during July and August in communities around the parks and in communities holding special events.

For those who enjoy bed and breakfast travel, Montana has a growing number of distinctive homes that take in guests. **Bed & Breakfast Western Adventure** is a B&B reservation service representing more than 40 inspected B&Bs in Montana. For a free brochure or $5 directory, write P.O. Box 20972, Billings, MT 59104, or call 259-7993.

A partial listing of resorts, bed and breakfast homes, cabins, and condominiums appears below. Guest ranches are listed separately. Note that the telephone area code is 406 throughout Montana. For a more complete listing that includes motels, call Travel Montana (800-541-1447) to request a copy of the *Montana Travel Planner.*

B = Budget, under $35; M = Moderate, $35–50; L = Luxury, over $50

A B S A R O K E E
Oliver's; Main Street; 328-4813; historic bed and breakfast near Absaroka-
Beartooth Wilderness; M

ANACONDA

Fairmont Hot Springs Resort; 1500 Fairmont Road; 797-3241 or (800) 443-2381; between Butte and Anaconda; L

BIGFORK

Burggraf's Countrylane; Rainbow Drive; 837-4608; on Swan Lake; L

The Gustin Orchard; East Lake Shore; 982-3329; on Flathead Lake; L

Marina Cay Resort; 180 Vista Lane; 837-5861 or (800) 433-6516; lake resort and convention center on Flathead Lake; L

O'Duach'ain Country Inn; 675 Ferndale Drive; 837-6851; between Flathead Lake and Swan Lake; L

BIG SKY

Big Sky Ski and Summer Resort; 995-4211 or (800) 548-4486; in Gallatin Canyon north of Yellowstone National Park; hiking, riding, fishing, golf, tennis, downhill and cross-country skiing; L

Golden Eagle Management; Meadow Village; (800) 548-4488; condominiums at Big Sky Ski & Summer Resort; L.

Triple Creek Management; 47650 Gallatin Road; 995-4847 or (800) 548-4632, condominiums at Big Sky Ski & Summer Resort; L

Montana's ranch culture and sense of humor manifests itself along highways and in hay fields.

BIG TIMBER
The Grand; 139 McLeod; 932-4459; historic bed and breakfast hotel near Boulder River and Yellowstone rivers and Absaroka-Beartooth Wilderness; M

BILLINGS
Feather Cove Inn; 5530 Vermilion Road; 373-5679; bed and breakfast inn 15 minutes from downtown; M

Sanderson Inn; 2038 S. 56th St. West; 656-3388; bed and breakfast in a renovated farmhouse on five acres west of the city; M

BOZEMAN
Bozeman Hot Springs; 133 Lower Rainbow Road; 587-3030; RV camping; B

Silver Forest Inn; 15325 Bridger Canyon Road; 586-1882; bed and breakfast home near Bridger Bowl Ski Area; L

Torch & Toes; 309 S. 3rd; 586-7285; historic bed and breakfast home; M

Voss Inn; 319 South Willson; 587-0982; a beautiful bed and breakfast home; L

CAMERON
Madison Valley Cabins; 682-4890; on the Madison River; B

Wade Lake Resort; 682-7560; cabins near Madison River and Yellowstone National Park; fishing, boating, hunting, cross-country skiing; lots of birds and watchable wildlife; B–M

CHOTEAU
Harvest Home; 36 4th Avenue SW; 466-5809; lovely bed and breakfast home near Bob Marshall Wilderness; M

CLINTON
Colonial House; 14265 Turah Road; 258-6787 or 259-7993; lovely bed and breakfast home near Missoula; L

COLUMBIA FALLS
Mountain Timbers; 5385 Rabe Road; 387-5830; near Glacier National Park; M

CONDON
Holland Lake Lodge; (800) 648-8859; near the Bob Marshall Wilderness; horseback riding, hiking, fishing, boating, hunting, cross-country skiing, snowmobiling; M–L

COOKE CITY
All Seasons Inn; 838-2251; close to Yellowstone National Park; M

CORVALLIS

Teller Wildlife Refuge; 1200 Chaffin Road; 961-3507; restored homestead on a
private wildlife refuge; wildlife watching, fishing, floating, hiking, birding,
duck hunting; L

DARBY

Nez Perce Ranch; West Fork Rt.; 349-2100; two log homes near the Selway-
Bitterroot Wilderness; L

Triple Creek Guest Ranch; West Fork Stage Route; 821-4408; deluxe lodging and
dining in the Bitterroot Mountains; horseback riding, hiking, swimming,
tennis, mountain-bike riding, snowmobiling, cross-country skiing; L

West Fork Meadows Ranch; Coal Creek Road; 349-2468; Deluxe cabins and
gourmet dining on the West Fork of the Bitterroot River; horseback riding,
floating, fishing, hiking, gourmet cooking lessons, snowmobiling, downhill
and cross-country skiing; L

EAST GLACIER

Backpackers' Inn; 29 Dawson Ave.; 226-9392; near Glacier National Park

ESSEX

Izaak Walton Inn; 888-5700; historic railroad inn near Glacier National Park;
hiking, fishing, cross-country skiing; L

EUREKA

Grave Creek Bed and Breakfast; Grave Creek Road; 882-4658; near Ten Lakes
Scenic Area; M

Trail's End; 57 Trail's End Road; 889-3486; M

GALLATIN GATEWAY

320 Ranch; 205 Buffalo Horn Creek; 995-4283 or (800) 243-0320; cabins and
lease homes on a working stock ranch in the Gallatin Canyon near Yellowstone
National Park and Big Sky resort; fishing, hunting, riding, downhill and cross-
country skiing, snowmobiling; M–L

Gallatin Gateway Inn; 763-4672; beautifully restored railroad inn near Bozeman,
fine dining; L

GARDINER

Absaroka Lodge; 848-7414; overlooks Yellowstone River, continental breakfast; L

GLACIER NATIONAL PARK

Belton Chalets, Inc.; Box 188, West Glacier, MT 59936; 888-5511; hike-in chalets, including three meals; L

Glacier Park Inc.; East Glacier, MT 59434; 226-5551; hotels, motor inns, lodges, and cabins in Glacier and Waterton national parks (summer only); B–L; between September 15 and May 15, use the following address for reservations: Greyhound Tower, Station 1210, Phoenix, AZ 85077; (602) 248-6000 *207-6000*

GREAT FALLS

The Chalet; 1204 4th Avenue N.; 452-9001, bed and breakfast home across from C. M. Russell Museum; M

Three Pheasant Inn; 626 5th Avenue N.; 453-0519; Victorian bed and breakfast near C. M. Russell Museum; M–L

HAMILTON

Sleeping Child Resort; 363-6250; in the Sapphire Mountains; M

HARDIN

Kendrick House Inn; 206 N. Custer; 665-3035; Victorian bed and breakfast located near Custer Battlefield and the Bighorn River; M

HELENA

Feathered Pipe Ranch; 442-8196; cabins and yurts in mountains west of Helena; educational workshops on holistic health, yoga, and psychology; gourmet vegetarian dining; L

The Sanders; 328 N. Ewing; 442-3309; historic bed and breakfast near downtown and Original Governor's Mansion; L

Upcountry Inn; 2245 Head Lane; 442-1909; bed and breakfast in a rural setting close to town; M

KALISPELL

Ballymurry; 206 4th Avenue E.; 755-7080; bed and breakfast; M

Brick Farmhouse; 1946 Whitefish Stage; bed and breakfast; 756-6230; M

Peaceful Bay Condominiums and Resort; 150 Sherry Lane; 752-4783; luxury condominiums on Flathead Lake; L

Vacation Farm; 566 Creston Road; 756-8217 or (800) 882-8217; furnished farm home in Flathead Valley; swimming, lawn games; L

LIVINGSTON

Talcott House; 405 W. Lewis; 222-7699; historic bed and breakfast; L

L O M A
Virgelle Merc; Star Rt. l, Box 50; 378-3110; bed and breakfast rooms and cabins on the remote Wild and Scenic Missouri River; canoe rentals, shuttle service; B

M I S S O U L A
Birchwood Hostel; 600 S. Orange; 728-9799; B
Goldsmith's Inn; 809 E. Front; 721-6732; lovely rooms on the Clark Fork River, in town; L

N O X O N
Bighorn Lodge; 710 Bull River Road; 847-5597; combination country inn and hunting lodge in Bull River Valley; trail rides, hiking, fishing, snowmobiling, cross-country skiing; L

P A R A D I S E
Quinn's Hot Springs; 826-3150; on the Clark Fork River between St. Regis and Paradise in western Montana; B

P O L E B R I D G E
North Fork Hostel; 756-4780; near Glacier National Park; B

P O L S O N
Bayview; 1221 Bayview Drive; 883-6744; bed and breakfast home on Flathead Lake; M
Hidden Pines; 792 Lost Quartz Road; 849-5612; near Flathead Lake; M

P R A Y
Chico Hot Springs Lodge; 333-4933; near Yellowstone River and Yellowstone National Park; M–L
Davis Creek B & B; Route 38; 333-4353; bed and breakfast home near Yellowstone River in Paradise Valley; M

R E D   L O D G E
Bear Mountain Guest House; 606 S. Broadway; 446-2207; private home, sleeps six; near Beartooth Highway and Red Lodge Ski Area; M
Creekside Cottages at the Red Lodge Resort and Golf Club; 2108 Broadwater; 656-0510 or (800) 444-8977; furnished townhouses and studio units on private golf course; L
Pitcher Guest House; 2 S. Platt; 446-2859; restored lodging house, sleeps eight; near Beartooth Highway and Red Lodge Ski Area; L

Rock Creek Resort; US 212 S; 446-1111; deluxe lodging, dining, conference facilities, and condominiums south of Red Lodge; tennis, swimming, hiking, horseback riding, biking, fishing; L

Willows Inn; 224 S. Platt; 446-3913; Victorian bed and breakfast home near Rock Creek, Beartooth Highway, and Red Lodge Ski Area; M

ROUNDUP

Ryan's Homestead Inn; 75 Turley Road; 323-2347; bed and breakfast horse ranch in Bull Mountains; M

SACO

Sleeping Buffalo Resort; Star Route 3, Box 13; 527-3370; B

SEELEY LAKE

Double Arrow Lodge; 677-2777 or (800) 468-0777; rooms, cabins, and RV sites in the Seeley Swan Valley; horseback riding, wagon and sleigh rides, hiking, fishing, hunting, swimming, tennis, cross-country skiing; M–L

SILVER GATE

Park View Cabins; 838-2371; near northeast entrance to Yellowstone National Park and Beartooth Highway; B

Pine Edge Cabins; 838-2222; near northeast entrance to Yellowstone National Park and Beartooth Highway; B

Whispering Pines Cabins; 838-2228; near northeast entrance to Yellowstone National Park and Beartooth Highway; B

SOMERS

Osprey Inn; 5557 US 93 S; 857-2042; on Flathead Lake, birders welcome; L

SULA

Broad Axe Lodge; 1151 East Fork Road; 821-3878; four cabins on East Fork of Bitterroot River; L

Lost Trail Hot Springs Resort; 821-3574; near Lost Trail Powder Mountain Ski Area; M

THREE FORKS

Sacajawea Inn; 5 N. Main; 285-6934; historic hotel near Headwaters State Park and Lewis and Clark Caverns; M

VIRGINIA CITY

Virginia City Country Inn; 115 E. Idaho; 843-5515; historic bed and breakfast home in a historic town; M

WEST GLACIER

Glacier Wilderness Resort; 888-5664; luxury log homes near Glacier National Park, M–L

WEST YELLOWSTONE

Firehole Ranch; 11500 Hebgen Lake Road; 646-7294; fly-fishing lodge; L

Madison Hotel Youth Hostel; 139 Yellowstone; 646-7745 or (800) 521-5241; near Yellowstone National Park

Sportsmen's High; 750 Deer Street; 646-7865 or (800) 272-4227; bed and breakfast home, fly-fishing spoken here; L

Yellowstone Cabins; 506 US 20; 646-9350; near Yellowstone; M

WHITE SULFUR SPRINGS

The Columns; 19 E. Wright Street; 547-3666; historic bed and breakfast home near Smith River and the Little Belt Mountains; M

WHITEFISH

Anapurna Properties; 3840 Big Mountain Road; 862-3687 or (800) 243-7547; condominium and private home rentals on The Big Mountain; L

Bay Point Estates; 300 Bay Point Drive; 862-2331 or (800) 327-2108; luxury condominiums on Whitefish Lake, near Glacier National Park and The Big Mountain; L

Big Mountain Ski and Summer Resort; 862-3511 or (800) 858-5439 or (800) 637-7574 (in Canada); near Glacier National Park; hiking, riding, mountain biking, downhill and cross-country skiing; L

The Castle; 900 S. Baker; 862-1257; L

Crestwood Resort; 1301 Wisconsin; 862-7574 or (800) 766-1181; condominium rentals near Glacier National Park and The Big Mountain; L

The Edelweiss; Big Mountain Village; 862-5252 or (800) 662-2270; luxury condominiums on The Big Mountain; L

The Garden Wall; 504 Spokane Avenue; 862-3440; lovely home in center of town; L

Grouse Mountain Lodge; 1205 US 93 W; 862-3000 or (800) 321-8822; on the Whitefish golf course, and near Glacier National Park and The Big Mountain; golf, tennis, cross-country skiing; L

The Lodge at Whitefish; 455 Blanchard Lake Drive; 862-2662; luxury home near golf course; L

WISE RIVER

Sundance Lodge; 689-3611; lodge and cabins near the Big Hole River; fishing, hiking, riding, hunting, cross-country skiing; M–L

YELLOWSTONE NATIONAL PARK

TW Recreational Services; Yellowstone National Park, Wyoming 82190; (307) 344-7901; advance reservations required at the park's lodges and cabins; M–L

ZORTMAN

Buckhorn Cabins; 673-3162; in the historic Little Rocky Mountains of north-central Montana; B

■ GUEST RANCHES

Montana's most distinctive accommodations are its many guest ranches, where Western hosts offer vacations with a flair and rooms with a view. No two ranches are alike, and rates vary widely, but most include lodging, meals, and activities. Many take guests only on a weekly basis. The ranches are listed below alphabetically by region. Write or call for detailed information and rates.

EASTERN MONTANA RANCHES

Bar Y Seven; Brusett, MT 59318; 557-6150; in the heart of the Big Open, near Fort Peck Lake and the C. M. Russell National Wildlife Refuge; horseback riding on working cattle ranch, hiking, fishing, hunting.

Hell Creek Guest Ranch; Box 325, Jordan, MT 59337; 557-2224; in the heart of the Big Open, near Fort Peck Lake and the C. M. Russell National Wildlife Refuge; working cattle ranch, fossil hunting, big-game hunting.

Schively Ranch; Box 281, Pryor, MT 59066 (summer); 1062 Road 15, Lovell, WY 82431 (winter); (307) 548-6688; near the Pryor Mountains and Bighorn Canyon National Recreation Area; serious horseback riding on a working cattle ranch; cattle drives and roundups.

CENTRAL MONTANA RANCHES

Circle Bar Ranch; Utica, MT 59452; 423-5454; Judith River Valley of central Montana; horseback riding, fishing, hunting, cross-country skiing, snowmobiling.

Elk Canyon Ranch; White Sulphur Springs, MT; 547-3373; on the Smith River, west-central Montana; horseback riding, fly-fishing, float fishing, swimming, tennis, trap and skeet shooting.

G Bar M Ranch; Clyde Park, MT 59018; 686-4687; in the foothills of the Bridger Mountains north of Livingston; horseback riding on a working cattle ranch; fishing.

JJJ Wilderness Ranch; Box 310, Augusta, MT 59410; 562-3653; near the Sun River Canyon and Bob Marshall Wilderness; horseback riding, fishing, hiking.

Klick's K Bar L Ranch; Box 287, Augusta, MT 59410; 467-2771 or 264-5806; near Bob Marshall Wilderness and Sun River Game Preserve; horseback riding, fishing, hunting.

Lazy AC Ranch; Box 460, Townsend, MT 59644; 547-3402; in the foothills of the Grassy Mountains near Townsend; horseback riding, fishing, square dancing.

Pine Butte Ranch; HC 58, Box 34C, Choteau, MT 59422; 466-2158; a Nature Conservancy property on the east slope of the Rocky Mountains near the Bob Marshall Wilderness; horseback riding, fishing, hiking, naturalist-guided tours, and workshops.

Seven Lazy P Ranch; Box 178, Choteau, MT 59422; 466-2044; on the Teton River and next door to the Bob Marshall Wilderness; horseback riding, fishing, hunting, cross-country skiing.

South Fork Lodge; Box 56, Utica, MT 59452; 374-2356; in the Judith River Valley of central Montana; horseback riding, fishing, hunting, snowmobiling, cross-country skiing.

YELLOWSTONE AREA RANCHES

Beartooth Ranch; Nye, MT 59061; 328-6194 or 328-6205; south of Columbus, near the Absaroka-Beartooth Wilderness; horseback riding, fishing, hiking.

Boulder River Ranch; McLeod, MT 59052; 932-6406; south of Big Timber, near Absaroka-Beartooth Wilderness; horseback riding, fly fishing, hiking.

Burnt Leather Ranch; West Boulder Road, McLeod, MT 59052; 222-6795 or 932-6155; south of Big Timber, near Absaroka-Beartooth Wilderness; horseback riding, cattle roundups, fly fishing, hiking, hunting.

CB Ranch; Box 604, Cameron, MT 59720; 682-4954; Madison River Valley near Ennis; fly fishing, horseback riding.

Diamond J Ranch; Box 577, Ennis, MT 59729; 682-4867; Madison River Valley near Ennis; horseback riding, fly fishing, hiking, trap and skeet shooting.

Hawley Mountain Guest Ranch; Box 4, McLeod, MT 59052; 932-5791; south of Big Timber near the Absaroka-Beartooth Wilderness; horseback riding, fishing, hiking, hunting.

Lazy K Bar Ranch; Box 550, Big Timber, MT 59011; 537-4404; in the foothills of the Crazy Mountains north of Big Timber; horseback riding on a working ranch; fishing, hiking, square dancing.

Lone Mountain Ranch; Box 69, Big Sky, MT 59716; 995-4644; near the Gallatin River, the Spanish Peaks, and Yellowstone National Park; horseback riding, fly fishing, Yellowstone tours, cross-country skiing.

Mountain Sky Guest Ranch; Box 1128, Bozeman, MT 59715; 587-1244 or (800) 548-3392; in the Paradise Valley north of Yellowstone National Park; horseback riding, fishing, hiking, tennis, swimming.

Nine Quarter Circle Ranch; Taylor Fork Road, Gallatin Gateway, MT 59730; 995-4276; north of Yellowstone National Park in the Gallatin Canyon; horseback riding, fly fishing.

Parade Rest Ranch; 7979 Grayling Creek Road, West Yellowstone, MT 59758; 646-7217; near the west entrance to Yellowstone National Park; fly fishing, horseback riding.

Rocking J Ranch; Park City, MT 59063; 633-2222; near the Yellowstone River west of Billings; horseback riding on a working cattle and registered quarter-horse ranch.

63 Ranch; Box 979, Livingston, MT 59047; 222-0570; south of Livingston near the Absaroka-Beartooth Wilderness; horseback riding, fly fishing, hiking, photo workshops.

Sweet Grass Ranch; Box 161, Big Timber, MT 59011; 537-4477 (summer) or 537-4497 (winter); in the Crazy Mountains north of Big Timber; horseback riding on a working cattle ranch, cattle roundups, fishing.

WESTERN MONTANA RANCHES

Blue Spruce Lodge and Guest Ranch; 451 Marten Creek Road, Trout Creek, MT 59874; 827-4762; in the foothills of the Bitterroot Mountains and near Noxon Reservoir in northwestern Montana; trail rides, float fishing, boating, hunting, cross-country skiing, and snowmobiling, all wheelchair accessible.

Double Diamond Guest Ranch; Box 501, Condon, MT 59826; 754-2351 or (800) 367-3612; in the Seeley Swan Valley between the Mission Mountains and Bob Marshall wilderness areas; horseback riding, hiking, fishing, cross-country skiing, snowmobiling.

Flathead Lake Lodge; Box 248, Bigfork, MT 59911; 837-4391; on the northeast shore of Flathead Lake; horseback riding, tennis, fishing, water sports.

Hargrave Guest Ranch; Star Rt., Marion, MT 59925; 858-2284; Thompson River Valley west of Kalispell; horseback riding on a working cattle ranch, fishing, hiking, cross-country skiing.

Laughing Water Guest Ranch; Box 157, Fortine, MT 59918; 882-4680 or (800) 444-3833; between Glacier National Park and Lake Koocanusa; horseback riding, fishing, hiking, swimming.

■ RESTAURANTS

The following Montana restaurants, cafés, and roadhouses provide a good cross section of the state's diverse eateries. The area code is 406 throughout Montana.

> B = Budget; under $10 per person, excluding drinks
> M = Moderate; $10–20 per person, excluding drinks
> L = Luxury; over $20 per person, excluding drinks
> (R) = Reservations advised.

A L D E R
Alder Steak House; 842-5159; beef is taken seriously at this out-of-the-way eatery; B–M

A N A C O N D A
Barclay II, 1300 E. Commercial; 563-5541; tenderloin steaks are the specialty; also seafood, spaghetti, ravioli, and lots of extras; dinner only, nightly; B–M; (R on weekends)

Jim & Clara's Dinner Club; 509 E. Park; 563-9963; traditional supper club specializing in seafood, plus steaks, spaghetti and ravioli, and lots of extras; M

B A K E R
Sakelaris' Kitchen; 778-2208; homemade soups, cinnamon rolls, pies and much more, all good, for breakfast, lunch and dinner; B

B E L T
Girdle Mountain Summer House; 277-3367; yet another one of Montana's surprise dining rooms in unlikely places; dinner only, *prix fixe,* b.y.o.b.; advance reservations a must; M

BIGFORK

Bigfork Inn; in the village; 837-6680; beef, including an excellent prime rib, plus seafood, pasta, chicken, and light dinners, all served in a rustic atmosphere; B–M (R)

Coyote Riverhouse; 600 Three Eagle Lane (north of Ferndale); 837-1233; fine dining on the Swan River; enjoy elegantly prepared steaks, pasta, and Mexican cuisine; M–L (R)

Coyote Roadhouse; 8083 Montana State Highway 35, north of the village; 837-4250; specializing in Cajun, Sicilian, and Mexican cuisine; *Travel and Leisure* declared it Montana's finest; M–L (R)

ShowThyme; next door to the Bigfork Summer Playhouse; 837-0707; have dinner before the show and desserts after; fresh pasta, seafood, and chicken entrées; substantial salads and desserts that speak for themselves, as in "Death by Chocolate Brownie Pie," M–L (R)

BIG SKY

Andiamo; Mountain Village; 995-2220; fine Italian cuisine; M (R)

First Place; Meadow Village; 995-4244; fine dining featuring regional American and continental cuisine; M (R)

Lone Mountain Ranch; 995-4644; gourmet dining in a rustic atmosphere; sleigh-ride dinners in winter; M (R)

BIG TIMBER

The Grand; 139 McLeod; 932-4459; elegant dining; M–L (R)

BILLINGS

Bruno's; 1233 N. 27th; 248-4146; authentic, affordable Italian cuisine; B–M

DeVerniero's; 513 N. 32nd; 252-9199; Italian cuisine for lunch and dinner; B–M (R)

Golden Belle; First Avenue N and Broadway; 245-2232; one of the few dining rooms in the state where blue jeans won't do; elegantly prepared and served entrées, appetizers, salads, and desserts; Billings' finest; M–L (R)

The Granary; 1500 Poly Drive; 259-3488; beef, seafood, chicken, and a great salad bar served in a restored flour mill; outdoor patio in summer; M (R)

Great Wall; 1309 Grand; 245-8601; Mandarin, Szechwan, and Cantonese for lunch and dinner, well prepared and served; B–M

Jade Palace; 2021 Overland; 656-8888; specializing in Mandarin and Cantonese gourmet cuisine for lunch and dinner; B–M (R)

Juliano's; 2912 7th Avenue N; 248-6400; fine continental cuisine served in an intimate atmosphere; lunch and dinner, plus gourmet take-out and tempting desserts; B–M (R)

Pug Mahon's; 3011 First Avenue N; 259-4190; good Irish stew, Reubens and other traditional Irish fare for lunch and dinner; B–M

The Rex; 24th & Montana; 245-7477; the best in beef, seafood, chicken and pasta, plus tempting appetizers and desserts; M–L (R)

Thai Orchid; 20 N. 27th; 256-2206; authentic Thai dinners and buffet lunch; B

Torres Café; 109 5th Street W; 248-5900; authentic Mexican food that reflects the influence of Montana's largest Hispanic population; B

B O Z E M A N

Bistro; 242 E. Main; 587-4100; imaginative menu, casual atmosphere; breakfast, lunch, and dinner; B–M

Ira's on Main; 233 E. Main; 587-9999; changing menu features new American cuisine for lunch and dinner; B–M

New Asia Kitchen; 1533 W. Babcock; 586-0522; Chinese and Thai food prepared with fresh ingredients; B–M

O'Brien's; 312 E. Main; 587-3973; fine cuisine, excellent wine list; M

Rocky Mountain Pasta Company; 105 W. Main; 586-1315; fine Italian cuisine; B–M

B R O A D U S

Montana Bar & Café; 436-2454; where the cowboys gather for coffee, homemade rolls, and pie, or a morning eye-opener from the bar; B

B U T T E

Gamer's Confectionery; 15 W. Park; 723-5453; no longer a confectionery but still a Butte tradition, right down to the Cornish pasties; owner-greeter-host Carl Rowan will make your day; B

Joe's Pasty Shop; 1641 Grand; 723-9071; these meat pies arrived in Butte with immigrant Welsh and Cornish miners; Butte lore has it that when a miner found a pasty in his lunch bucket, he referred to it affectionately as "a letter from 'ome"; pasties have endured as part of the Butte ethnic tradition; B

Lydia's; 5 Mile Harrison Avenue; 494-2000; traditional supper club with good service and lots of extras; the steaks and ravioli are memorable; M

M & M Bar & Café; 9 N. Main; 723-7612; a Butte classic, with a diner's counter on the right, bar on the left, and poker tables in the rear; B

Pekin Noodle Parlor; 117 S. Main; 782-2217; dating back to Butte's mining heyday, this no-frills walk-up is as popular for its atmosphere as it is for its pork noodles and boiled won ton; B

Uptown Café; 47 E. Broadway; 723-4735; arguably Montana's finest dining room, serving elegantly prepared seafood, poultry, veal, beef, and pasta; also great for lunch; M–L

C H A R L O

Allentown Restaurant; U.S. Route 93; 644-2588; enjoy views of the Mission Mountains and Ninepipe National Wildlife Refuge while dining on beef, seafood, pasta, soups, and sandwiches; B–M

C H E S T E R

Red Onion; U.S. Route 2; 759-5335; spaghetti is the standout here; choose a traditional red sauce, or try the white with shrimp, oysters or scallops; also, small steaks cooked just right; B–M

C O N R A D

Mom's Country Cooking; 319 S. Main; 278-5436; huge buttermilk and sourdough pancakes, plus homemade syrup, rolls, cakes, soups, and a full dinner menu (kids under eight eat dinner for under $1.75); open daily; B–M

C O O K E   C I T Y

Joan and Bill's Restaurant; 838-2280; family-style meals and famous homemade pies. B–M

D A R B Y

Karen's Montana Cafe; U.S. Route 93; where loggers and locals gather for good home cooking and perpetual coffee; breakfast and lunch; B

West Fork Meadows Ranch; West Fork Rt., Coal Creek Road; 349-2468; European cuisine prepared by nationally known chef Greg Patent and served in rustic elegance; one of Montana's finest dining rooms; L (R)

D E L L

Yesterday's Calf-A; about 60 miles south of Dillon; take the Dell Exit; 276-3319; you won't know if you don't go; aim for the Sunday buffet; B

DILLON

Bannack House; 33 E. Bannack; 683-5088; Italian cuisine, plus locally grown veal, lamb, and beef; large selection of imported and domestic beers and wines; lunch and dinner; B–M

EAST GLACIER

Glacier Village Restaurant & Dining Room; 266-4464; wide variety for all budgets, just outside of Glacier Park; B–M

EKALAKA

Ekalaka Locker; Main St.; 775-6260; homemade soups and breads for lunch; also a popular gathering spot in the morning for coffee and rolls; B

EMIGRANT

Livery Stable; 333-4688; prime rib is the specialty, plus steaks, BBQ ribs, and chicken; dinner only, nightly, luncheon buffet on Sunday; B–M

Chico Hot Springs Lodge; 333-4933; one of Montana's most distinctive dining rooms in a most unlikely spot; M–L (R)

ENNIS

Continental Divide; next door to Jack Creek Saloon; 682-7600; fresh seafood, thick steaks, Cajun cuisine, fine desserts and wines; M–L (R)

Grizzly Bar & Grill; between Ennis and West Yellowstone on U.S. Route 287; 682-7118; half-pound burgers, steaks, and chicken with all the trimmings (especially good after a day on the Madison River); B–M

FORSYTH

Blue Spruce Café; 109 S. 10th; 356-7955; butchers its own beef to assure quality; breakfast, lunch, and dinner served daily, with good specials; B–M

GALLATIN GATEWAY

Gallatin Gateway Inn; 763-4672; seasonal menus and fresh ingredients bring out the best in seafood, beef, poultry, and lamb; the restored, Spanish colonial-style inn was built by the Chicago, Milwaukee & St. Paul Railway in 1927 as a hotel-depot for tourists en route to Yellowstone National Park; M–L (R)

GARDINER

The Ranch Kitchen; U.S. Route 89, 7 miles north of Gardiner; 848-7891; owned and operated by the Church Universal and Triumphant; great menu featuring fresh-baked breads and desserts, organically grown vegetables and meats, vegetarian entrees; B–M

The Loft; upstairs from Town Café; 848-7322; All-American food with a great view; B–M

GLASGOW

Sam's Supper Club; 307 First Avenue N; 228-4614; Hi-Liners travel miles for the steaks, seafood, walleye, and many other lunch and dinner specialties; B–M

GLENDIVE

Jordan Coffee Shop; 223 N. Merrill; 365-5655; don't miss the Klapmeier agate collection and the original J. K. Ralston mural and paintings; B–M

GREAT FALLS

Borrie's; 1800 Smelter (in Black Eagle); 761-0300; traditional Italian and American fare served in a festive, friendly atmosphere; B–M

Eddie's; 3725 2nd Avenue N; 453-1616; popular supper club known for its "campfire" steaks (arguably the best in Montana), burgers and homemade ravioli; there's also a coffee shop; B–M

Jake's; 1315 8th Avenue N; 727-1033; steaks, prime rib, fresh seafood and salads served in a classy dining room, once an iron works plant; M

Mama Cassie's; 319 First Avenue N.; 454-3354; Italian sandwiches, pastas, soups; deli-style sandwiches and salads, and desserts to die for; B

Morning Light Coffee Shop; 900 2nd Avenue N; 453-8443; a good place to start the day with fresh coffees, breakfast rolls, and soft music; B

Peking Gardens Restaurants; 801 Smelter; 727-3913, or 2408 10th Avenue S; 727-2194; best Chinese/Szechwan in town; eat in or take out; B

HAMILTON

Haigh's Hideway Deli; 163 2nd S; 363-4433; good deli selection; B

Mustard Seed; 149 Cherry St.; 363-3801; Asian; B

Signal Bar & Grill; 131 W. Main; 363-4648; burgers and steaks; B–M

HARDIN

Purple Cow; north end of town; 665-3601; popular breakfast spot; homemade soups, sandwiches, salad bar, buffet; B

HAVRE

The Lunch Box; 213 Third Avenue; 265-6588; choose from 69 different sandwiches, plus soup, cookies, and desserts, all homemade; B

Nalivka's Pizza Kitchen; 439 W. First; 265-5426; pizza and traditional Italian pasta dishes, plus sandwiches, soups, and salads; B

HELENA

Morning Light Coffee Roasters; 44 S. Park; 442-5180; breakfast rolls to accompany your fresh-ground coffee, espresso, cappuccino; B

On Broadway; 106 Broadway; 443-1929; regional Italian cuisine in a fine dining atmosphere; M

The Parrot; 42 N. Last Chance Gulch (on the downtown walking mall); 442-1470; the lunch menu says chili and tamales but it's the hand-dipped chocolates, chocolate malteds, chocolate parfaits, sodas, and sundaes that have kept people coming into this old-fashioned soda fountain and confectionery since 1922; B

Pasta Pantry; 1218 11th; 442-1074; eat in or take out fresh pasta, variety of sauces, soups, salads, light dinners, and elegant desserts; B

The Red Fox; 2245 Head Lane; 442-1909; dinners served *prix fixe* Friday and Saturday nights at the Upcountry Inn; M–L; in the afternoon, brewed teas are served with scones, tarts, and assorted tea sandwiches; B. Both by reservation only.

Windbag; 19 S. Last Chance Gulch; 443-9669; popular saloon that serves a variety of burgers, homemade soups, quiche, and light dinners; B–M

HUNGRY HORSE

Huckleberry Patch; 8858 U.S. Route 2 E; 387-5670; here is the place to sample western Montana's purple delicacies in the form of muffins, cookies, hotcakes, milkshakes, and more; B

Mike & Aggie's Hide-a-Way; 9050 U.S. Route 2 E; 387-5997; where the locals meet for hearty dinners featuring Montana beef and homemade desserts; B–M

INGOMAR

Jersey Lilly Bar & Café; 358-2278; this is a period-piece business; in fact, the only business in town; the owner and his signature pinto beans are legendary throughout the state; B

JORDAN

QD Café; 557-2301; this is the place to get a short stack or a steak sandwich and study the sociology of the Big Open; B–M

KALISPELL

1st Avenue West; 139 First Avenue East; 752-5757; fresh seafood, pasta, chicken, beef, and dinner salads, good wine selection; lunch, too; B–M

Moose's Saloon; 173 N. Main; 755-2337; lunch and dinner served in a lively Western bar, complete with swinging doors and sawdust on the floor; B–M

Sykes Grocery & Market Restaurant; 202 2nd Avenue West; 257-4306; home of the 10-cent cup of coffee and three affordable square meals a day, all homemade; if you need to know anything about Kalispell, this is the place to start; B

LEWISTOWN

Bar Nineteen; Fairgrounds Road; 538-3250; watch your steak, chicken, or seafood charbroiled to perfection, then head for the dance floor to learn the cowboy jitterbug; B–M

Whole Famdamily; 206 1/2 W. Main; 538-5161; a pleasing and nutritious menu features homemade soup, sandwiches, desserts, and dinner specials; B

LIBBY

Adam's Rib & Seafood; 1207 Utah; 293-3129; steak, seafood, prime rib, and chicken, served in a restored, turn-of-the-century church, complete with stained glass and pews; M

LIVINGSTON

Livingston Bar & Grille; 130 N. Main; 222-7909; a good-times bar with a serious kitchen, savory specials and wide selection of imported beers; B–M

The Sport; 114 S. Main; 222-3533; Western bar specializing in BBQ and jumbo burgers; B

LOGAN

Land of Magic Dinner Club; Exit 283 from Interstate 90; 284-3794; great steaks and prime rib; M–L

LOLO

Guy's Lolo Creek Steak House; 6600 U.S. Route 12 W; 273-2622; open-pit cooking, fresh ingredients, and a rustic atmosphere make this the best steak house in the valley; B–M

MILES CITY

600 Café; 600 Main; 232-3860; where the cowboys meet before dawn, and the kitchen keeps serving all day long; B

MISSOULA

Alley Cat Grill; 125 1/2 W. Main; 728-3535; imaginative menu offers French to Indonesian and Thai, and lots of seafood specials; lunch and dinner; B–M (R)

Casa Pablo's; 147 W. Broadway; 721-3854; authentic, affordable Mexican; B

The Depot; 201 W. Railroad; 728-7007; fresh seafood, choice beef, Cajun specialties; M (R)

Ekstrom's Stage Station; Rock Creek Road off Interstate 90, 20 miles (32 km) east of Missoula; 825-3183; family-style meals featuring homemade soups, breads, pies; lunch and dinner, summer only; B–M

Freddy's Feed & Read; 1221 Helen; 549-2127; gourmet and health food deli adjoining one of Missoula's best bookstores; heaven can wait; B

Goldsmith's; 809 E. Front; 721-6732; homemade ice cream is the draw; also a good stop for breakfast and lunch; B

Iron Wok; 2700 Paxson; 549-3965; Asian cooking prepared on tableside grills; prepared and served by members of Missoula's Hmong community; B–M

Kadena's; 231 W. Front; 549-3304; "gourmet take away" menu is small but imaginative; B

Mammyth Bakery Café; 131 W. Main; 549-5542; homemade breads, pastries, soups, sandwiches, and specialty desserts; a great place to ease into the day; B

Mustard Seed; 419 W. Front; 728-7825; "Fireworks Chicken" and "Tsing-Tsing Tofu" are just two selections on this original Asian menu; fresh ingredients, light sauces, and reliably good; B

Old Town Café; 127 W. Alder; 728-9742; healthful, whole grain cooking for breakfast, lunch and dinner; popular weekend breakfast spot; B

The Oxford; 337 N. Higgins; 549-0117; every university student has been to the Ox at least once for brains 'n' eggs or browns 'n' gravy; old-timers meet here for a beer, a game of poker, and an affordable meal; B

The Shack; 222 W. Main; 549-9903; one of Missoula's favorite breakfast places; beloved for its "browns," omelets, and hotcakes; lunch and dinner, too; B

Torrey's; 1916 Brooks; 721-2510; good, affordable, health-conscious home cooking; B

Zimorino Bros. Red Pies over Montana; 424 N. Higgins; 549-7434; giant, thick-crust pizza, plus spaghetti, ravioli, lasagne, and Italian sausage, all homemade; B

Zorba's; 420 S. Orange; 728-9259; authentic, affordable Greek cuisine in a casual atmosphere; lunch and dinner; B–M

M O N A R C H

Lazy Doe; 236-9949; renowned for the quality of its beef, plus occasional crab and lobster feeds, and imaginative salads; B–M

NORRIS

Schoolhouse Restaurant; U.S. Route 287; 685-3200; homemade Mexican food is the specialty here; B

NOXON

Bighorn Lodge; 710 Bull River Road; 847-5597; private guest lodge, open to the public for dining on weekends; prime rib is tops, plus seafood, chicken, pork, and lamb; M (R)

OLNEY

Point of Rocks; U.S. Route 93; 881-2752; steaks and seafood, plus trout, pork, and chicken; combos are a specialty; so are the quality and generous portions; B–M

PENDROY

The Rose Room; County Route 219; 469-2205; well-prepared shrimp and Montana beef are the specialties at this popular, out-of-the-way supper club, open nightly; B–M (R)

POLSON

China Garden; Jct. 93 & 35; 883-4048; enjoy Chinese or American fare and a close-up view of Flathead Lake; B–M

RED LODGE

Bearcreek Saloon; east of town on County Route 308; 446-3481; Mexican dinners served on weekends, but the big draw is the entertainment: pig races, Memorial Day through Labor Day; lizard races in winter; B

Bogart's Pizza; 11 S. Broadway; 446-1784; Mexican, too; B

Kalico Kitchen; 412 N. Broadway; 446-2568; this is a bakery that turns out good soups for lunch; B

Natali's Café and **Pius' International Room;** 115 S. Broadway; 446-3333; gourmet burgers and German, Austrian, and Italian cuisine, plus seafood specials and a memorable Caesar salad; B–L (R)

17 Broadway; 105 S. Broadway; 446-1717; gourmet-style, New American cuisine Friday and Saturday evenings; also, homemade soups, salads, and a delicatessen; B–M

ROSCOE

Grizzly Bar; 328-6789; a great place to stop for steaks or burgers en route to East Rosebud Lake; B–M

ROUNDUP
Busy Bee; Junction of U.S. Route 12 and 87; 323-2204; open 24 hours for truckers, hunters, locals, and visitors; extensive menu with lots of specials; B

ST. MARY
Johnson's of St. Mary; U.S. Route 89; 732-5565; down-home cooking served family-style, plus menu choices, at the east edge of Glacier National Park; B–M

SCOBEY
Cozy Café; 15 Main; 487-5370; extensive Chinese/American menu offers everything from biscuits and gravy to Peking duck; B–M

SEELEY LAKE
Seasons Restaurant; at the Double Arrow Lodge; 677-2777; seasonal products and fresh ingredients; dinner features imaginative variations on seafood, beef, chicken, and pasta; M–L (R)

STANFORD
Pump Bar; 71 Central; 566-9914; Rocky Mountain oysters served year-round, with a free oyster feed every fall; B

STEVENSVILLE
Marie's; 4040 S. U.S. Route 93; 777-3681; well-prepared Italian cuisine and tempting desserts; B–M

SULA
Broad Axe Lodge & Restaurant; 1237 East Fork Road; 821-3878; view bighorn sheep from the dining room of this rustic lodge; steaks, seafood, chicken, and prime rib; B–M

TOWNSEND
Rosario's Pizzeria; 316 N. Front; 266-3603; authentic Italian cuisine and pizza, steaks, seafood, and sandwiches; B–M (R)

UTICA
Oxen Yoke Inn; 423-5530; here, the burgers are all beef, and they're so big, they're called "haystacks"; B

WEST GLACIER
Glacier Highland Motel & Restaurant; U.S. Route 2 E; 888-5427; wide variety of well-prepared food, breakfast, lunch, and dinner, just outside Glacier Park; B–M

WEST YELLOWSTONE
Alice's; 1545 Targhee Pass Highway; 646-7296; German/American; B–M

WHITEFISH
The Bistro; 307 E. 2nd; 862-8922; pleasing combination of good food and contemporary art; breakfast, lunch, and dinner daily; B–M
Jimmy Lee's Chinese Restaurant; 6550 U.S. Route 93 S; 862-5303; imaginative menu that includes "Oriental Fajitas," "Shanghai Fire Pit," and "Buddha Pie"; a sure fix for anyone who loves Chinese; B–M

WOLF CREEK
Holter Lake Lodge; on Holter Lake; take the Recreation Road north of Wolf Creek; 235-4331; exceptionally well-prepared dinners Wednesday through Sunday; summer only; M

■ TOURS

The telephone area code is 406 throughout Montana.
The Fishing Widow; Box 548, West Yellowstone, MT 59758; guided tours and activities in and around Yellowstone National Park for non-fishing spouses or partners.
Montana Board of Outfitters; 1424 9th Ave., Helena, MT 59620; 444-3738; directory of licensed outfitters who provide hunting and fishing trips, trail rides, whitewater raft trips, scenic floats, and other guided outdoor trips.
Montana Outfitters and Guides Association, Box 1339, Townsend, MT 59644; 266-5625; another organization to contact for guiding information.
Off the Beaten Path; 109 E. Main, Bozeman, MT 59715; 586-1311; personalized itineraries by travel consultants who match clients' interests with outfitters, guest ranches, ski resorts, and tour operators.
TW Recreational Services; Yellowstone National Park, WY 82190; (307) 344-7901; horseback and stagecoach rides, bus tours, and guided fishing trips in summer; guided ski and snowcoach tours in winter.
Wilderness Walks; Montana Wilderness Association, Box 635, Helena, MT 59624; 443-7350; one-day and extended hikes led by Wilderness Association members into Montana's roadless backcountry.
Yellowstone Tour & Travel; Box 369, West Yellowstone, MT 59758; (800) 221-1151; full package summer and winter tours of the Yellowstone

National Park area, including bus tours, snowmobile tours, and guest ranch stays.

BIKE TOURS

Backcountry Bicycle Tours; Box 4029, Bozeman, MT 59772; 586-3556; van-supported, inn-to-inn mountain bike tours of Glacier, Yellowstone, and the Bozeman area; most tours on secondary and dirt roads.

Backroads Bicycle Touring; Box 1626, San Leandro, CA 94577; (800) 533-2573 or (415) 895-1783 (in California); van-supported tours of Glacier National Park.

Bikecentennial; 113 W. Main, Missoula, MT 59801; 721-1776; maps, itinerary assistance, and guided bicycle tours.

BOAT TOURS

Bighorn Canyon Boat Tours; S-S Enterprises, Box 717, Cowley, WY 82420; (307) 548-6418; 2-hour tours from Horseshoe Bend near Lovell, WY.

Far West; 857-3203; daily excursions on Flathead Lake in a 64-foot (20-m) cruise ship, departing from Somers on the north shore of the lake.

Gates of the Mountains; Box 478, Helena, MT 59624; 458-5241; cruise a portion of the Lewis and Clark route along the Missouri River north of Helena.

Glacier National Park SceniCruises; Box 5262G, Kalispell, MT 59903; 732-4430 (seasonal); daily tours of St. Mary, Many Glacier, McDonald, and Two Medicine lakes.

Lewis and Clark Cruises; 1414 Front St., Fort Benton, MT 59442; 622-5537; half-day to extended boat tours of the Upper Missouri River.

Port Polson Princess; 883-2448; daily cruises on the south end of Flathead Lake aboard a 41-foot (12-m) tour boat departing from Polson.

Questa; Flathead Lake Lodge, Bigfork, MT 59911; 837-5569; daily sailing excursions on Flathead Lake in a 51-foot (16-m) racing sloop.

WAGON TRIPS

Bozeman Trail Wagon Train; Box 36, Reedpoint, MT 59069; (800) 962-7483; four-day wagon trips along the historic Bozeman Trail in south-central Montana.

Old West Adventures; Box 1899, Whitefish, MT 59937; 752-5167 or 862-3511; 3- and 4-day horse and wagon trips in the Flathead.

Wagons West; Box 483, Broadus, MT 59317; 436-2350; six-day horse and wagon trips through southeastern Montana.

■ NATURE STUDY VACATIONS

The telephone area code for Montana is 406.

Elderhostel; Flathead Valley Community College, 777 Grandview Drive, Kalispell, MT 59901; 756-3836; week-long field study courses in and around Glacier National Park for people age 60 and over; April through October.

Glacier Institute; Box 1457, Kalispell, MT 59903; 752-5222; one-day to one-week summer field seminars on Glacier National Park geology, botany, wildlife, history, and photography, conducted by professional staff and instructors; college credit available.

Museum of the Rockies; Montana State University, Bozeman, MT 59715; 994-5257; one-day to two-week paleontology and archaeology field trips with professional scientists; college credit available.

Pine Butte Guest Ranch; HC58 Box 34C, Choteau, MT 59422; 466-2158; week-long natural history tours and workshops on birding, mammal tracking, photography, paleontology, and backcountry horsepacking at this Nature Conservancy property along the Rocky Mountain Front.

Rocky Mountain Front Exploratory Workshops; Seven Lazy P Guest Ranch, Box 178, Choteau, MT 59422; (406) 466-2044; week-long natural history tours and workshops on birds, plants, and grizzly bear ecology; hiking and horseback riding.

Yellowstone Institute; Box 117, Yellowstone National Park, WY 82190; (307) 344-7381; grizzly bear ecology, wilderness writing and photography, llama trekking, catch-and-release fly fishing, and kids' camping are just some of the more than 80 field courses conducted each year in Yellowstone National Park; college credit available.

■ CAMPING

Montana has much to offer campers and RV travelers, especially during summer and early fall. In addition to many private campgrounds located in cities and towns and near major attractions, Montana has hundreds of public campgrounds in national forests and state parks, as well as in the more crowded national parks. Whether it is near a mountain lake or a wilderness trailhead, by a trout stream, or next door to a wildlife refuge, each merits an entry in your Montana travel journal.

For a complete listing of public and private campgrounds, request a copy of the *Montana Travel Planner* from Travel Montana (800-541-1447). The U.S. Forest Service, National Park Service, and Bureau of Land Management can provide more detailed information about campgrounds. See "Useful Addresses" below for specifics.

■ MUSEUMS AND HISTORIC HOMES

Nearly every Montana county has a historical society, and most communities maintain a historic house or museum where visitors can learn about the people and events that shaped the area. Many charge no admission. A partial listing of notable historic homes and museums follows. The telephone area code throughout Montana is 406.

Aerial Fire Depot and Smokejumper Visitor Center; 5765 Highway 10 West; 329-4934; history of smokejumping.

Bighorn County Historical Museum and Visitor Center; Hardin; 665-1671; restored buildings, cultural exhibits about the homestead era.

C. M. Russell Museum Complex; 400 13th St. North, Great Falls; 727-8787; original paintings, bronzes, illustrated letters, and memorabilia of cowboy artist Charlie Russell in a gallery next door to his log cabin studio; also original works by many of his contemporaries.

C. W. Clark Mansion; 321 West Broadway, Butte; 723-7600; chateauesque-style mansion built in 1898 for William Clark's oldest son, Charles; now houses the Arts Chateau.

Carter County Museum; Ekalaka; 775-6886; impressive collection of fossils and artifacts from the dinosaur country of southeastern Montana.

Cascade County Historical Museum; Paris Gibson Square, 1400 1st Ave. North, Great Falls; 452-3462; rotating exhibits and lectures on homesteading, farming, mining, and railroading.

The Castle; 4th Ave. and Jefferson, White Sulphur Springs; 547-3744; stone mansion built in 1892 by rancher-businessman Byron Sherman; furnished with antiques from families throughout the area; now houses the Meagher County Museum.

Chief Plenty Coups Museum; Pryor; 252-1289; Crow Indian artifacts and history; the museum is part of a state park that preserves the home and burial site of Plenty Coups, last chief of the Crows.

Conrad Mansion; Woodland Ave. between 3rd and 4th streets, Kalispell; 755-2166; three-story, 23-room, Norman-style mansion built by the city's founder, Charles E. Conrad.

Copper King Mansion; 219 West Granite, Butte; 782-7580; three-story, 30-room Elizabethan-style residence owned by William A. Clark.

Copper Village Museum and Art Center; 401 Commercial, Anaconda; 563-2422; Anaconda Copper Company mining history.

Daly Mansion; East Side Highway, Hamilton; 363-6004; three-story, 42-room, Georgian Revival residence built by Butte copper king Marcus Daly.

Daniels County Museum and Pioneer Town; Scobey; 783-5691; restored, early-1900s town with 40 buildings, vintage machinery, cars, and tractors.

Fort Peck Museum; Fort Peck; 526-3431; impressive fossil collection and history of Fort Peck Dam.

Four Winds Historic Village; St Ignatius; 745-4336; history and culture of the Flathead Indians; historic buildings; railroad history.

Frontier Gateway Museum; Belle Prairie Road, east of Glendive; 365-4123; farm and ranch history, Plains Indian history and culture, and a frontier main street in miniature.

Grant-Kohrs Ranch; Deer Lodge; 846-2070; the ranch house at this national historic site was built in 1862, enlarged in 1890, and decorated over several decades with the finest furnishings available.

H. Earl Clack Memorial Museum; Fairgrounds, west of Havre; 265-9913; history and archaeology of north-central Montana; tours of Fort Assiniboine and a nearby bison kill site.

Historical Museum at Fort Missoula; 31st St. and South Ave., Missoula; 728-3476; history of the fort, built in 1877 for the protection of white settlers, plus history of Missoula County, forest management, and timber production in western Montana.

Livingston Depot; 200 West Park, Livingston; 222-2300; history, culture, and art of the Yellowstone region.

McCone County Museum; Circle; 485-2414; eastern Montana's ranch and homestead history; vast collection of machinery and artifacts.

Mehmke's Antique Farm Machinery Museum; Highway 87/89, east of Great Falls; 452-6571; large collection of tractors and antique farm machinery.

Mineral Museum; Montana Tech campus, West Park St., Butte; 496-4414; more than 1,300 mineral specimens on display.

Miracle of America Museum; US 93, Polson; 883-6804; 200 years of American history in artifacts and art.

Mondak Heritage Center; 120 3rd Ave. Southeast, Sidney; 482-3500; area history and art, turn-of-the-century street scene, and a Winchester rifle collection.

Montana Agriculture Center and Museum of the Northern Great Plains; Fort Benton; 622-3278; Montana's official museum of agriculture includes a homestead-era village and covers three generations of farming.

Montana Historical Society; 225 North Roberts, Helena; 444-2694; Montana Homeland exhibit uses 2,000 artifacts and works of art to illustrate Montana's past; also, the art of C.M. Russell and photographs of F. Jay Haynes.

Moss Mansion; 914 Division St., Billings; 256-5100; turn-of-the-century French Gothic mansion built by banker-developer Preston B. Moss; mixed interior styles include a Louis XVI French parlor, English Tudor dining room, and Moorish entry.

Museum of Fly Fishing; 200 Yellowstone Ave., West Yellowstone; 646-9541; part of the Federation of Fly Fishers' International Fly Fishing Center; history, art, and practice of the sport.

Museum of the Plains Indian and Craft Center; Browning; 338-2230; Northern Plains Indian history and culture; large collection of Blackfeet Indian artifacts.

Museum of the Rockies; Kagy Blvd. and Greek Way, Bozeman; 994-2251; four billion years of history and pre-history, plus a world-class dinosaur exhibit and planetarium.

Old Montana Prison; 1106 Main, Deer Lodge; 846-3111; built by convicts in 1871, it was one of the first prisons constructed in the Western U.S. and served as the Montana State Prison until 1979.

Old Trail Museum; Junction of US 89 and US 287, Choteau; 446-5332; fossils and Indian artifacts; fossil location and identification field trips.

Original Governor's Mansion; 304 North Ewing, Helena; 444-3115; Queen Anne-style, brick mansion built as a private residence in 1888 by entrepreneur William Chessman; served as Montana's official executive residence from 1913 to 1959.

Oscar's Dreamland; Route 9, west of Billings; 656-0966; antique farm machinery—including 500 tractors—and a dozen old buildings.

Range Riders Museum; US 10/12 West, Miles City; 232-4483; 400-piece gun collection, 1880s-era main street scene, military and cowboy memorabilia, Indian artifacts, and pioneer photographs.

Towe Ford Museum; 1106 Main, Deer Lodge; 846-3111; antique Ford car collection.

Western Heritage Center; 2822 Montana Ave, Billings; 256-6809; exhibits, tours, classes, and workshops emphasize the culture and history of the Yellowstone River Valley.

World Museum of Mining; West Park and Granite St., Butte; 723-7211; Hell Roarin' Gulch, a reconstructed, turn-of-the-century mining camp on the site of the old Orphan Girl Mine, with mining equipment and copper king memorabilia.

■ TOP MONTANA EVENTS

JANUARY

Montana Winter Fair, Bozeman. Week-long celebration featuring livestock shows and sales, commercial exhibits, cooking and crafts, draft horse pulling contests, sheep shearing, and many more events.

Professional Rodeo Cowboys Association Circuit Finals, Great Falls. This national organization is divided into 12 competitive regions, or circuits; this is the final round of competition for the Montana circuit.

FEBRUARY

Montana 500 Sled Dog Race to the Sky, Helena-Holland Lake. A five- to six-day trek along the Continental Divide makes this second-only to the Alaska Iditarod in length.

Whitefish Winter Carnival, Whitefish. Three-day celebration features torchlight skiing, races, winter games, parade, fireworks, and a formal ball.

Yellowstone Art Center's Annual Art Auction, Billings. Montana's largest auction of contemporary art features up to 100 pieces of juried art by top regional artists (sometimes held in early March).

MARCH

National Gelande Jump Championship, Montana Snowbowl. Alpine ski jumping competition.

C. M. Russell Auction of Original Western Art, Great Falls. Widely recognized as the nation's largest and finest Western art auction, this is a four-day binge of auctions, quick-draws, seminars, receptions, and sales by about 100 exhibitors.

St. Patrick's Day, Butte. Easily Butte's biggest annual event, this Irish celebration draws upwards of 50,000 residents and visitors for a mid-day parade through uptown Butte, preceded by the annual Friendly Sons of St. Patrick's Day banquet and Shillelagh Shindig.

Western States Junior Olympics, Red Lodge Mountain. Week-long ski racing competition features top 16- to 18-year-old racers in the Western U.S.

APRIL

International Wildlife Film Festival, Missoula. Top wildlife films from around the world are screened during this week-long event, which also offers workshops, lectures, and seminars.

MAY

Intermountain Opera, Bozeman. One of Montana's most distinctive cultural events draws on considerable local talent and top professionals to create two nights of classical opera.

Miles City Bucking Horse Sale, Miles City. This cowboy classic features three days of bucking horse action, pari-mutuel horse racing, wild horse races, street dances, and a parade.

JUNE

Adult Chamber Music Festival, Bozeman. Professional musicians coach workshops during the day and perform nightly concerts.

American Legion Rodeo, Augusta. One of Montana's biggest small-town rodeos.

College National Finals Rodeo, Bozeman. Five nights of rodeo competition for college scholarships.

Montana Traditional Jazz Festival, Helena. Three-day party of outdoor concerts, jam sessions, and dancing on the city's downtown walking mall.

Red Bottom Celebration, Frazer, on the Fort Peck Indian Reservation. Traditional Indian celebration commemorating the Lower Band of the Assiniboine; dancing, contests, and hand games.

Red Lodge Music Festival, Red Lodge. A full week of evening performances by seasoned classical musicians who spend their days coaching young students.

JULY

Arlee Powwow, Arlee, on the Flathead Indian Reservation. Combined celebration of the Salish and Kootenai tribes over July 4th weekend; competitive dancing, stick games, horse racing, and rodeo.

Arts in the Park, Kalispell. Three-day summer fair features 65 artist booths, food, demonstrations, and entertainment.

Bannack Days, Bannack State Park. Horse and buggy rides, black powder rifle shooting, gold panning, frontier arts, crafts, music, and food at one of Montana's foremost historic parks.

Big Sky Arts Festival, Big Sky. Four outdoor concerts performed by the New World Symphony of Miami at the orchestra's summer residence.

Flathead Festival, Flathead Valley. Regional and world-class musicians perform everything from classical to jazz, and New Age to opera, during a two-week series of concerts.

Fourth of July Rodeo, Ennis. Another popular July 4th weekend rodeo, this one is organized by the National Rodeo Association.

Home of Champions Rodeo, Red Lodge. One of several July 4th rodeos, this three-day PRCA event is located at the base of the Beartooth Highway, en route to Yellowstone Park.

Last Chance Stampede, Helena. Three nights of rodeo featuring nationally known cowboys and professional entertainment.

Livingston Roundup, Livingston. Another July 4th PRCA rodeo, this one features three days of rodeo competition, plus a parade, fireworks, skits, and other entertainment.

Logger Days, Libby. Professional loggers use the tools of their trade to compete for prizes; games and contests for kids, too.

Montana State Fiddlers' Contest, Polson. Top fiddlers of all ages come together for two days of competition and jam sessions in this pleasant lakeside community.

Native American Indian Days, Browning, on the Blackfeet Indian Reservation. Highlights of this major Blackfeet celebration are dancing, singing, drumming, rodeo, parade, and games.

Northern Cheyenne Powwow, Lame Deer, on the Northern Cheyenne Indian Reservation. Annual celebration of the Morning Star People, also held July 4th weekend; parades, dance contests, drumming, singing, and feasting.

Summerfair, Billings. Regional arts and crafts fair featuring 90 artists in a juried show and sale on the campus of Rocky Mountain College; ethnic foods and entertainment add to the festive atmosphere.

Taste of Bozeman. Local restaurants serve their specialties to hundreds of guests on Main Street, which is closed to traffic (sometimes held in early August).

Wild Horse Stampede, Wolf Point. Located on the Fort Peck Indian Reservation, this event grew out of traditional Indian powwows and bucking contests. Wild horse races and other events draw a large crowd to the "granddaddy" of all Montana rodeos.

AUGUST

Crow Fair, Crow Agency, on the Crow Indian Reservation. One of the nation's premier native cultural celebrations, Crow Fair draws Native Americans and spectators from throughout North America. Hundreds of teepees rise from the banks of the Little Bighorn River, making this the "Teepee Capital of the World" for five days of parades, rodeos, dancing, singing, feasting, gambling, horse races, and relays.

Festival of Nations, Red Lodge. Nine-day festival celebrating the European immigrants who built this once-booming mining community. Popular events are the international cooking pavilion, evening programs, street dances, craft demonstrations, and All Nations Day Parade.

Fiesta, Billings. Montana's largest Hispanic community combines Cinco de Mayo (May 5) and Mexican Independence Day (September 16) into a single, two-day celebration featuring Mexican music, dancing, games, and traditional foods.

Montana Cowboy Poetry Gathering, Lewistown. Two days of rhymes and recitations, jam sessions, music, and dance. This is no ersatz imitation or goopy reminiscence; this is the real thing.

Sweet Pea Festival, Bozeman. Headline musicians, artists' booths, kids' crafts and entertainment, a parade, sporting events, and a ball make this one of Montana's most festive summer weekends.

Western Rendezvous of Art, Helena. Three-day exhibition and sale of works by a select group of Western artists; includes receptions, auctions, and a popular quick-draw atop nearby MacDonald Pass.

SEPTEMBER

Herbstfest, Laurel. Initiated by the area's Russian German community as a harvest festival, this celebration has grown to include other ethnic groups, and two full days of music, dancing, drinking, and feasting.

Jaycee Rodeo, Dillon. Montana's largest Labor Day rodeo features top national and Montana cowboys and cowgirls in two days of competition, plus dances, a parade, and barbecue.

Nordicfest, Libby. Three-day celebration honors the Scandinavian peoples who settled this logging community in Montana's northwest corner. Highlights include crafts, food, dances, and sporting events.

Threshing Bee and Antique Show, Culbertson. Farm celebration and antique show with large display of old-time tractors and farm equipment.

OCTOBER

Northern International Livestock Exposition, Billings. Indoor rodeo at season's end brings some of the nation's top contestants to this growing event, which also features a stock show and commercial exhibits.

C. M. Russell Museum Benefit, Great Falls. A classy evening featuring the show and sale of up to 100 pieces of mostly Western art, and a formal reception attended by many of the artists.

NOVEMBER

U.S. Nordic and Biathlon Training Camps, West Yellowstone. Top U.S. athletes come here for their early season training.

DECEMBER

Christmas in Bigfork. Thousands of lights, greenery, carolers, sleigh rides, and special events make this attractive lakeshore community a festive destination from Thanksgiving to Christmas.

Christmas Stroll, Bozeman. Downtown heralds the season by closing the streets for two days of celebration and cheer.

■ USEFUL ADDRESSES

The telephone area code for Montana is 406.

AMTRAK; (800) 872-7245

Beaverhead National Forest; 610 N. Montana, Dillon, MT 59725; 683-3900

Bitterroot National Forest; 316 N. Third, Hamilton, MT 59840; 363-3131

Custer National Forest; 2602 1st Ave. North, Billings, MT 59103; 657-6361

Deerlodge National Forest; Federal Building, Butte, MT 59703; 496-3400

Flathead National Forest; 1935 Third Ave. East, Kalispell, 59901; 755-5401

Gallatin National Forest; Federal Building, Bozeman, MT 59715; 587-6701

Glacier National Park; West Glacier, MT 59936; 888-5441

Helena National Forest; Federal Building, Helena, MT 59626; 449-5201

Kootenai National Forest; 506 US 2 West, Libby, MT 59923; 293-6211

Lewis and Clark National Forest; 1101 15th St. North, Great Falls, MT 59403; 791-7700

Lolo National Forest; Fort Missoula, Missoula, MT 59801; 329-3750

Montana Arts Council; 48 N. Last Chance Gulch, Helena, MT 59620; 444-6430

Montana Board of Outfitters; 1424 9th Ave., Helena, MT 59620; 444-3738

Montana Department of Fish, Wildlife & Parks; 1420 E. 6th, Helena, MT 59620; 444-2535

Montana Department of Highways; 2701 Prospect Ave., Helena, MT 59620; 444-6200

Montana Historical Society; 225 N. Roberts, Helena, MT 59620; 444-2694

Montana Outfitters & Guides Association; Box 1339, Townsend, MT 59644; 266-5625

National Weather Service; 449-5204

Travel Montana; 1424 9th Ave., Helena, MT 59620; (800) 541-1447; this is the primary source of statewide tourist information for Montana

U.S. Bureau of Land Management; Box 36800, Billings, MT 59107; 255-2882

U.S. Forest Service, Northern Region; 200 E. Broadway, Missoula, MT 59807; 329-3511

Yellowstone National Park; Yellowstone National Park, WY 82190; (307) 344-7381

Montana chambers of commerce offices with visitor information centers:

Anaconda Chamber of Commerce; 306 E. Park, Anaconda, MT 59711; 563-2400

Billings Chamber of Commerce; Box 31177, Billings, MT 59107; 245-4111

Bitterroot Valley Chamber of Commerce; 105 E. Main, Hamilton, MT 59840; 363-6518

Bozeman Chamber of Commerce; Box B, Bozeman, MT 59715; 586-5421 or (800) 228-4224

Butte-Silver Bow Chamber of Commerce; 2950 Harrison Ave., Butte, MT 59701; 494-5595

Columbia Falls Chamber of Commerce; Box 312, Columbia Falls, MT 59912; 892-2072

Dillon Chamber of Commerce; Box 830, Dillon, MT 59725; 683-5511

Fort Benton Community Improvement Association; Fort Benton, MT 59442; 622-3761

Glasgow Chamber of Commerce; Box 832, Glasgow, MT 59230; 228-2222

Glendive Chamber of Commerce; Box 930, Glendive, MT 59330; 365-5601

Great Falls Chamber of Commerce; Box 2127, Great Falls, MT 59403; 761-4434

Hardin Chamber of Commerce; 204 N. Center Ave., Hardin, MT 59034; 665-1672

Havre Chamber of Commerce; Box 308, Havre, MT 59501; 265-4383

Helena Chamber of Commerce; 201 E. Lyndale, Helena, MT 59601; 442-4120

Lewistown Chamber of Commerce; Box 818, Lewistown, MT 59457; 538-5436

Malta Chamber of Commerce; Drawer GG, Malta, MT 59538; 654-1776

Manhattan Chamber of Commerce; Box 606, Manhattan, MT 59741

Missoula Chamber of Commerce; Box 7577, Missoula, MT 59807; 543-6623

Plentywood Chamber of Commerce; Box 4, Plentywood, MT 59254; 765-1810

Red Lodge Chamber of Commerce; Box 988, Red Lodge, MT 59068; 446-1718

Scobey Chamber of Commerce; Box 91, Scobey, MT 59263; 487-5961

Sidney Chamber of Commerce; 909 S. Central Ave., Sidney, MT 59270; 482-1916

West Yellowstone Chamber of Commerce; Box 458, West Yellowstone, MT 59758; 646-7701

Whitefish Chamber of Commerce; Box 1120, Whitefish, MT 59937; 862-3501

Wibaux Chamber of Commerce; Box 260, Wibaux, MT 59353

Wolf Point Chamber of Commerce; Box 237, Wolf Point, MT 59201; 653-2012

■ BOOKSTORES

The following booksellers (listed alphabetically by town) support Montana's literary tradition with strong regional sections and occasional book-signing parties to promote new releases. The telephone area code is 406 throughout Montana.

Montana Valley Bookstore; Railroad Avenue, Alberton; 722-4590; used and rare books.

Beyond Necessity; 401 E. Commercial, Anaconda; 563-3218.

Bay Books and Prints; Grand Street, Bigfork; 837-4646; used and rare books.

Electric Avenue Books; 490 Electric Avenue, Bigfork; 837-6072.

Big Timber Book Nook; 216 McLeod, Big Timber; 932-5514.

B. Dalton Booksellers; Rimrock Mall, Billings; 652-4200.

Broken Diamond Books; 19 N. Broadway, Billings; 259-3440; used and rare books.

Thomas Minkler Art and Books; 2907 Second Avenue N, Billings; 245-2969; used and rare books.

Country Bookshelf; 28 W. Main, Bozeman; 587-0166.

Graham/Timmer Books; 109 S. Fourth Avenue, Bozeman; 586-8032; used and rare books.

Museum of the Rockies; Kagy Blvd. & Greek Way, Bozeman; 994-2251.

Vargo's Books; 1 E. Main, Bozeman; 587-5383; used and rare books.

Books & Books; 206 W. Park, Butte; 782-9520.

Plaza Books; 3100 Harrison, Butte; 494-5817.

Second Edition; 129 W. Broadway, Butte; 723-5108; used and rare books.

The Bookstore; 26 N. Idaho, Dillon; 683-6807.

C. M. Russell Museum; 400 13th Street N, Great Falls; 727-8787.

Hastings Books & Records; 1017 10th Avenue S, Great Falls; 727-9550.

Chapter One; 219 Main, Hamilton; 363-5220.

Rocky Mountain House Bookstore; 140 N. Second, Hamilton; 363-2662; used and rare books.

Big Sky Books; 525 Second Ave., Havre; 265-5750.

Little Professor; 331 Last Chance Gulch, Helena; 443-0260.

Montana Historical Society Museum Store; 225 N. Roberts, Helena; 444-2694.

Blacktail Mountain Books; 42 First Avenue W, Kalispell; 257-5573; used and rare books.

Books West; First & Main, Kalispell; 752-6900.

Village Book Shop; Gateway West Mall, Kalispell; 752-8041.

Don's; 120 Second Avenue S, Lewistown; 538-9408.

Gallery Books & Cards; 508 W. Main, Lewistown; 538-7209.

Sax & Fryer's; 109 W. Callendar, Livingston; 222-1421.

The Bookmark; 907 Main, Miles City; 232-7776.

The Bird's Nest; 219 N. Higgins, Missoula; 721-1125; used and rare books.

Fact and Fiction; 216 W. Main, Missoula; 721-2881.

Freddy's Feed and Read; 1221 Helen, Missoula; 549-2127.

Great Northern Book Company; 133 N. Higgins, Missoula; 721-3311.

Sidney's Used Books; 518 S. Fourth Avenue W, Missoula; 543-5343; used and rare books.

Broadway Bookstore; 13 S. Broadway, Red Lodge; 446-2742.

The Book Peddler; 104 Canyon, West Yellowstone; 646-9358.

Bookworm; 14 Canyon, West Yellowstone; 646-9736.

Bookworks; 110 Central, Whitefish; 862-4980.

RECOMMENDED READING

There is a lifetime of good reading about Montana. Recognizing that there may be more to life than reading about Montana, here is the short list.

■ HISTORY

Abbott, E. C. and Helena Huntington Smith. *We Pointed Them North: Recollections of a Cowpuncher.* University of Oklahoma Press, 1955. One of Montana's best storytellers recounts the glory days of the open range.

Alderson, Nannie T. and Helena Huntington Smith. *A Bride Goes West.* University of Nebraska Press, 1969. One of the finest records of a woman's life on the Montana frontier.

DeVoto, Bernard, editor. *The Journals of Lewis and Clark.* (abridged) Houghton Mifflin, 1953. Meriwether Lewis and William Clark were better explorers than they were writers, but the journals they kept as they traveled up the Missouri and across the Northern Rockies are delightful reading for anyone following the same route, either by car or canoe.

Garcia, Andrew. *Tough Trip Through Paradise.* Comstock Editions, 1976. A lively account by a mountain man of life among the Indians.

Glasscock, C. B. *The War of the Copper Kings.* Bobbs-Merrill, 1935. Much of Montana's history was written in the mining city of Butte, and no one has written a more colorful account than this one.

Malone, Michael, Richard Roeder, and William Lang. *Montana: A History of Two Centuries.* University of Washington Press, 1991. The standard text on Montana history.

Rolvaag, O. E. *Giants in the Earth.* Harper & Row, 1965. You will taste the dust and dread the wind by the time you finish this classic about the homestead experience.

Russell, Charles M. *Trails Plowed Under.* Doubleday, 1937. Colorful yarns about the West by Montana's famed cowboy artist.

■ NATIVE AMERICANS

Brown, Mark H. *The Flight of the Nez Perce.* University of Nebraska Press, 1982. The definitive work on the Nez Perce War of 1877.

Bryan, William L., Jr. *Montana Indians: Yesterday and Today.* American Geographic Publishing, 1985. Words and photographs illustrate the diversity, cultural traditions, and contemporary issues of Montana's Indian tribes.

Bullchild, Percy. *The Sun Came Down.* Harper & Row, 1985. A collection of Blackfeet Indian stories acclaimed as one of the finest ever published of traditional Native American literature.

Deloria, Vine, Jr. *Custer Died for Your Sins: An Indian Manifesto.* University of Oklahoma Press, 1985. A witty and incisive polemic about this nation's dismal relationship with its native inhabitants.

Farr, William E. *The Reservation Blackfeet, 1882–1945: A Photographic History of Cultural Survival.* University of Washington Press, 1986. A graphic illustration of the impact of Euro-American civilization on native culture.

■ REMINISCENCES AND ESSAYS

Doig, Ivan. *This House of Sky: Landscapes of a Western Mind.* Harcourt Brace Jovanovich, 1978. A gifted Montana writer explores his connections to the land and the people who shaped his values.

Duncan, Dayton. *Out West.* Viking, 1987. Follow the same route Lewis and Clark did through the eyes of a modern explorer.

Frazier, Ian. *Great Plains.* Farrar Straus Giroux, 1989. From Custer and Crazy Horse to MX missiles, Frazier gives his readers a new look at America's heartland.

Kittredge, William, editor. *Montana Spaces.* Nick Lyons Books, 1988. Original essays about the land and the people of Montana by some of the West's finest writers.

Kittredge, William and Annick Smith, editors. *The Last Best Place.* University of Washington Press, 1988. The best in history, poetry, and literature, all wrapped up in one 5-pound (two-kg) volume.

Maclean, Norman. *A River Runs Through It and Other Stories.* University of Chicago Press, 1976. Humor and tragedy blend in this American classic about living and fishing in the Blackfoot River country of Montana.

McFadden, Cyra. *Rain or Shine.* Alfred A. Knopf, 1986. The daughter of a famous Montana rodeo announcer and dancer-turned-trick rider recounts her childhood on the rodeo circuit.

Stegner, Wallace. *Wolf Willow.* University of Nebraska Press, 1980. One of the West's great writers explores his boyhood on the plains of southern Saskatchewan, just north of the Montana border.

■ POETRY

Hugo, Richard. *The Lady in Kicking Horse Reservoir.* Norton, 1973. Before his death in 1982, this poet was mentor to many of Montana's leading writers as director of the University of Montana's creative writing program.

Keeler, Greg. *American Falls.* Confluence Press, 1987. Fishing is the metaphor for this poetry by a delightfully offbeat professor-writer-musician-angler.

McRae, Wallace. *It's Just Grass and Water.* Oxalis, 1986. One of Montana's favorite cowboy poets talks of life on the range.

Zarzyski, Paul. *Roughstock Sonnets.* Lowell Press, 1989. A refreshing and contemporary twist on cowboy poetry.

■ FICTION

Doig, Ivan. *Dancing at the Rascal Fair.* Atheneum, 1987. A chronicle of the American experience, beginning in Scotland in 1889 and ending three decades later on the Rocky Mountain frontier.

Dorris, Michael. *A Yellow Raft in Blue Water.* Warner Books, 1988. A sensitive and spellbinding portrait of three generations of contemporary Indian women.

Guthrie, A. B., Jr. *The Big Sky.* Houghton Mifflin, 1947. The best known of several historical novels by Montana's Pulitzer Prize winner.

Johnson, Dorothy. *A Man Called Horse* and *The Hanging Tree.* Ballantine, 1953, 1957. Two of the late Montana author's short stories that became motion pictures.

Welch, James. *Fools Crow.* Viking Penguin, 1986. A fictional account of the impact of white civilization on a band of Blackfeet Indians.

■ GUIDEBOOKS

Alt, David and Donald Hyndeman. *Roadside Geology of the Northern Rockies.* Mountain Press, 1927. An authoritative but non-technical explanation of the violent natural forces that shaped the landscape we see today.

Fischer, Carol and Hank Fischer. *Montana Wildlife Viewing Guide.* Falcon Press, 1990. Practical information on more than 100 easily accessible wildlife viewing sites.

Van West, Carroll. *A Traveler's Companion to Montana History.* Montana Historical Society, 1986. A motorist's guide to the past and its influence on today's landscape and communities.

■ GLACIER AND YELLOWSTONE
NATIONAL PARKS

Depending on your field of interest (hiking, sightseeing, wildflowers, wildlife, natural history, geology, etc.), there are many guidebooks about Glacier and Yellowstone national parks available through each park's natural history association. For a complete list of field guides, general books, and maps, write **Glacier Natural History Association,** Box 327, West Glacier, MT 59936, (406) 888-5756, and **The Yellowstone Association** Box 117, Yellowstone National Park, WY 82190, (307) 344-7381.

■ MAGAZINES

Montana Magazine, American Geographic Publishing, Helena, MT. People, places, and lots of color photography (bimonthly).

Montana: The Magazine of Western History, Montana Historical Society, Helena, MT. Widely regarded as one of the nation's best history magazines (quarterly).

Montana Outdoors, Montana Department of Fish, Wildlife and Parks, Helena, MT. For sportsmen and all who love the outdoors (bimonthly).

I N D E X

DISCOVER AMERICA
WITH COMPASS AMERICAN GUIDES

WRITTEN FOR THE "LITERATE TRAVELER," this series of guides conjures up the images, explores the myths and legends, and reveals the spirit of the cities and states of the Great American West and Canada. Each title gives voice to the place in such a way that these books are less destination guides than guides to the people, landscape, communities, and cultures that shape the character of North America.

Superb color photography commissioned from internationally acclaimed photographers captures what is contemporary, while archival illustrations bring the past alive.

Meticulous maps and extensive indexes provide an easy-to-use reference guide. An informative back section in each guide covers accommodations, dining, tours, and other tips essential for the traveler.

Compass American Guides are available in general and travel bookstores, or may be ordered directly from the publisher by sending a check or money order, including the cost of shipping and handling, payable to: Compass American Guides, Inc., 6051 Margarido Dr., Oakland, CA 94618. Tel. (415) 547-7233. Or ask your bookseller to order for you.

Shipping & Handling Charges: Domestic UPS or USPS 1st Class (allow 10 working days for delivery): $3.50 for the 1st book, 50¢ for each additional book. California residents should include 6% sales tax.

Booksellers: Compass American Guides are distributed to the trade by Publishers Group West, and are also available from Ingram, Baker & Taylor, Gordon's, Pacific Pipeline, and other regional wholesalers.

Prices: All prices are subject to change.

CITIES

San Francisco and the Bay Area San Francisco has something for everyone, whether your taste runs to cappuccino or dim sum, to downtown honky tonk or Davies Symphony Hall. Special emphasis on the surrounding Bay Area, from the wine country of the Napa Valley to the markets of the East Bay.
Author: Barry Parr—Photographer: Michael Yamashita
ISBN 1-878867-00-8; 396pp.; Price $14.95

Las Vegas Deke Castleman's rollicking introduction to the capital of glitz, with a tale of fifty hotels, a celebration of tacky museums, a guide to quick weddings and sign language, and, of course, a system for playing slots, craps, blackjack, poker, and other games of chance.
Author: Deke Castleman—Photographer: Michael Yamashita
ISBN 1-878867-01-6; 302pp.; $12.95

WESTERN STATES

Wyoming High, wide and handsome, a land where tales of Indians, pioneers, gun slingers, cattle barons, cowboys and other characters of the Old West still cling to life. Nat Burt, son of pioneering dude ranchers, roams the state where the myth of the cowboy was born.
Author: Nathaniel Burt—Photographer: Don Pitcher
ISBN 1-878867-04-0; 396pp.; Price $14.95

Utah Unspoiled as the day Brigham Young proclaimed "this is the right place," this land of redrock canyons and snow-capped mountains offers glorious scenery and a glimpse of the magnificent cliff-dwellings of the ancient Anasazi Indians. Special emphasis on outdoor recreation.
Authors: Tom & Gayen Wharton—Photographer: Tom Till
ISBN 1-878867-09-1; 364pp.; Price $14.95

Arizona From hidden canyons to museums of archaeology, from the civilized pleasures of Phoenix to jagged wildlands, author Larry Cheek reveals Arizona's scenic, cultural, and historical attractions and colorful eccentricities.
Author: Larry Cheek—Photographer: Michael Freeman
ISBN 1-878867-08-3; 320pp.; Price $14.95

Colorado Breathtaking photography and author Jon Klusmire's irreverent commentary guide travelers to the heart of the Rockies (a real Rocky Mountain High). Join the jet-setting crowd of Aspen or the prehistoric inhabitants of Dinosaur National Monument in this natural wonderland. Special section on Ski Country USA.
Author: Jon Klusmire—Photographer: Paul Chesley
Available August 1991; ISBN 1-878867-07-5; 302pp.; Price $14.95

Montana Love of land and sky runs deep in Montana. Mountain ranges with names like the Crazies, Snowies, and Sapphires. Legendary rivers—the Madison, Big Hole, Yellowstone, and Missouri. Curiouser creeks—Froze-to-Death, Stinking Water, and Hellroaring. High plains, once home to herds of buffalo, still offer wide vistas to the eye and soul. This Land of the Big Sky may well be the last best place.
Author: Norma Tirrell—Photographer: John Reddy
ISBN 1-878867-10-5; 304pp.; Price $14.95

New Mexico Space, light, purity—New Mexico has cast a magical spell of mystery over its inhabitants for centuries. Native Americans expressed their reverential relationship with the land through their art. In more recent times, artist Georgia O'Keeffe and writer D.H. Lawrence settled here hoping to capture the seemingly indescribable. In spite of their efforts, and those of many others, there is only one way to appreciate New Mexico—by experiencing it.
Author: Nancy Harbert—Photographer: Michael Freeman
Available Fall 1991; ISBN 1-878867-06-7; 288pp.; Price $14.95

CANADA

Canada Veteran journalist Garry Marchant approaches the second largest country in the world as not one, but six different nations. Special sections on the Inuits, Canadian sports, rail hotels, Quebecois culture and the Calgary Stampede.
Author: Garry Marchant—Photographer: Ken Straiton
ISBN 1-878867-12-1; 320pp.; $14.95

■ ABOUT THE AUTHOR

Born and raised in Montana, Norma Tirrell brings to this guide a native's first-hand knowledge of the state and an insider's view of its travel industry. For six years, as publications specialist for Travel Montana, a division of the Montana Department of Commerce, she wrote and produced the state's official travel guides. A graduate of the University of Montana School of Journalism, her first book, *We Montanans,* was published in 1988 by American Geographic Publishing. She and her husband, Gordon Bennett, enjoy exploring Montana from their home in Helena, centrally located on the east slope of the Rocky Mountains.

■ ABOUT THE PHOTOGRAPHER

John Reddy, based in Helena, has been photographing landscapes and people since 1974. Reddy earned a degree in photography from Montana State University's Film and Television Production Department in Bozeman and subsequently lectured there for two years. He is widely published in Montana. His work has been seen in publications such as *American Heritage, Historic Preservation, Psychology Today, Sunset Magazine,* and the *Smithsonian Guide to Historic America.* Reddy has many commercial clients, but prefers working on books and magazines featuring outdoor subjects. In his free time, he enjoys spending his time with his family and continually strives to capture on film the many splendors of his beloved Montana outdoors.